"You don't really own your property. Under 'emi[...]
cians can seize it for their purposes, and toss you a[...]
goodness that Steven Greenhut, one of the stars of American journalism,
has exposed this evil as never before, and shown us the way out."

> — Llewellyn H. Rockwell Jr., President of the
> Ludwig von Mises Institute, Auburn,
> Alabama, and editor of LewRockwell.com

"Steven Greenhut beautifully vivifies how eminent domain turns politicians
into tyrants. *Abuse of Power* is must reading for anyone who wants to understand the pervasive plundering committed by governments across this nation.
Not recommended for incurable idealists and other damn fools."

> — James Bovard, author of *Terrorism and Tyranny*,
> *Feeling Your Pain*, *Freedom in Chains* and *Lost
> Rights*

"The power of eminent domain is no longer used for strictly government
purposes, but increasingly to transfer private property from one owner to
another. Steven Greenhut's probing analysis clarifies the central issues
regarding this controversial practice, and in doing so he has performed a
valuable public service. *Abuse of Power* should be read by every judge, leg-
islator, council member and reporter, and by every American who cares
about constitutional rights."

> — Steven B. Frates, senior fellow, Rose Institute
> of State and Local Government

"This thoughtful and valuable book exposes the extreme abuses of eminent
domain that are typical of urban renewal and redevelopment schemes. That
these schemes have only made our cities worse demonstrates that respect
for property rights *is* good city planning."

> — Supervisor Chris Norby, Orange County,
> California, and founder of Municipal Officials
> for Redevelopment Reform

"Steven Greenhut knows how to research and tell these well-documented
stories of flagrant abuses of government power. My students and colleagues in planning and architecture will do well to pay heed and note how

precious freedoms and individual rights are too often being sacrificed for tax returns, private profit and niceties of design. Those seeking to preserve their neighborhoods can learn also how the system works and how to prevail against the odds. A very readable and important book for those who cherish living in 'the land of the free.'"

> — Frank Hotchkiss, architect and former director of planning at the Southern California Association of Governments

"A hard-hitting expose of another of Big Brother's tricks, and one you probably haven't thought much about: declaring your real estate 'blighted,' seizing it under the power of 'eminent domain,' paying you less than it's worth, and then handing it over to some pet businessmen to 'redevelop' as part of a grandiose 'urban renewal' scheme. If that doesn't make you grind your teeth, nothing will."

> — William A. Rusher, former publisher of *National Review*

"Greenhut offers the most compelling case I've read against the misuse of eminent domain."

> — Jim Doti, President of Chapman University and Donald Bren Distinguished Chair of Business and Economics

"Government should not be diametrically opposed to market principles. They can and should operate together. Greenhut clearly documents what can happen when governments lose sight of the bigger, more important principles."

> — Mayor Curt Pringle, Anaheim, California

"It was a shock when the local redevelopment agency attempted to seize our church's property through the use of eminent domain. It not only made us realize that it could happen to anyone, we soon found out that similar situations were occurring throughout the country. Some of the stories of other churches, businesses and individuals that were the victims of eminent domain abuse that came to our attention were nothing less than heart-wrenching. *Abuse of Power* addresses a subject that every property owner and every American needs to be aware of."

> — Pastor Bayless Conley, Cottonwood Christian Center, Los Alamitos, California

ABUSE OF POWER:
How the Government Misuses Eminent Domain

Steven Greenhut

SEVEN LOCKS PRESS

Santa Ana, California

Seven Locks Press
P.O. Box 25689
Santa Ana, CA 92799
(800) 354-5348

Individual Sales. This book is available through most bookstores or can be ordered directly from Seven Locks Press at the address above.

Quantity Sales. Special discounts are available on quantity purchases by corporations, associations, and others. For details, contact the "Special Sales Department" at the publisher's address above.

Printed in the United States of America
Library of Congress Cataloging-in-Publication Data
is available from the publisher
ISBN 1-931643-37-7

Cover and Interior Design by Heather Buchman
Page x: Photo by Bruce Harkness, Walter P. Reuther Library, Wayne State University
Pages 14–15: Photos by Mark Timieski, Committee for Lakewood
Page 51: Photo by Steven Greenhut
Page 164: Drawing courtesy of Cottonwood Christian Center

To my dad, Kurt Greenhut, 1928–2002.
We never agreed on politics,
but I always admired his sense of justice.

TABLE OF CONTENTS

A government which robs Peter to pay Paul can always count on the support of Paul.

— George Bernard Shaw[1]

A family prepares to leave the Poletown neighborhood, forced out by eminent domain to make way for a General Motors factory.

FOREWORD
Eminent Domain Abuses Will Come to Haunt Us

Anyone who loves liberty cannot but be grateful to Steven Greenhut for taking a critical look at the way governments abuse eminent domain, in clear violation of the takings clause of the U.S. Constitution. This is an extremely important topic, and this wonderful book offers a very astute and up-to-date treatment of it.

Greenhut shows, among other things, that, contrary to widespread academic and journalistic dogma, it's often big business, in cahoots with government, that violates the principles of the free market all around us, to our great detriment, especially as owners and patrons of small businesses.

Just consider: Many critics of the capitalist features of America cite the case of General Motors' treatment of Poletown, where in the 1980s city officials conspired with General Motors to knock down an entire neighborhood in order to build a new assembly plant. This was done in the name of the "greater good" of encouraging economic development in a depressed region.

The bulk of the criticism over the destruction of the Poletown neighborhood (which Ralph Nader helped to organize) centered on GM's abuse of its economic power and on the evils of corporate America. The far greater evil of government's trampling on property rights was ignored.

In his book Greenhut shows, with numerous brilliant examples, how private property rights are actually the best way to protect those with little political power against those, such as GM, with a great deal of clout with the politicians.

This basic issue of property rights is something Greenhut discusses with far more astuteness than those from the Left, with their constant refrain about corporate power—what about the plain fact that government is not supposed to cave in to such power, any more than a judge or juror is supposed to cave in to a bribe? And his principled treatment is far more convincing than the occasional bellyaching from the Right about the high cost to big business of government interference. Greenhut doesn't act as a mouthpiece for those corporate interests that do not hesitate to use government even as they pay lip service to free enterprise. He defends freedom for us all.

The outrage in Poletown is that GM didn't just buy some land up for sale—it took the land from others with the aid of government, and the plant never even lived up to its grandiose economic-development promises.

Yet, few critics of the Poletown case called attention to this fact when it was a media item. Mostly what they stressed, not only in their writings but also in a film about the taking, is that General Motors, a private business, has immense power to influence politics. Greenhut's book brings to light the real issue: the importance of private property rights to all Americans and how unbound government is the real threat, especially when it's so chummy with big business.

Properly grasped, the eminent domain law concerns government's taking private property for public purposes. That would involve taking such land, paying for it at the going market price, and using it for what is the properly limited public interest, such as building a courthouse or police station.

This law is entirely perverted when the purpose for which private property is taken is not related to bona fide public tasks but to special interests such as General Motors' economic progress. There is nothing in the U. S. Constitution that authorizes such use of the "takings clause" however much some apologists may cry, "But it will generate taxes for us." The very idea of private-property rights—one of the basic human rights imposing limits on governmental power and explicitly mentioned in the takings clause of the Fifth Amendment to the U.S. Constitution—is threatened by such abuse of eminent domain powers.

The eminent domain tradition, interpreted honestly and correctly, concerns the need of governments to do their proper, limited jobs as they go about securing our rights, the task that the Declaration of Independence clearly identifies as the proper one for government. So, the building of courthouses, police stations, prisons, military facilities, roads and some other purposes may be served by eminent domain, but under no stretch of the imagination would it authorize government to violate the property rights of citizens so as to collect more taxes. If taxes are needed, in America they are supposed to be assessed through the legislative process, not by driving people off their property so that the property can be given to a new owner with a more lucrative use for the land.

The government should have no authority to use eminent domain to do favors for special groups, especially at the expense of other citizens.

Alarm over this abusive practice of governments, urged on by all too many unprincipled big businesses, is timely. Some notice has already been taken of it, for example, by CBS-TV's *60 Minutes* program, and it is now vital to get a more detailed, more principled and sharper discussion of what exactly is being perpetrated here.

Unless the trend is reversed and eminent domain is kept within its proper bounds, anyone at all could become a victim of this abuse. In time anyone may be told by some local or national bureaucrat: "We think your property can be used better by someone else, someone who will pay higher taxes to us, so get out."

— Tibor R. Machan

Tibor R. Machan is professor of business ethics at Chapman University in Orange, California; professor emeritus of philosophy at Auburn University, Ala.; research fellow at Hoover Institution, Stanford University and author of The Right to Private Property *(Stanford: Hoover Institution Press, 2002).*

ACKNOWLEDGEMENTS

This book would never have come about without the support and encouragement of so many people. My wife, Donna, and my daughters, Teresa, Diana and Laura, gave me their love and understanding, allowing me to shirk my family responsibilities for several months. I offer thanks to my employer, the *Orange County Register*, and especially to Editorial Page Editor Cathy Taylor for giving me free rein to write about eminent domain and redevelopment in my work at the newspaper, and for enabling me to pursue this side project. I greatly appreciate the many experts in the field of eminent domain who shared their expertise and advice with me. I especially want to thank attorney and professor Gideon Kanner, one of the nation's foremost experts on eminent domain, and attorney Susan Trager, another expert in the field, for kindly reviewing this manuscript and giving me helpful suggestions to improve it. My colleague, Editorial Writer John Seiler, also gave me helpful suggestions. Thanks also to Chris Sutton, Bob Ferguson, John Murphy, Andrew Guilford and Sean O'Connor, and the Institute for Justice's Dana Berliner, John Kramer and Scott Bullock, all of whom have energetically represented the interests of property owners and shared their ideas with me. I owe a debt of gratitude to Orange County (California) Supervisor Chris Norby, who introduced me to the subject of redevelopment and eminent domain abuse several years ago. A steadfast opponent of such abuses, Chris Norby is proof that a politician can be both principled and effective. His brother and chief of staff, Eric Norby, also has been a source of constant advice and support to me on this issue. My admiration goes out to the individual property owners who have fought city hall to protect the rights guaranteed to them in the U.S. Constitution. This includes people such as pastors Bayless Conley and Mike Wilson of Cottonwood

Christian Center; Jim and JoAnne Saleet of Lakewood, Ohio; Dick and Nancy Saha of Coatesville, Pennsylvania; Steven Strooh of Des Moines, Iowa; Manny Ballestero of Garden Grove, California; and all the other fighters in this long and unfinished battle.

1. INTRODUCTION:

EMINENT DOMAIN IS THEFT BY ANOTHER NAME

Eminent Domain: *The power of the state to take private property for public use upon compensating the owner.*

Mention the term "eminent domain" to the average American, and you'll be greeted by one of two responses. The first, and most common, is for the person's eyes to glaze in utter boredom. This does not initially sound like a sexy topic, and most people would prefer to be anywhere else than with someone who wants to talk at length about an arcane legal doctrine. The second response is for people to say, "Oh, yeah, that's what government sometimes does when it builds a highway or prison." Those people who know what it means understand why a victim of eminent domain might be annoyed at the process or might have reason to fight for better compensation, but they rarely doubt the legitimacy of eminent domain. After all, how could public projects get built if property owners, on certain occasions, couldn't be forced to sell their property to the government?

Only the rare person understands, however, that eminent domain these days is not just about the government taking property for public works. For various reasons, reviewed in the following chapters, governments increasingly use eminent domain to take property from one private owner in order to give it to another private owner. Typically, the victimized party is a small-business owner, a homeowner or some average Joe minding his own business, living the American dream in his own particular way. Then along comes a city manager or government attorney who informs him that he must surrender his home or business because a wealthy developer—perhaps a big campaign contributor and mover and shaker in the community, or an out-of-town corporation promising an expanded tax base for the city—has bigger and better plans for it.

Incredulity is the next usual response. People who learn about how eminent domain is abused can't believe it is a common process. Victims of these increasingly common "takings" simply cannot believe that they are being forced to leave their home or business, not for a highway, but for a Home Depot, a Wal-Mart or a privately owned business park or sports stadium. They are shocked to learn the legal process is rigged against them. They get little if any legal notice, no due process, and, mainly, all they can do is fight in court to get a better financial settlement. No one believes this can happen in America until it happens to them.

Well, at least the victimized property owners get just compensation, right? Even that is not true. Almost always, the government tries to lowball the property owner, in many cases offering a fraction of the property's value. The victim must hire an expensive lawyer to argue for the "just compensation" the U.S. Constitution promises to eminent domain's victims. Even the U.S. Supreme Court admits that property owners are not fully compensated when they are victims of eminent domain, yet the court has washed its hands of the matter, refusing to set things right.[2]

This hardly sounds like America. But this scenario is no aberration. In thousands of documented recent cases[3] and many more that haven't received any publicity, property owners are being forced to sacrifice their dreams to government agents acting on behalf of big developers, gambling casinos, large retail stores and multibillion-dollar corporations. Even when eminent domain isn't ultimately used, the mere threat of it convinces many property owners to sell their properties at less-than-ideal terms. This abusive practice, in fact, distorts the entire real estate market by adding uncertainties and political factors in what should be market decisions. For instance, prospective property owners cannot think about investing in an older or up-and-coming area without at least considering the possibility that city officials might have a redevelopment plan in store for the area.

Eminent domain creates an avenue for corruption, as government officials get to play God with other people's neighborhoods and businesses, and can therefore punish enemies and reward friends. Eminent domain limits the freedoms we all have to pursue our own economic futures. I think of the family that had planned for years to eventually sell their sewing-machine and vacuum-cleaner repair shop in Brea, California, and use the money to retire. But after their business was placed in a redevelopment area where it was subject to eminent domain, it lost most of its value. No one would buy it under the conditions. Their lives were placed on hold, their future diminished. As the *Orange County Register* reported October 2, 2002, Jim and JoAnn Cossack spent twelve years trying to rebuild the small shop after "redevelopment pushed them out of Brea's old downtown in 1990." The city targeted them again, in their new site at the edge of downtown. The city bought the strip mall where their business was located for some future redevelopment.

"At that time, the Cossacks were trying to sell their business—its name, inventory and years of good will—and retire on the proceeds," wrote Eric Carpenter. "They were in escrow when they got the news: Their buyer had fled.

"No other buyer has come forward.

"So the Cossacks' retirement plans are on hold," the article reported.[4] This is unfair, especially considering that the property was most likely earmarked for a developer's use, not the public's use.

When told about such outrages, many listeners assume that eminent domain can only happen by stealth. Once the truth is revealed, they think, judges won't permit it, and the powers that be will rally to the side of the abused property owners. Justice will prevail. But this rarely is the case. Usually, the political powers don't lift a finger to help the victims. The influential people in the community typically rally behind the Great New Project that promises new tax revenue and good-paying jobs. Surprisingly, the courts treat eminent domain victims with disdain, acting as if they are the guilty party seeking to subvert the public good.[5] The victims are portrayed as greedy obstructionists. This is bad enough when the project is designed for a genuine public use, but it is unconscionable to treat property owners this way when the project is private in nature.

Wall Street Journal editorialist John Fund refers to the civic boosters of such government-backed "redevelopment" projects as Leaders Of Our Town, or LOOT.[6] That says it all, yet it always surprises eminent domain's victims that no one with any power rallies to their side. They are left alone, with mounting debt, after their business is shut down. They must muster the resources and courage to fight the city's deep-pocketed lawyers, who often use techniques that are eerily reminiscent of those used by a Mafia family.

This wanton abuse of property rights is an incredible injustice, and it happens over and over, in every state and in scores of cities and suburbs. It happens in every region of the country, in big cities, suburbs and even rural areas. Often, the targeted businesses and homes are owned by those on the lower and middle rungs of the economic ladder, although these days the properties are as likely to be well-kept as they are to be rundown. Increasingly, governments eye perfectly good vacant land. I've seen newer shopping centers and handsome strip malls declared blighted. In one case discussed in a later chapter, a Southern California city attempted to declare as blighted and then use eminent domain to take one store on behalf of its next-door neighbor. Both buildings were among the finest retail buildings in town. They were built as part of the same project and were practically identical. The only difference between the "good" building and the "blighted" one is that the blighted one was coveted by the other store, and the city feared that this store would flee for another city if it wasn't granted its neighbor's property at a bargain-basement price.[7]

Older neighborhoods and businesses, especially those owned by immigrants, elderly people and middle-class folks who lack the means to fight back bear the greatest brunt of eminent domain's abuses. That's because cities rarely understand the vitality that goes on in older areas, preferring instead modern, look-alike national chain stores that pay high amounts of tax revenue along prime commercial areas. Government officials are taught at their League of Cities meetings and at planning seminars how to improve the tax cash flow and other conditions of their communities. So officials use their power to drive out those homes and businesses that they don't like and replace them with the types of housing and businesses that they prefer. They are picking economic winners and losers, interfering with the natural process by which communities improve themselves, and doing it in the name of promoting economic development by cleaning up blight. Author Jane Jacobs, whose groundbreaking book on urban life is discussed in Chapter 5, had a wonderful saying: "New ideas must use old buildings."[8] But such new ideas can never take root in a world where eminent domain is pre-eminent because the government is too busy driving away the people with those new ideas in order to bulldoze their buildings and replace them with cookie-cutter projects. A new idea doesn't have a chance in this world. This abuse of eminent domain stifles creativity, and is wholly inappropriate in a society that values individual freedom rather than central planning.

Eminent domain's use for private advantage is so outrageous because it strikes at the root of American freedom. We are not particularly free if our life's labors can be taken on the whim of a government official, acting on behalf of another private party. In fact, the more special the property is and the more it is lovingly restored, the more it might be coveted by someone else who has a "better" idea for it. This is eerily reminiscent of the Soviet Union, where people who had, say, a nice apartment had to hope that some apparatchik didn't notice how nice it was.

In recent decades, property rights have become the bastard stepchildren of the Bill of Rights: the rights the courts and elected officials don't like to parade before the neighbors. The abuses described in this book are the result of that downplaying of a fundamental right. The secure ownership of property is the reason America's economy has flourished while other nations' economies haven't. In order to invest and expand a business, for instance, the owner has to feel secure that he will reap the reward of that investment. If the property can be taken at any time and for any reason, such security is diminished. This is the basic point of property, yet it's something U.S. officials increasingly ignore. They have their reason to do this.

OTHER PEOPLE'S PLANS

Property rights get in the way of *Other People's Plans.* Governments are beholden to the political winds that happen to be blowing. When the fad is to renew rundown urban neighborhoods, government agencies craft plans to do that. When the fad is to create sales-tax-paying retail centers to help city budgets, they do that, too. Whatever the plan is, it is far easier to use government police powers to scrape away existing properties than it is to follow the rule of law and the rules of the marketplace and negotiate with people in good faith. Sure, it might be frustrating when a homeowner or small-business owner gets in the way of a project that promises to revive an older part of town. But that's the price of freedom. It's a small price to pay, when you consider the abuses inflicted on people in other lands where individuals must do whatever the authorities tell them. One of the foundations of American society, and any free society, is the right to say "no." When that right is stripped away, citizens are far less free than they think they are.

Eminent domain denies people the right to say "no." That's why the founders allowed it only in the most limited circumstances, for "public" uses, after "due process" is afforded, and only if "just compensation" is paid. We'll look at the legal reasoning that has brought America to the current, sorry state in the fourth chapter. But suffice it to say that America is built on the idea of individual liberty, and the Constitution and other founding documents are designed to keep government out of individual lives. The founders would be shocked at the degree to which eminent domain—one of the ultimate forms of government muscle-flexing—is abused today. The whole Constitution seems to have been turned on its head. The rights of government, even though governments are not supposed to have rights, take pre-eminence in such matters over the rights of individuals.

Really, what's happening today shouldn't even be called eminent domain, in a technical sense. As the dictionary definition explained,[9] eminent domain refers to the taking of private property for *public* use. Despite the twisting of the term "public," and the courts' acquiescence in that matter, the cases this book discusses rarely have anything to do with public projects. And so often the property owners do not receive just compensation, for reasons discussed in Chapter 3. What's going on is a simple abuse of power, allowed by weak politicians and courts more interested in preserving the prerogatives of government than in doing their job and protecting the rights of law-abiding individuals.

Put yourself in the position of a small restaurant owner targeted by a city for "redevelopment." Or in the place of an owner of a well-kept tract house whose entire neighborhood is deemed "blighted" by city planners, and slated for demolition and replacement with a theme park. The courts first require governments to declare as blighted the area slated for redevelopment. You know your business or home isn't blighted, at least not by any normal definition of that term, but that doesn't matter to officials. They can call anything they want blighted, based on a laundry list of irrelevant factors. It's part of the scam. Even advocates of using eminent domain to transfer properties from one set of owners to another often admit that the blight finding is a legal fiction designed to satisfy the courts, and nothing more. Everyone pretends the transfer of property is done to eliminate blight, which the courts have long deemed a public purpose. The way around the legal restraint is to declare virtually anything as blight—peeling paint, "underutilization," a lack of utilities on vacant land. The concepts have gotten more far-fetched as the years have progressed, a testament to the cleverness of city attorneys and the laziness of courts that, until recently, have granted the widest possible latitude in defining blight.

In one charming older neighborhood in Lakewood, Ohio, slated for the wrecking ball by city officials who wanted to hand the prime park-front location to a condominium developer, the city declared that the lack of attached garages was enough to justify the blight moniker. The mayor, speaking to a *60 Minutes* reporter, admitted that even her own home fit the definition of blight, and that blight doesn't really mean blight in the dictionary sense of the word.[10] We've entered the world of *Alice in Wonderland*, where legal interpretations are based on nonsense, and the clear words of the Constitution are ignored.

It's bad enough that you will lose your home once a city decides to target it for redevelopment. Even worse, the process could last years. You could be stuck waiting, year in and year out, for the next shoe to drop. Often, these big projects dreamed of by city planners never come to fruition. The financing doesn't come through, or a developer pulls out of the deal months or years into the plan, or the city administration changes and the plans change. But once a home or a business is called "blighted," it is nearly impossible to sell it or to plan for the future. The owner must simply wait until officials get their act together. Once the shoe drops, and the condemnation proceedings begin, owners often get thrown into a long and costly legal tangle. Cities often try to buy the land on the cheap, dragging out court proceedings for months or even years if the homeowners don't like the deal they have been offered. And cities only must pay the value of the property. Business good will—the term for crucial intangibles such as a business' reputation—must only be paid in a few states. Even in the states where the payment of good will is required, government attorneys have ways to evade that requirement. Many a business moved from its site by eminent domain goes belly up soon afterwards. It's too difficult for many people to go through the start-up process again. For those who do give it a try, the clientele doesn't always follow the business to the new location. Almost always, the victimized owner loses significant amounts of money.

Eminent domain is far from the only assault on property rights in America today. Myriad environmental and regulatory provisions severely limit what individuals can do with their land.

In many cases, for instance, laws demanding the preservation of open space, or protecting so-called endangered species, put such strict limits on private-property ownership that land often, in essence, is stolen. A person might own a twenty-acre tract of farmland and be planning to develop it into a subdivision, which would yield a tidy profit—enough to secure a comfortable retirement. But after an open-space preservation law is passed, or an endangered-species habitat is discovered, the land can no longer be used as planned. Perhaps only one or two houses can be built there, rather than the desired subdivision. But unless the land's value is completely taken, the courts rarely require the government to pay compensation for the loss. Such regulatory "takings" are making property ownership far more tenuous and unpredictable than it used to be.

The story of eminent domain abuse has some similarities with those sorts of regulatory takings. When a property is put in a redevelopment area, which is an area in which government gains the power to use eminent domain on some future project, individuals lose options and freedoms. Sometimes it is worse than the actual taking itself, because no compensation is paid until the title of the land is actually transferred. Such government-driven projects can drag on for years. The loss of value, in the meantime, is the owner's problem. It's one thing to use such an extreme form of government power to deny a person his property so the government can build a freeway, but quite another when that person loses his rights, his options, his freedoms, so that someone else can gain them in his place.

Property rights are what protect the little guy from the designs of the rich and powerful. They also are what protect the rich and powerful from the designs of the jealous mobs. They are what help most Americans secure a source of wealth, stability and personal liberty. How free would any of us be if we couldn't own property? We would not be very free at all. The right to own property isn't about avarice, but about the right to control one's life and one's economic future. Property roots people in their communities and promotes public spiritedness and other enduring values. As author Ayn Rand argued, "Without property rights, no other rights are possible. Since man has to sustain his life by his own effort, the man who has no right to the product of his effort has no means to sustain his life. The man who produces while others dispose of his product is a slave."[11]

In fact, some might argue that the right to own property is the most important right that human beings have. Those with protected property rights can say what they please, worship whom they choose and do whatever they please—provided they don't directly tread on someone else's rights. At first glance, it may be hard to understand why so many Americans don't stand up for property rights the way they might be expected to stand up for the freedom of speech or the freedom of religion. But after years of anti-property-rights indoctrination, most Americans are oblivious to the real situation in America today. We think we are free and masters of our own lives and property, yet don't understand that, increasingly, American governments and the courts are recognizing property rights in the same way that the king used to think about property rights back in not-so-Merry Old England, before the colonists got fed up and declared themselves a free and independent nation. The foundations of the American political experiment are summed up in the Declaration of Independence: "We hold these truths to be self-evident, that all men are created equal, that they are endowed by their Creator with certain unalienable Rights, that among these are Life, Liberty and the pursuit of Happiness."[12] Essential to the pursuit of happiness was the ownership of property.

But when government can take property from anyone for virtually any reason and give it to anyone else, there's no way that anything approaching the founders' vision of freedom still exists. These days, the government is not doing what it is supposed to do, which is protect the guaranteed liberties of individual American citizens and ensure a fair legal playing field. Instead, it is making central plans and intervening in the market to favor some people over others. It is robbing Peter, paying Paul, and distorting the sense of fairness that is the bedrock of a true, market-oriented, democratic and freedom-protecting society.

Eminent domain may at first sound like a boring concept. Advocates of its misuse count on most Americans tuning out when discussions about it are raised. But it is not boring at all. The story of eminent domain in modern America is a story about the abuse of government power, about the abuse of authority to benefit the rich and powerful at the expense of the poor and powerless. It is a story of untrammeled greed, of the influence of special interests, of the undermining of traditional American constitutional concepts and their replacement with a system more reminiscent of the old Soviet Union. It is a story of personal hardships and abuse, and, finally, a story of individuals who have put everything on the line to fight for their homes and businesses. It is my hope that this book presents the subject in a way that interests more Americans. Only through widespread outrage can we build a big enough movement to secure reforms that protect Americans from such abuses.

A STORY OF ORDINARY HEROES

The story isn't an entirely discouraging one. Often, governments face little opposition when they try to take property. But sometimes heroes emerge, who organize their community and beat back the eminent domain plan. One person is all it takes to spark a revolt, which can spread across a neighborhood, and an entire city, like a wildfire.

In the Lakewood, Ohio, case mentioned earlier, an older couple, Jim and JoAnne Saleet, started a grass-roots revolt that saved their neighborhood, changed the power structure in the city and sent a big developer packing. It was a classic David v. Goliath story. The neighborhood in which the Saleets lived was a well-kept, historic, middle-class enclave near a beautiful park along the Rocky River. "As my husband said, developers discovered our view," said JoAnne Saleet.[13] "But we found it first."

City officials—in fact, the entire Lakewood political establishment, including the business community and the Cleveland Democratic Party, according to the Saleets—were eager to find ways to bring in new development and new tax revenue. Developers coveted the parkfront neighborhood, so city officials planned to wipe away sixty-six lovely older homes, five apartment buildings and numerous small businesses. The developer planned to build 200 upscale condominiums and a retail center on the site. There wasn't anything that appeared blighted in the area, but the city wanted more affluent residents and businesses in such a fine location. In its view, it was a waste to have such prime property occupied by middle-class houses.

Initially, the city produced a consultant's report identifying the neighborhood as the ideal spot to bring in national chain stores, along with condos that would overlook the park. The report called the neighborhood blighted, pointing to the small size of the homes and the lack of attached garages. Eventually, a Cleveland developer, CenterPoint Properties, proposed a plan that promised to bring in $30 million more in tax revenue to the city than the current neighborhood produced. The mayor pledged to use eminent domain against any property owners who wouldn't sell out to CenterPoint.[14]

Unfortunately, the Ohio Constitution specifically allows eminent domain for economic development, which is a key reason that eminent domain abuses are rampant in Ohio, and far less common in Arizona, where the Constitution strictly limits private benefit from eminent domain.

Officials told residents that the entire future of their city was on the line. Without the new, tax-generating project, they argued, Lakewood would begin a slow decline into the abyss. This is a standard ploy. Redevelopment backers always say their proposed plan is the future of their city. Without it, residents might as well roll up the sidewalks and start looking for a new place to live. As *Cleveland* magazine noted in a January, 2004 article, "Their forecasts were so bleak that even . . . a pro-West End councilman had to disagree. 'If it doesn't pass, is it going to be the death knell of Lakewood? No. Lakewood will be fine.' "[15]

When officials announced their plan in 2002, they told the Saleets the bulldozers would be coming in two to three months. There was nothing they could do about it. Most neighbors, JoAnne Saleet said, were resigned to sell out and move on. But Jim Saleet was stubborn. He said he wouldn't move. The couple is retired and they decided to spend their days battling to save their home. Their first strategy was

The city of Lakewood called these charming homes "blighted" to justify the transfer of the park-front neighborhood to a developer.

Neighbors held a Blighted Block Party and marched in the July 4th parade to rally support to save their homes.

to get the support of other neighbors who shared a priceless view along the park. Once those neighbors had vowed to fight, many other neighbors decided to stand firm.[16]

"When Jim says something, he means it," said JoAnne Saleet. "The others saw that we could fight. But we weren't well-organized. We had no money." So they collected enough money to get some advice from a lawyer. His advice was to first try to stop the plan by community organizing. That's what the couple did. The Saleets and their neighbors got to know officials at City Hall. They spoke at every public meeting. They told their story in heartfelt ways. It was tough. During the battle, the Saleets' youngest granddaughter came down with leukemia, so they had a family emergency to deal with along with their problems with the city.

"We were just hanging on," JoAnne Saleet said. The most news coverage they had gotten was a line or two in the *Cleveland Plain Dealer*. Then, all of a sudden, their fortunes improved. During one council meeting, Jim Saleet made an emotional pitch to save his neighborhood. He was quoting from the U.S. Constitution and quoting past presidents, JoAnne Saleet explained. A *Plain Dealer* reporter was moved by the meeting, and he sent a photographer to Lakewood to photograph the Saleets standing by their house with the gorgeous park view in the background. The story was printed, front page, on a Sunday, and it took up two-thirds of the jump page. The story was picked up on the Internet, and then a Washington, D.C.-based legal organization that defends property rights, Institute for Justice, contacted the Saleets and came out to meet with them.

The couple got thirty-five to forty neighbors together in their living room and met with Institute for Justice attorneys. That was December, 2002. The institute offered the families much free legal advice, and then in June, 2003 agreed to file a lawsuit on their behalf, on a pro bono basis. The institute also offered extensive help in community organizing and public relations. The tables started to turn.

City officials could no longer count on the neighbors running out of money and energy in their fight. The neighbors were energized. They printed fliers, attended meetings, read every related document put out by the city. They tried some successful and innovative strategies. For starters, they kept their message simple and relevant to other Lakewood residents: "It Could Happen To You Next!"[17]

The Saleets invited all the council members to tour their home and neighborhood. In fact, they gave tours to anyone interested in taking one. They wanted people to see that their home was charming, and that their neighborhood was not blighted, JoAnne Saleet explained in an interview. They hosted a Blighted Block Party. They built a float for the Fourth of July parade. It was handmade. They painted part of the Constitution on a large muslin cloth. They installed a music system on the float that blasted patriotic music. The most touching moment, JoAnne Saleet said, was when elderly war veterans lined up along the parade route and saluted, and pledged support for their cause.[18]

The enthusiasm for protecting the neighborhood started to spread. Another organization, called Committee for Lakewood, sprung up and placed an initiative on the ballot. It put the specific development plan before a citywide vote in November, 2003. The Saleets and their neighbors made their case across the city, spending a fraction of what the developers and project supporters were spending. In the end, they won by forty-seven votes after a recount.[19] They also succeeded in voting in a new mayor to replace the old one, who had been the prime advocate for the project.

After the November 2003 vote, as the *Cleveland Plain Dealer* reported on January 12, 2004, CenterPoint cancelled its offer to buy land in the neighborhood. The developer sent cancellation notices to those citizens who had agreed to sell their homes and apartment buildings.[20] One apartment-building owner told the newspaper he was "near financial collapse," given that he had been unable to rent out the apartments after the eminent domain plan was announced, but now he would receive no compensation from the developer or the city for his losses. But most property owners the *Plain Dealer* interviewed were thrilled that their ordeal seemed to be over. The city pledged to move forward with a smaller project that would not require forcing property owners out of their homes. Too bad no one thought of that in the first place. The referendum went well, and having one sure beat doing nothing. But it's troubling to have to put one's property rights to a public vote.

The project had unraveled, although residents feared that, at any time, the city could create a new project in their officially "blighted" neighborhood. So the Saleets, their neighbors and their supporters pushed forward a second initiative, called Issue 10, to remove the blight designation from the neighborhood. On March 2, 2004, the city voted overwhelmingly—63 percent to 37 percent—to remove the designation. The nightmare was over. As of March 2003, the Institute for Justice's lawsuit was still pending; it wouldn't be dropped until the city officially removed the area's blighted status. But the end was near for Lakewood's heavy-handed redevelopment plans. The victory was the result, in part, of the institute's efforts and the publicity generated by a *60 Minutes* special featuring the Lakewood situation. But victory would not have been achieved without the Saleets' heroic fight.

Ironically, the deposed former mayor, Madeleine Cain, started teaching urban development at Cleveland State University. "Keep your children away," is how JoAnne Saleet jokingly put it.[21]

The Saleets are real-life heroes. As *Cleveland* magazine wrote: "An elderly Lakewood couple and their neighbors save their homes and bring down a mayor, with a little help from some Washington lawyers and *60 Minutes*."[22] Not bad, given the odds the Saleets were up against.

Chapter 2 deals with the efforts by the city of Garden Grove, California, to take an entire middle-class neighborhood of about 400 homes and 1,000 residents and turn it into a theme park. The lightning rod in that community was a newcomer to the neighborhood named Manny Ballestero. He did many of the same things as the Saleets: going door-to-door, organizing neighbors, attending City Council meetings, talking with city officials and threatening to gather signatures for a referendum to overturn the city's blight plan. As described in the next chapter, it was the outpouring of opposition to the plan that caused the supportive council members to back away from it.

Ballestero, a school teacher who had moved to the neighborhood just before the city tried to redevelop it, jumped into action after neighborhood residents received a letter from the city discussing the redevelopment plan. It was difficult to understand what the letter meant, and few residents were concerned about it. Ballestero called the city and was told the letter was just a formality, but he continued his investigation until he figured out that a plan to use eminent domain was being hatched in City Hall. I review the details in Chapter 2. But Ballestero was a true hero. He was persistent. He consulted with an attorney, and got pledges from the affected neighbors to raise the $350,000 that would be needed to fight a legal fight. He met with local politicians and invited residents to an organizing meeting at a local church.

"I looked at the map of the affected area," Ballestero said in an interview. "I divided up the area and named a captain for each of the streets. The captain would know the neighbors, and we met on a weekly basis."[23]

He wanted to stay under the radar screen so the city wouldn't realize that opposition was organizing. So each council meeting, only five residents would show up, rather than dozens. They took notes and learned as much as they could, but quietly. They learned whom they could trust, and whom they couldn't. They gained help from the media and were building a community organization that would spring into action at the appropriate time. But Ballestero wasn't banking on political activism alone. He and his neighbors amassed $75,000 in a legal war chest (the additional amount of money was in the form of pledges), in case they had to go to court, and he was consulting with an attorney who was explaining exactly what to do to pave the way for a legal challenge. Residents must follow a specific technical process for challenging a redevelopment plan, so it was crucial to work in concert with an attorney who understands the deadlines and legal requirements.

"I told them, don't lose your temper, don't be emotional," Ballestero said. But it was tough. Elderly people in particular were scared about being driven from their homes. Some residents were angry, others wanted to cut a deal with the city. But Ballestero kept them on board, kept hundreds of people closely following his playbook. He told the residents who wanted to negotiate with the city on their own that they certainly could do so, but that if they did they would never be allowed to join the neighborhood lawsuit if it came to that. Most everyone stayed on board. "It was very empowering for the people," he added. "It left a lasting impression with all of us. You can beat City Hall. But you must do it a certain way. You don't win with rhetoric, but by creating a plan and implementing that plan."[24]

In Chapter 7, we see how Pastor Bayless Conley of Cottonwood Christian Center in Cypress, California, refused to accept the city's unfair terms for taking his church property to hand over to Costco. Conley was up against a remarkably unscrupulous city government that claimed to be negotiating in good faith but at every turn was doing nothing more than trying to take the property and stop the church project. Most impressive, perhaps, was the pastor's restraint.

He represents a large congregation, and many church members showed up at council meetings, but Conley never unleashed the fury of his congregation on the city. He plodded along, pursuing his rights calmly and charitably. Once, when the city offered to give him another piece of property in exchange for his, he refused the deal because it would have required that the city use eminent domain against another property owner. If it was unfair for the city to use it against Cottonwood, he said, it was unfair to use it against anyone else. He turned the other cheek when the city pulled out all the stops to malign the church as a narrow, special interest.

In Crystal Heights, Minnesota, Bob Smith of the Libertarian Party of Minnesota gave local residents moral support and much-needed publicity as they fought to save their World War II-era homes from the wrecking ball. The seventy-eight mostly well-kept properties were targeted for a more upscale multi-unit housing project because they were older and had large lots. Unlike residents in Lakewood, the Minnesota residents got no national attention for their plight. But, according to Smith,[25] residents organized their neighbors, turned out as many as eighty people to council meetings, set up an effective Web site and managed to get the redevelopment agency to meekly back down. That was quite a turnaround. In the early days of the project, city officials treated homeowners with disdain, even using police to keep residents from speaking longer than their allotted time during a public meeting.

Smith captured the Big Brother nature of the project by printing on his Web site the words from the publicly funded redevelopment report:

"The study was conducted to propose a solution to the difficult process of revitalization in the Crystal Heights neighborhood. More than 90 percent of the neighborhood's seventy-eight houses were built as post-World War II structures that do not meet current building-code standards and have since experienced limited renovation and repair.

City staff and decision makers undertook the feasibility study to understand the potential for complete neighborhood redevelopment."[26]

As Smith observed, all the report was saying was the homes are old, of the sort that are common throughout the country. The city didn't want old homes in its midst, so it proposed a plan to bulldoze them and turn the property over to a developer that would build a more upscale project. Smith and his allies used the same argument used successfully by Conley, Ballestero, the Saleets and others: "It can happen to you next!"

On January 15, 2004, the Crystal City Council voted against the plan. As the suburban Minneapolis *Sun Post* newspaper reported the following week, "A standing-room-only audience burst into applause and cheers last week when the Crystal Economic Development Authority (EDA) unanimously voted to stop its long-discussed redevelopment plans for the Crystal Heights neighborhood."[27] Planning officials suggested that the EDA not move forward with the plan, citing a lack of financial resources to begin the project.

But opponents of the plan are sure their efforts contributed to the decision. Of course, the city can reverse itself at any time. "While the city will not be redeveloping the entire area, it will continue to work to redevelop properties one house at a time," the newspaper reported. Which leads me to wonder: Doesn't anyone believe in leaving anyone else alone? Does every neighborhood have to be brand-new before officials will stop abusing eminent domain and subsidies?

"It's important to get organized quickly," Smith said in an interview. "That's why cities do this underground. They are ready do roll by the time anyone finds out about it." Smith and the Libertarian Party of Minnesota have developed a task force with the goal of monitoring cities and agencies that might be proposing such plans, in order to get the information out to residents as soon as possible. Smith's goal is to cultivate friendly officials in every city who might alert the public to any pending redevelopment plan early enough for the public to organize to oppose it. "It doesn't take a lot," Smith added. "You have to convince people that this can happen to them. Most people think they're safe because their house is a little nicer than others."

In the Lake Elsinore, California, redevelopment project described in Chapter 9, a local factory worker, Les Poppa, used his savings to start an ultimately successful battle against a county redevelopment plan. He organized 200 residents to drive to the county seat to oppose the plan, and wasn't dissuaded when the supervisors who wanted to level his neighborhood gave all of them a collective three minutes to speak.

The key to ultimate victory, Poppa said in an interview,[28] was that he and his neighbors conducted their own physical study of the neighborhood showing the small amount of blight. The county hadn't conducted its own physical blight study, and ultimately the judge used that fact to rule in the neighbors' favor. Poppa and his neighbors raised the money to keep attorney Bob Ferguson of Claremont, California, going. A judge tossed out the neighbors' lawsuit twice and was overturned at the appeals-court level twice. Eventually, Ferguson, Poppa and the neighbors agreed to a settlement that had everything in it that they were looking for. The neighborhood would be protected from eminent domain, the county would not be allowed to abuse code enforcement to drive out residents, and all the new tax dollars generated in the area would be used for street lights, curbs and other infrastructure.[29]

Without Poppa's efforts, he and his neighbors would probably have been moved off of their properties by now.

These are tough battles, especially when one's home or business is at stake. Often the battles are fought against all odds, yet sometimes the homeowners win. At the least, as we see in Chapter 3, determined property owners can assure that they get a more reasonable financial offer from the condemning agency, which often tries to get properties on the cheap. These fighters are the heroes of this book. The heroes, too, are the increasing number of judges who are starting to hold agencies to stricter standards and are even recognizing that the Constitution's simple words mean what they say.

UNITING RIGHT AND LEFT

Eminent domain is an issue that promises to unite people of greatly varying ideologies and backgrounds. Liberals understandably get upset at the thought of special interests and big corporations flexing their political muscle to deprive working people of their homes and livelihoods. They also should be upset at the way eminent domain is sometimes used as "ethnic cleansing"—to clear away poorer, predominantly minority neighborhoods so that the properties can be redeveloped in uses that benefit the wealthy. Conservatives and libertarians get upset also at the way government authorities abuse their power, build their budgets and strip away the founders' property-rights protections. The making of a grand coalition to stop eminent domain abuses is out there. But those who benefit financially from the process, along with those ideologically committed to government planning or government-driven economic development, have successfully thwarted reforms. Only recently have the media begun doing their part in telling this story.

Supporters of the system have their rationales and excuses. They are only doing what the law allows, they insist. Their plans are making life better for the "greater good," they say. Often they pretend not to know what all the fuss is about. Many officials claim they have never or rarely used eminent domain to acquire properties. They conveniently forget that the threat of eminent domain is as significant as its actual use. It's like a mugger saying, "I never have shot anyone when I have robbed them."[30] Well, he doesn't have to. The loaded gun pointed at the victim's forehead is all that's usually needed to get the victim to hand over his wallet.

Absurdly, supporters of this system carry on the pretense that the projects they use eminent domain to pursue are genuine public uses. In a March 9 letter to the editor in the *Orange County Register*, Lawrence Hoffman, professor emeritus of real estate economics at Long Beach City College, captured the absurdity:

"In your editorial of March 7 entitled 'Wal-Mart, the source of all evil,' you made the statement that '[c]ities will even use eminent domain to acquire property from private owners and turn it over to Wal-Mart. . . . . Such actions of course are wrong.'

"Contrary to your opinion, it is not wrong. If eminent domain were not used, municipal progress would be impossible. It is a rare occasion that a city will condemn private property that is not in a state of functional or economic obsolescence. These properties are most often a blight on the city, or in direct disagreement with growth and city planning."

The letter gives new life to the term, "ivory tower." The ugly truth is that American cities (and other government entities) understand that they can take anything they want for any reason. "Public" use is anything they say it is. Increasing the tax base is a justification for taking a privately owned shopping center and giving it to a big campaign contributor who wants to build a mega-mall. Developers are thrilled, given how time-consuming and expensive it is to negotiate for property the old-fashioned, free-market way. Redevelopers get to buy the condemned land after the city clears it, for a lot less than what the city paid for it with taxpayer funds. It's called "land write-down." Sometimes redevelopers pay only a token one dollar.[31] Often, it's the little guy who gets taken for a ride. The big companies have high-priced lawyers on retainer to protect their rights, but the owners of mom and pop businesses don't have such resources at their disposal. Some critics have compared the current system to mercantilism, in which big business and big government work hand-in-hand to advance common interests. Those interests, of course, are rarely the interests of average property owners. As Chapter 8 explains, an entire industry has emerged around redevelopment and the abuse of eminent domain. There are special attorneys, consultants, pollsters and bond dealers who profit mightily from the eminent domain industry. Many retailers and corporations have become adept at leveraging cities' land-clearing abilities to gain a competitive edge. Of course, without the willingness of government officials to abuse their powers, no Costco, nor Home Depot, nor General Motors could take what isn't theirs.

Although the Eminent Domain Industry has been dealt a handful of unfavorable court rulings in the last few years, it presses on largely undeterred. There are too many profitable deals to be made for the consultants, too many below-market properties to be obtained for the big-box retailers, and too much new tax revenue to be gained by governments. Congress has so far shown no interest in acting to stop the abuse by reaffirming the Constitution, so the fight is waged on myriad fronts by myriad property owners. There are political battles, public relations battles and state and federal court battles, but no united front.

As property rights erode, so does the freedom and quality of life enjoyed by Americans. As Chapter 4 explains, property rights are human rights. Property is not about greed and avarice, but about giving individuals choices, freedoms, the ability to create their own economic futures. The right to property is fundamentally a human right. The loss of property rights is a slow erosion—so slow most of us don't even notice. We don't notice, that is, until agents of the government decide they want to take our family homestead and turn it over to a developer to build newer houses that pay higher rates of property tax. We don't notice until our church is driven off its land because it doesn't pay as much in taxes as a retail center. We don't notice until our dreams must give way to the dreams of the planners.

THE EMINENT DOMAIN MATRIX

In the popular science fiction movie, *The Matrix*, the hero Neo is first learning that the world in which he lives is not what it appears to be. A computer programmer who works in a downtown office and lives in a seedy apartment, Neo is about to have all his assumptions challenged by Morpheus, whom he meets as a result of his late-night computer hacking.

Morpheus is going to tell Neo about the Matrix.

"Do you want to know what it is?" Morpheus asks. "The Matrix is everywhere. It is all around us, even now in this very room. . . . It is the world that has been pulled over your eyes to blind you from the truth."

"What truth?" asks Neo.

"That you are a slave, Neo," responds Morpheus. "Like everyone else, you were born into bondage, born into a prison that you cannot smell or taste or touch. A prison for your mind."

Morpheus then asks Neo to make a choice: "You take the blue pill, the story ends; you wake up in your bed and believe whatever you want to believe. You take the red pill, you stay in Wonderland, and I show you how deep the rabbit hole goes. Remember, all I'm offering is the truth, nothing more." Neo, of course, takes the red pill, and he learns the unthinkable. His entire world is a computer creation implanted into the minds of human beings.

This is where readers have a choice: Take the blue pill, close the book and go back to your comfortable illusions. Or take the red pill, keep reading further, and see how far down the slippery slope our nation has traveled. Nothing is what it seems, at least when it comes to property rights. But learning the truth is the first step toward restoring our laws to where they should be.

2. WE'RE FROM THE GOVERNMENT
AND WE'RE HERE FOR YOUR PROPERTY

Property is private and enterprise is free until and unless outcomes do not conform to the preconceptions of big government planners or big industry planners. In that case, any means are deemed permissible to make reality conform.

> — Llewellyn Rockwell Jr.,
> President of the Ludwig von
> Mises Institute, Auburn,
> Alabama[32]

Homeowners in a large well-kept neighborhood in Garden Grove, California, a working-class suburb of about 170,000 people thirty-four miles south of Los Angeles, labored under the same delusion that most Americans labor under. They believed, quite simply, that as American citizens they were free to chart their own lives, to invest in their property as they desire, to raise their children in the neighborhood they choose, and to live their lives without molestation by government officials—provided they pay their taxes, keep their property from falling into dramatic disrepair, and live as law-abiding citizens.

Then, one warm day in April, 2002 hundreds of Garden Grove residents learned firsthand that they, along with Americans in virtually every state, are not quite as free as previously thought. Their future, their economic investments, their homes and their businesses, are theirs only as long as government officials decide they can keep them. Welcome to the world of eminent domain, as practiced today.

The residents say their nightmare started when a state senator gave them a copy of a map the city manager, community development director and mayor had been shopping around to potential investors. A large neighborhood with about 400 houses was encircled. Stamped across the area were the words: "theme park." Apparently, city officials had targeted the area for a new use. They were still developing their plans, but city leaders figured the 1960s-era tract houses south of the city's core should be bulldozed and turned into a tax-generating theme park, or some other private use. There was no developer in mind, just an idea in the head of the city's top planners and bureaucrats. They were going to do what they had been doing on a smaller scale across the city: play land developer by condemning property, then trying to market the acquired tracts to some big out-of-town development company.[33]

Residents of the neighborhood couldn't believe their eyes. Could this be legal? they wondered.

City officials acted shocked that homeowners would react the way that they did. The city first tried twisting the facts, arguing that there were no specific plans for the property. Then they claimed the theme park was just one concept created by consultants.[34] Mainly, officials argued that the "map wasn't ready for public viewing just yet," as community development official Matt Fertal put it in an *Orange County Register* article. It was almost unbelievable: Their only apparent concern was how the document was leaked from the city offices.

"We are coming down Harbor Boulevard to develop the city; that's no secret," Mayor Bruce Broadwater, known throughout the city as "the Bulldozer" for his abuses of eminent domain, said. "But these are just ideas. We haven't implemented anything. People are panicking over nothing."[35] Harbor is the main drag that leads from Disneyland, which is located in Anaheim, just north of the Garden Grove city limits.

City officials insisted that the "theme park" designation was premature. There are all sorts of developments that could go into that area, they said. The city simply is looking for some type of "anchor development," Fertal added.[36] Officials were too oblivious to community concerns, too immersed in their world of government-run redevelopment, to grasp the idiocy of what they were saying. Earth to Garden Grove: The targeted residents didn't care whether a theme park or an auto mall or a nuclear waste dump was slated for their development. No one doubted that the theme park was just one early idea. No one thought the city had final plans for the area—under state law, the city couldn't ink a deal without a host of notices and public hearings. But local residents, who had viewed the city's many heavy-handed redevelopment efforts before, knew that whatever was going to happen was going to be bad for them. It was going to change their lives forever.

The "anchor development" could be a theme park or a shopping mall or an entertainment district similar to failed projects proposed on other locations by the city at other times. It didn't matter. Whatever would go there would mean the current owners and renters would have to vacate their homes. Residents were shocked that city officials could begin the process of taking their property not for a public use, but for a private one. And they could do so without any project in mind, but on speculation. City officials had become land speculators, except none of the officials or even the city budget was subject to risk. They were speculating on the backs of the current, mostly working-class homeowners. As the city would shop around the property, the property owners' lives would be placed on hold. Their homes would be rendered worthless, given that no one in their right mind would buy a house that was sooner or later targeted for demolition.

There would be no just compensation for the owners of the properties—at least not until a final deal was inked. That could take, by the mayor's own admission, five years or more. There's nothing to worry about, the mayor said. Just ideas, long-term plans. But who could retire or sell their property? Who would make investments in their homes given the uncertainty? Who could go on with their lives?

THE LETTER

Three months before the "theme park" map made its way out of City Hall prematurely and into the hands of concerned citizens, city officials had sent a letter to the area's residents warning them about what was to come. It didn't spark much concern. That's because city officials did everything they could to make the letter sound as innocuous as possible. Verla and Leo Lambert, residents of the neighborhood since 1956, ignored it until their new neighbor, Manny Ballestero, referred to in Chapter 1, alerted them to its substance.[37] Verla thought it was a similar letter to the one she had received years earlier offering free paint jobs to people in the city.

Titled, "Notice of Second Project Area Committee Election and Related Public Meetings," the January 28, 2002, letter offered this unintelligible information:

"In connection with the proposed amendment to the Redevelopment Plan (the 'Amendment') for the Garden Grove Community Development Project (the 'Project') being prepared by the Garden Grove Agency for Community Development (the 'Agency'), the Planning Commission and the Agency approved preliminary boundaries for the area proposed to be added to the Project (the 'added Territory'). Thereafter, in January 2002, the preliminary boundaries of the Added Territory were modified by the Planning Commission and Agency, which modified Added Territory boundaries are shown on the accompanying map."[38]

In English, this mumbo-jumbo is saying that the redevelopment area has been expanded to include homes in the neighborhood of those receiving the letter, and that, in accordance with state law, elections are held for a committee representing those who live in the targeted areas.

One would need to be a lawyer to understand the letter, which is designed to meet legal requirements, not inform residents in plain language that their homes are going to be placed in a redevelopment area and subjected to a government taking. It was a reminder of the level of subterfuge that was behind the city's effort.

Other required letters were even more misleading. In May 2002 the city sent homeowners a letter informing them that the expanded redevelopment area was about to come before the City Council for final approval. Here's how the agency worded it: "The Amendment is intended to be a tool to enable the Agency to continue its efforts to promote and implement community development projects and programs which lessen or eliminate existing blight and prevent the spread of new blight within the Existing Project and to initiate similar community development activities within the Added Territory."

How exciting. The city is targeting blight and using all the tools available to it. Residents should be happy about that. At least that was the tone of the letter. Only problem—the blight is the resident's home, the resident's neighborhood. The city plans to stop the spread of blight by leveling the resident's property and marketing the land to a theme-park developer, or to some other big developer who would build some sort of "anchor development."

Here was my interpretation of the letter from June 2002, from my *Orange County Register* column:[39]

> Dear (soon to be ex-) Garden Grove resident:
>
> The city of Garden Grove wants to invite you to participate in an exciting once-in-a-lifetime opportunity. In fact, it's such a great opportunity that it's one we won't let you refuse.
>
> You have been selected to be part of our Expanded Redevelopment Area. That's a fancy way of saying that Mayor Bruce Broadwater and other city officials such as City Manager George Tindall and Community

Development Director Matt Fertal have targeted your neighborhood for extinction. As the Monty Python troupe might put it, your neighborhood will soon be an ex-neighborhood. But we know this is no time for humor.

As our letter points out, your inclusion in the redevelopment area will mean an elimination of existing blight and "construction of new and upgrading of existing public facilities and infrastructure, promoting and facilitating economic development and job growth, providing additional affordable housing opportunities, and generally helping to improve the quality of life for residents and businesses . . ..

That's great, isn't?

Here's the rub: The existing blight we are referring to is your homes, your businesses, and your neighborhood. Yes, through massive tax subsidies and outrageous debt spending, city officials will try to provide some improvements to the quality of life. Unfortunately, it won't be your lives whose quality will have been improved.

Sorry, but you'll be off somewhere in the Inland Empire [a lower-cost inland area thirty miles or more away in Riverside and San Bernardino counties], which will probably be the only place you'll be able to afford to live once we take your properties and give you what our appraisers deem to be fair-market value. Look on the bright side. When this is all said and done, you'll like living in Hemet more than you ever thought you would.

As Mayor Broadwater told the *Orange County Register* recently, the city of Garden Grove is marching

down Harbor Boulevard, with the intention of bulldozing businesses, homes and entire neighborhoods—
anything that gets in the way of what city officials
believe is progress.

Just because you bought your home fair and
square, have lived there for forty years or so and have
made deep and lasting friendships with your neighbors doesn't give you any special claim to your
property.

You need to understand this reality: Under redevelopment law, private-property rights no longer
really exist. The concept of willing buyers and willing
sellers is history. Under redevelopment, cities have
the broadest power to take properties by force and
give them to any favored developer, for virtually any
reason officials choose.

Get over it.

Regular old neighborhoods like yours may be
well-kept and safe places to raise kids, but they do
not bring in much revenue, and they aren't too
impressive-looking to the tourists who take a wrong
exit from the 22 Freeway when they're looking for
Disneyland.

So your neighborhood needs to go. The way we
can legally take your property depends upon our
ability to call it blighted.

It's not really blighted under a *Webster's Dictionary*
definition, but the law allows us to deem as blighted
virtually anything—and there's always a consultant
willing to produce the necessary blight finding. It's a
complicated process, and we don't expect any of you
to understand how it works. We've been doing this

for a very long time. So it's far easier to do what the Planning Commission suggested recently, and simply trust us to do what's best for you.

Our real constituents, developers, love us for our land-clearing services and generous subsidies. Imagine how hard it would be for them to operate in a free market and actually have to negotiate with individuals to buy their land. You need to have more compassion.

We need to take your homes for the health of the entire city. You see, the mayor, staff and council majority have big plans for Garden Grove. They don't like that it is a nice, working-class city filled with people like you who work hard and play by the rules.

It's not very impressive to be the mayor of Garden Grove when one travels to League of Cities meetings. It's far more impressive to be the mayor of a big-shot city with world-class resorts and hotels, fancy shopping malls, sports teams and big budgets. We want to be more like Anaheim, where officials get to hobnob at ballparks and Mickey Mouse theme parks. To implement all of the big plans means that some people—that's you, in case you're not following—have to make sacrifices for the good of everyone. You don't want to be viewed as selfish. . . .

There's a practical side also.

Unless redevelopment agencies keep floating more debt (such as the $23 million bond we just floated, using city properties as collateral) and taking more properties in the hopes of developing bigger and better projects, they cannot keep servicing their previous debt.

Unfortunately, a pesky school teacher named Manny Ballestero has organized hundreds of residents to oppose our plan. He keeps reminding his neighbors that once their homes are in a redevelopment zone the homes lose value, and that redevelopment puts their lives on hold indefinitely. The city might take their properties, or it might not, which means it's hard to make plans for the future, or make investments in the property while the wrecking ball hangs over their heads.

He's correct, but he's not looking at the big picture. Doesn't he want his grandkids to have a nice, modern roller-coaster to ride on right here in the middle of Garden Grove?

We've done everything we can to encourage this troublemaker to get with the program, but he insisted that a deal we offered residents—no eminent domain for five years—isn't legally binding. We even gerrymandered the proposed redevelopment zone to eliminate opponents of the project from the Project Area Committee, yet opposition continues to grow.

Honestly, we're frightened by a referendum Mr. Ballestero is organizing. If he can get enough signatures to put our plan on a citywide ballot, we know we're in trouble. Redevelopment always loses at the polls, and these battles often have broader political consequences. Many a council member has lost a seat over eminent domain squabbles.

It would be so much nicer if you, the targeted (soon to be ex-) residents of Garden Grove, simply do what people do in other countries: Accept the dictates of the officials and forget about lawyers, constitutional rights and the referendum process. Those things just get in the way of responsible planning. Just accept your fate like decent folk and everyone will be happy. Then we can get back to the next business before us—targeting other neighborhoods for new redevelopment schemes.

Sincerely,
Your Friendly Officials at the Garden Grove
Department of Community Development

BLIGHT IS MIGHT

In Garden Grove, and throughout the United States, redevelopment agencies have the right to use eminent domain to promote new development. Various states have various names for the process and for their agencies, but the concept is the same. Because redevelopment law originally was designed to help cities clean up decrepit areas, the beginning of the process of using the eminent domain tool is the designation of blight. Cities must go through a formal process of calling the targeted area "blighted." Once the area earns that designation, it cannot easily be removed.

Garden Grove is an older working-class city developed mostly in the 1950s and 1960s. The city had only about 5,000 residents as late as 1941. From then on, the area—like much of the Southern California region—boomed. As the *Garden Grove Journal* explained in a November 30, 2003 article,[40] "The war created a tremendous land boom in Southern California. Many servicemen and defense workers who had come to the area during the war fell in love with the region—especially Orange County—and the rush was on. In the 1950s, the growth became explosive. Developers bought up orange orchards and subdivided them into neat rows of suburban homes." The city's population soared to 84,000 by 1960, and then to nearly 170,000 today.

Over the years, the city changed from a predominantly white community to a heavily immigrant one. Garden Grove, along with neighboring Westminster, is home to Little Saigon—the largest Vietnamese population outside Vietnam. The first Vietnamese settled in the area after being airlifted out of South Vietnam following the Vietnam War. They landed at the nearby El Toro Marine Corps Air Station. Many who fled in other ways (i.e., as boat people) also settled in the area. The city has become a cultural mix, as large influxes of Koreans, Mexicans and Arabs also turned the commercial strips into vibrant centers of international restaurants, grocery stores, shopping plazas. Some critics refer to this older city, which is less upscale in its appearance than many wealthy nearby Orange County communities, as Garbage Grove. City officials used that unkind moniker as evidence why their so-called blight removal activities are so important. In reality, Garden Grove is a nice community, with little significant blight—at least by the standards of older East Coast and Midwest cities.

Although Garden Grove doesn't look brand new, it mostly is a vibrant place filled with small businesses—especially those for people on their first rung up the economic ladder. One can find amazing delicacies and unusual businesses throughout the city. It's a place where families might not speak English, but can earn enough money by running a grocery store or dry cleaner to send their kids to the University of California at Berkeley or the University of Southern California. More often then not, then, the city's redevelopment efforts fall the hardest on the small businesses that are the backbone of the city's economy. They fall hardest on those businesses owned by immigrants who aren't skilled at the English language, let alone at the complexities of the U.S. legal system. Critics complain that Garden Grove officials purposefully target those business owners who are least able to fight for their rights in court. City officials say that's nonsense, and say their efforts fall hardest on immigrants because the city has such a large immigrant population. Whatever the motives, the city hires some of the county's biggest, most prestigious private law firms to put these business owners/ "troublemakers" through the wringer.

The neighborhood targeted for the theme park doesn't look like blight to the naked eye, even though there are some rundown properties in the commercial areas around it. Even City Manager George Tindall told a group of people who live there it doesn't look like blight.[41] Blight, as advocates of redevelopment and eminent domain often point out, is a legal term rather than a descriptive term. That's another way of saying that lawyers, city officials and judges have twisted a perfectly good word to mean anything they want it to mean. In one failed Garden Grove redevelopment project, the city declared as blighted a shopping center that the agency already had redeveloped a few years earlier.

Blight now means an area a city wants to take by force. Nothing more. The city merely goes through a legal process (studies, hearings and a redevelopment agency vote) of designating it as blight and then, voila, it is blighted. The abuse of this word has gotten to be too much even for courts that typically have allowed local officials to get away with just about anything. In *Beach-Courchesne v. City of Diamond Bar*, involving an eastern Los Angeles County city that tried to declare a commercial area blighted, a state court ruled that such a finding was inappropriate. In its official publications, the city bragged about what an upscale place it is, but then it called its commercial areas blighted when it wanted to create a redevelopment area to subsidize new commercial tenants. The court found that the city's idea of blight included such horrors as chipping paint and issued a ruling requiring far more extensive blight studies before blight can be declared. The decision was striking for its rarity.[42] "To make a finding of blight, a consultant is hired to conduct a study," according to the book, *Redevelopment: The Unknown Government*,[43] a guide published by a California-based organization opposed to government-backed redevelopment programs that foster eminent domain abuse. "New redevelopment areas are largely driven by city staff who choose the consultant with the approval of the city council. Consultants know their job is not to determine if there is blight, but to declare blighted whatever community conditions may be.

"Once the consultant's blight findings are ratified, a city may create or expand a redevelopment area. Voter approval is never asked. . . . A growing number of law firms specialize in redevelopment. . . . Their livelihood depends on the aggressive use of redevelopment and increasingly imaginative definitions of blight."[44]

The Lamberts' house, where a dozen neighbors gathered to talk to this columnist and to organize the fight against the redevelopment plan, is a well-maintained tract house on a tree-lined street surrounded by other well-maintained tract houses. The next-door neighbors had just sunk $80,000 into a total renovation of their property. There are scattered exceptions, but the sense is one of a nice, older neighborhood, albeit one where the properties are about forty years old.

If this is blight, then most of America is blighted. City officials know that, so they tried to intimidate the local residents. Organizer Manny Ballestero said the mayor told him: "There is the nice Mayor Broadwater and the one that isn't very nice. I can be that if I need to."[45] He then called Ballestero a mischief-maker. Ballestero shrugged off the threat and the name-calling and responded this way: "It's nothing personal, but this is about our homes. You want to take our homes, and we're not going to let you."

How did it come to this?

DEBT, TAXES, HOTELS

Most observers would have to wonder, "Why in heavens would a city want to displace hundreds of its residents and replace a neighborhood with a theme park?" It doesn't make obvious sense at quick glance. But there are a few reasons. Two of them are most significant. Number one is the quest for new tax revenue. Number two is the love of central planning, a temptation well understood by any observer of government abuses.

First, city officials are always trying to increase revenue to their general fund. Residences, older businesses, churches and many of the traditional things found in most cities don't pay significant amounts of taxes. In California, property taxes are capped thanks to Proposition 13, a tax-limiting constitutional amendment passed in 1978 to keep people from being taxed out of their homes as property values soared. In other states, property taxes aren't limited, but it is politically unpopular for localities to keep hiking the tax rates or inflating the property valuations. Rather than cut spending, or hold the line on pensions for public-employee unions, city officials look for ways to maximize tax generation on private property. That typically means trying to lure Wal-Mart, Home Depot, Costco and other big-box retailers that pay phenomenal amounts of sales tax per square foot. Auto malls and national-chain hotels are other sought-after developments.

In Garden Grove, officials have been vocal about the need to find new sources of revenue. Because the city is located just south of Anaheim, home to Disneyland, Garden Grove has staked its future on gobbling up the crumbs from its big-city neighbor to the north. It has built one new hotel after another, running up enormous public debt to subsidize hotels that often go begging for tourists, given that most people would rather stay within walking distance of the Anaheim theme parks.

As to number two, even the best-intentioned officials often look at their cities like they are monopoly boards, promoting central plans to regenerate old downtowns or create the kind of business environment or neighborhoods preferred by the officials. They love to see new edifices—city buildings, shopping centers, whatever.

Garden Grove is redevelopment's perfect storm. There, officials combine the love of central planning with a need for tax revenue. Throw in the city's inferiority complex, and the stage is set for some of the most aggressive use of eminent domain in the country. City officials are proud of it. They have boasted in newspapers and in a city video of their aggressive redevelopment efforts. When he ran for re-election in 2002, Mayor Broadwater showed his pride in his nick-name, "the Bulldozer," by posing in a campaign photo next to a real-life bulldozer. He is proud of his role in knocking down old buildings and replacing them with new ones. The problem is, Broadwater and his council and staff allies are knocking down people's homes, their dreams, their businesses. They are driving away people who don't want to leave. They are ridding the city of its character and replacing it with unexceptional chain stores and hotels that will long be dependent on government subsidies to make their way in the marketplace.

In a taxpayer-funded video distributed by police officers to city residents prior to a public hearing on the theme-park plan, the city said that it needs to "find the right balance"[46] as it plans for the future. The city has a relatively low tax base, aging infrastructure and spreading blight, the video claims. Redevelopment—backed by the threat of eminent domain—is one of the only "tools" the city has to correct the problem, given that the city has little open land to lure new developments. That was the video spin, anyway.

The video bragged about the new hotels that have gone up along main commercial streets. It even included clips of residents removed from previous developments to make way for the new hotels. "They did me a big favor," said one man, photographed beside an oceanfront property. "They took my place in Garden Grove and gave me paradise." Said a woman also removed by the city from her longtime home:

"Thank God." She said she couldn't be happier. Forget about the surreal quality of the tape, or the echoes of totalitarianism—citizens
thanking the State for depriving them of their property. It's for the
greater good of Garden Grove, after all! What's astounding is what the
city did not say. It didn't explain that the bad economics of previous
redevelopment decisions put the city in a difficult fiscal situation.

"The proposed theme park is perhaps the most grandiose solution to a problem created by the city's effort to lure Disneyland
tourists into several hotels subsidized by taxpayers," wrote *OC
Weekly* in a June 14, 2002, article. "Since September 11, the tourists
haven't been coming in numbers sufficient to justify the huge
amount of money the city has invested in the project. Hence the
theme park—a redevelopment solution to a debt problem created by
redevelopment."[47]

Redevelopment requires cities to run up large debts to pay for
subsidies to big businesses and developers. Cities need to keep
enough funds rolling in to pay for the large debts they incur. If their
projections are off, officials might refinance a project, the way many
homeowners keep refinancing their homes to pay off an unsustain-
able level of credit-card debt. Redevelopment creates an endless
shell game as city officials become increasingly desperate to fund
new projects to pay off the debt on ill-performing old projects.

Garden Grove invested heavily in hotels, but then, by officials'
own admission, realized that the city needs its own attraction to
keep the hotels filled. So it looked for land to develop into a major
theme park or regional attraction. Previous efforts to create a
Riverwalk,[48] along an unattractive "river," came up dry, so the theme
park was the next goal of the central planners. Once bad decisions
are made, more bad decisions must be made to sustain the previous
bad decisions. That's an apt summary of redevelopment. Without
eminent domain, little of this would be possible. Homeowners
would simply tell city officials to take their grandiose plans and stuff

them. The agency could run up some debt if officials could assemble some parcels, but without the ability to use force to take property, officials would not be able to hatch the large schemes that have created so much fiscal and emotional ruin.

In the *Orange County Register* on September 3, 1998,[49] Tiffany Horan explains the fiscal conundrum in Garden Grove: "The (redevelopment) agency predicts a $2.2 million deficit in 2000. About $3.4 million of agency-owned land must still be sold to balance this year's budget. The agency is using $4.5 million in city money (which is separate from redevelopment money) for expenditures this year." Furthermore, the agency has tried to shortchange the local school district for the "pass-through" funds it owes. These are dollars agencies pay to schools given that redevelopment, through a complex financing scheme described later in this book, siphons dollars from more traditional government services. In 2002, the city floated a $23 million bond to cover its redevelopment debt, using city property— a golf course, parks, City Council chambers—as collateral. No wonder officials are so desperate to bring in more revenue to prop up their previous, failed schemes.

Even Mayor Broadwater, when he first ran for his post in the 1980s, understood as much. In a brochure with the banner headline, "BOONDOGGLE!," the then-mayoral candidate argued that his opponent "paved the way for passage of a controversial 450-room high-rise hotel after heavy lobbying . . . "[50] Then his opponent pushed forward a plan to use $8 million in public money to help pay for the hotel, which soon failed. Then the city provided a $2 million bailout, and it too failed. It was a damning account of redevelopment, and how good taxpayer money follows bad, yet soon enough the new boss would be the same as the old boss. It's an example of how difficult it is for officials to avoid the lure of redevelopment to prop up their budgets. And once they embrace this means of financing city operations, they must rely increasingly on bond debt and . . . on the use of eminent domain to take properties from unwilling sellers. It's a vicious cycle.

THE NEIGHBORS REVOLT

The June 2002 City Council meeting, at which Garden Grove officials were voting on whether to add the neighborhood to the redevelopment zone and thereby start the process of condemning hundreds of homes, was one of those events that restores one's faith in the average citizen—and makes one sick to one's stomach at the audacity of special interests, public employee unions and city officials.

The crowd of about 1,000 people flowed outside the council chambers. People carried "Save Our Homes" signs.[51] One after another, average, working-class residents implored the council to save their neighborhood. To believers in the founding principles of property rights, it was a disturbing spectacle. This isn't some tin-pot dictatorship or socialist republic. Why should people have to beg their leaders to leave them alone? Why should they have to listen to interested parties, who stand to gain financially from the theft of their property, talk about the Greater Good?

One resident of the doomed neighborhood could speak only in Spanish. But everyone could understand her talk about her "casa" and her "familia." "Where do we go?" asked another resident, speaking before the council chambers. "This is the Little City of Horrors, where they see only parcels. We are the city. We have the right to live in our city and to move when we choose to move. This is wrong. You might have the legal right, but not the moral right. Leave us alone."[52] That's a sentiment as old as America's founding: Leave us alone. City officials were unmoved. They droned on and on about the city's "fiscal deficiencies." The city manager talked about the costs of running the city and the amount of dollars siphoned from local government by the state. "We need to look for additional revenue sources," he said. Officials ranged from stone-faced to condescending. They appeared aggravated that they had to listen to all those pesky property owners.

A city-hired consultant from a firm called Urban Futures was booed repeatedly by the agitated homeowners as he talked deadpan, in bureaucratese, about his firm's "evidentiary record" pointing to blight in the neighborhood.[53] These were real people's homes and lives, but the consultant spoke as if the neighborhood was nothing more than a mass of boards and chipping paint. As he explained, "deleterious conditions" did not have to exist in all or most of the properties for the area to be labeled "blighted." But he did find that the area under examination was an example of "economic blight" because it was not as affluent as many other areas of the city.

Consider what he was saying. Any time an official could find an area or a property in a city that is below the average in value, then it could be declared economic blight and taken by force and given to a more "worthy" owner. If that's true, then property rights no longer exist.

There were other infuriating aspects of the evening. The public-safety officials who are charged with protecting the city's residents came down squarely on the side of the government. The police representative testified to the importance of the project to keep the city police budget funded, even though city police had no pressing funding problems. The Garden Grove Fire Fighters handed out a letter to people entering the meeting thanking the council members for their support. "We would like to remind the citizens of Garden Grove that it was not to [sic] long ago that our city was looking at the possibility of not being able to fund its own fire and paramedic service. . . . Thank you for having the courage to make the necessary choices to enable Garden Grove to be a safer place to live, work and play."[54]

The firefighters didn't come right out and support the abuse of eminent domain to take hundreds of homes, and the displacement of as many as 1,000 residents, but "wink, wink," it's not that hard to understand what fire officials were saying. Protect our budgets, and let property rights and freedom be damned.

Self-interest was evident everywhere. General managers of hotels, wearing designer suits that contrasted with the predominantly denim attire of the mostly working-class residents, sang the praises of redevelopment. Laura Archuleta, president of Jamboree Housing, a company that provides government-subsidized "affordable housing," supported the plan because redevelopment law in California requires that 20 percent of future property tax funds in the area are redirected to low-income housing. It was odd. As I wrote in the *Orange County Register* at the time, "Archuleta was backing a plan that would throw thousands of real people out of their affordable, non-subsidized homes so that government funds could be diverted to her company to develop subsidized affordable homes for other people."[55]

Welcome to the wacky world of redevelopment, where not all affordable housing counts as affordable housing, where blight doesn't mean what most of us think of as blight, and where property rights don't even register in discussions. Without eminent domain, very little of this insanity would be possible.

Garden Grove is represented by a state senator, an assemblyman and a U.S. congresswoman who are liberal Democrats, and who make frequent noises about standing up for the little guy against the big predators. Yet none of them was heard from in any significant way, although state Sen. Joe Dunn's office provided the initial map to the residents. None of these defenders of the working guy would lift a finger to help the residents. None of the Latino activist groups that have a field day accusing businesses and government agencies of discrimination against Latinos played any role in defending this heavily Latino neighborhood. The residents had to fight this battle themselves, yet they managed quite well.

In the end, the sheer force of the anti-redevelopment sentiment, born of the project's amazing overreach, combined with a threatened initiative (redevelopment and eminent domain almost always lose at the polls) and a coming election convinced all five council members, even the mayor, to remove the residential neighborhood from the redevelopment plan. Small businesses and apartment buildings were not exempt, and later efforts to slowly expand the redevelopment area proceeded.

The neighbors rejoiced in their victory, but basically packed up their bags and went home. They never turned their success into a movement, which left them vulnerable to future attacks by city officials who still covet more property to market to out-of-town developers. The mayor was re-elected and has not changed his basic philosophy of development. All the same problems still remain, even though the fight was well worth the effort. Any property saved from eminent domain is a small step forward for property rights and freedom. But this is one sleeping dog that's not going to lie quietly for very long.

THE LESSONS

Clearly, when citizens band together to fight eminent domain proceedings, they can get further than citizens who are unfortunate enough to be targeted by themselves or in small groups. Garden Grove officials failed in their naked land grab simply because they moved away from their typical strategy. Earlier victims of Garden Grove's redevelopment schemes weren't nearly so lucky, given that they and the properties they owned or leased were picked off one at a time. It is the "united we stand, divided we fall" maxim. Hundreds of angry people showing up at city council meetings and starting initiative drives have a way of getting a city council's attention, even a council that is committed to using redevelopment and eminent domain.

But an occasional disgruntled victim of a city's land-clearing policies, and an occasional news story buried in the local section of the
newspaper, don't register on the radar screen—especially when
news stories celebrate the opening of every brand new building.
When the renowned economist Frederic Bastiat wrote about government projects, he wrote about the concept of the "seen and the
unseen."[56] Everyone can see the bridge the government built and
can't imagine life without it. But people don't see the things that
weren't built because government took the money out of the pockets of people who would have invested it in myriad private ways.

The same economic principle is true for redevelopment. People
see the new hotels built on subsidies, and they see the auto malls and
big-box stores. They don't see the mountain of debt that finances the
charade, and the many ways those dollars would be put to oftentimes better uses. They don't see the future obligations that will be
committed to finance these projects when they don't perform as well
as expected. Most important, they don't see the business owners and
homeowners who have had their livelihoods and homesteads taken
from them by force. So many redevelopment projects are built on the
backs of these victims of eminent domain, but once the project is
completed, no one thinks about their sacrifices.

It is the essence of a free society that individuals—not government bureaucrats—get to navigate their own lives. That doesn't
mean anything goes. The basic premise of a free society is that as
long as you don't harm others or trample on others' rights, you are
pretty much free to do as you choose. The tort system is a check on
those who would harm others. And, of course, America has become
a highly regulated land, where government rules limit many of the
things we can do. I think we've gone far to the excess in terms of regulation. But even with an excess of government rules, Americans are
freer than most other peoples. We pride ourselves on a legal system
that still protects individuals against the ravages of the state, and in

an economic system that vests most choices in the hands of private citizens, not in the hands of central planners in government agencies. In America, the business chooses its own best location, not the city manager. The private owner, not the bureaucrat, gets to decide what to buy, when to sell, where to move and what terms are acceptable. Yet as cities abuse eminent domain and micromanage the development process, this tradition is eroded.

Garden Grove is a prime example of what is happening throughout the United States. Increasingly, government officials believe they should make the choices. They want Garden Grove to be different than it is. They want high-taxpaying national chain stores in the prime locations, not small, immigrant-owned businesses. They want to negotiate the terms and decide who does what, rather than leave these decisions to the marketplace. The marketplace is not some force of nature, as critics depict it. It is the sum total of the private decisions every individual makes. It is not cold and heartless, as some depict it. The market is us—and it's a far more reliable way to drive decisions, including those about the use of property and the type of business that should occupy a site, than letting central planners make them.

During the Soviet Union's existence, Russian citizens used to laugh at the way the central planners would overproduce certain items that nobody wanted, yet allow shortages in the things people needed. There's no way any individual, or group of individuals, no matter how wise or public-spirited could possess the proper amount of information needed to assure that the right products are produced at the right price in the right quantity and delivered to the right places.

Yet the market does make these decisions, billions of them every day. This is basic economics, but a rehash of it is necessary because the philosophy that allows an entire neighborhood to be deprived of its homes to make way for a city-proposed theme park is based more on the Soviet model than the traditional free-market American model. Individual homeowners and business owners should decide what to do with the land they own or lease. They should decide whether a location is acceptable or not. They should decide whether to stay in Garden Grove or to move somewhere else. The small businesses Garden Grove redevelopment officials are driving off their land are there because they have a willing clientele. By contrast, the city—like those Soviet bureaucrats—is creating subsidized hotels that can't stay filled, and it now must build a theme park to create potential guests to stay in them. This doesn't make sense.

It's dangerous to treat property rights so shabbily. As John Adams said, "The moment the idea is admitted into society that property is not as sacred as the law of God, and that there is not a force of law and public justice to protect it, anarchy and tyranny commence."[57]

The Garden Grove experience proves the enduring truth of this founder's words.

City officials wanted to bulldoze well-kept tract homes such as this one to make way for a theme park or other large development.

3. UNJUST COMPENSATION

Thou shalt not steal.

— Exodus 20:15

When discussing eminent domain horror stories with government officials and other defenders of the practice, one will often hear a refrain of this sort: "None of this is any big deal, really, because the victims of eminent domain must be made financially whole, under the law." But, just as the Constitution's clear requirement that government only take property for "public" use has been twisted and contorted so that a Costco is a public use, so too has its demand that governments pay "just compensation" been distorted so that woefully low offers are considered "just." Governments have found all sorts of ways to deny appropriate financial payments to homeowners and business owners, and even when a fair-market value eventually is paid, it's questionable whether anything can pay for the torment and tumult—often including months or years of court battles and business losses—the owner has been put through. Keep in mind that the courts define fair-market value as less than what would be paid in a voluntary transaction, so in any eminent domain proceeding the victim, by law, will not be made whole.[58]

"You have to pay dearly to be treated fairly," is how Steven Strooh, vice president of Des Moines Blue Print Co. Inc. in Des Moines, Iowa, puts it, after having had the business he works for taken by the city in 2000 to make way for a new downtown office building. "What they intended for evil has turned into good," Strooh explains. "That doesn't mean selling Joseph into slavery was the right thing to do, just because it all turned out okay."[59]

The story of Des Moines Blue Print is worth reviewing in detail because it is, from the property owner's standpoint, a relative success story. The business managed to find a decent new location, it managed to get a decent valuation, it managed to keep most of its clientele. In other words, the company's experiences are as good as it gets once a property owner is targeted by a government for eminent domain. And as good as things went, the process was still a nightmare from the owner's perspective—a process that required intense time and financial commitments to assure that he didn't get abused. Even so, the owner still lost tens of thousands of dollars in the process.

It was March 2000, and Strooh and company owner Leonard Ainsworth were sitting in the office going over the day's work. One of the company's employees knocked on the door and asked, "Have you seen the newspaper today? There's something about a new building, and it looks like it will go right where we are."[60]

"Lo and behold," said Strooh, "the map in the *Des Moines Register* shows three city blocks right over our premises. This wasn't a proposal, either. The City Council had voted to give Nationwide Insurance our property and the property of our neighbors. No one had told us about it. The article said the city would acquire the land for the company. We shook our heads in disbelief. We kept looking at the map and checking it, and checking the street signs. It was a surreal feeling. There was no way, as property taxpayers, we could comprehend that they would do this without notifying owners. If we were tenants it might make sense, but we were the owners. . . . Len and I couldn't believe it. We were incredulous."[61]

One of the problems with eminent domain is that city officials have no comprehension—or they don't care—about what is involved in building a business from scratch. They look at a business and figure it can easily be moved. No big deal. The appraiser comes in and makes an offer, and the company moves. From the outside, Des Moines Blue Print, like many of the small businesses around it on the western edge of downtown Des Moines, looked modest.

Although a nearby Art Deco office building had been lovingly restored, most of the businesses wouldn't look nearly as impressive as a high rise.

But Des Moines Blue Print wasn't just a business, it was the life's work of its owner and employees. It was the end result of years of dreams and investments, a successful business that had gone through good years and bad, a small manufacturing plant with specialized needs that could not be replaced with the snap of a bureaucrat's fingers.

The business had started at its location in the 1970s. Ainsworth bought it in the early 1980s, brought in new equipment, expanded the operation to the second floor and began expanding the company. It mainly provided blueprints, black and white photographic reproduction and signs for commercial clients. In 1994, Strooh moved from his native South Africa to Des Moines to take a job with the company, with the goal of building a new color printing operation. With computerization and digital equipment becoming the state of the art, the company's traditional black and white photography work was declining, so Ainsworth and Strooh decided to take a chance on an emerging market.

With so much overlap between the black and white business and the new color business, Ainsworth decided he needed to buy the building next door. To acquire it, he had to pay a premium—about $200,000 more than it would fetch on an appraisal. That's a crucial point. People will often pay more than the market value for properties if those properties suit a particular need. That's not an unwise thing to do. Had Des Moines Blue Print not been able to buy the building next door, the company would have been faced with extra ongoing expenses and hassles. Yet when eminent domain rears its ugly head, city appraisers refuse to compensate for these types of extra costs.

The new building was gutted completely and adapted to its new use. It meant providing new concrete flooring to hold the heavy printing equipment, special drainage systems and engineered designs to accommodate the machinery. By 2000, when Ainsworth and Strooh read about the city's plan in the newspaper, the color operation was still not making money. It was improving, and nine employees were working on the color side. But it was not yet profitable. "Everything hinges on the success of this color operation," Strooh said. "We were all learning as we went along. I moved to another country to make a go of this. The heat was on. In 1999, we were satisfied with the progress we made. We were not making a profit overall on the color side. We had great dreams for 2000, and that's when we opened the newspaper and saw this plan."

About an hour after opening the newspaper, Strooh and Ainsworth were still sitting in the office dumbstruck. "We were still debating what it means to us," Strooh said. "Reality is setting in. Then these two sheepish-looking city employees appear at the door. They were absolute dweebs. I still have this picture in my mind of those guys framed in the doorway peering around the corner, knowing they are going to walk into a hornet's nest. They said, 'We're from the city!' "

Strooh told them to have a seat. The officials then said: "Have you seen the newspaper this morning?" The officials told them they had until July 30 to get out of their building. It was incredible—a mere four months to move an entire manufacturing facility to another, yet-to-be-found location. "We were still quite numb," Strooh said. "It was like hearing you have a fatal disease and have only six months to live.

"They left us the paperwork and muttered something about the department of economic development," Strooh added. "They mentioned the term 'eminent domain,' which I had never heard of before, and then mentioned the word 'condemnation.' I felt dragged down by the weight of this. I wasn't listening to all the specifics. It was like the dying man not hearing the details of all the medical treatments. My mind was still reeling."

Ainsworth and Strooh thought it would be the end of the business. They were talking about selling out, closing up shop, laying off the thirty-one employees. Through an associate, Strooh found an attorney who specialized in eminent domain. The attorney, Dan Manning of the Connelly law firm in Des Moines, convinced them that there was no sense being distraught about the process: It was going to happen and the only thing they could do was to fight for the best possible deal in terms of "just" compensation. Rather than fight the condemnation, as some property owners do, they focused on getting up and running at a new site.

The location they had was perfect for them. It was downtown, near most of their clients, had plenty of parking, and even had a drive-through window facing an alley, so clients could drive by and pick up their blueprints. Yet they realized that those factors weren't really considered for the valuation. Des Moines Blue Print also learned that city officials had been planning to redevelop this part of downtown for several years, and had quietly been paving the way for the process. For instance, during the process, Strooh learned, the city had lowered the property valuations in the area in 1998. Officials said they were doing so because the buildings were getting older.

Cities typically don't offer to lower tax valuations. The real goal, Strooh believes, was to lower the values of the properties the city intended to condemn. But such efforts never made the newspapers. It's another example of the way government rigs the game in its favor. The city began the appraisal process soon after those dweebish city employees showed up at the company's doorstep, and from then, "we had to spend every waking moment trying to learn everything we could about eminent domain and condemnation hearings," Strooh said. "Plus, we were trying to run the business, plus we were trying to find a new location."

Cities often boast that they will help targeted businesses relocate. This, as Strooh found out, was a complete joke. "The department of economic development came up with a list of properties, each one significantly more stupid than the last one. They listed properties that had the same square footage, but they were clueless about what we did. They are bureaucrats, anyway, so what did they care?" They were following the letter of the law—providing new options—but had no interest in helping the company find a new location that would actually work for it.

Consider the ridiculously tight time frame. In about four months, the company would be forced from its location. But it did not know what the city was going to offer for the property. So the company didn't know how much money it would have for a new facility. "Then one day Dweeb No. 1 arrives at the office with a woman from the city named Sandy, and they have this appraiser with them," Strooh said. "They come into the front office and tell us they don't want to inconvenience us with the appraisal. I told them that was nothing compared to what they were already putting us through. 'If you really care about inconveniencing us, then turn around and leave us alone.' . . . They walked around saying, 'Wow, there's a lot going on here. You would never know it from the street.' "

Des Moines Blue Print was denied due process under the law. Under due process, the company could have made the case as to why its property should not be taken. It could have explained the extent of the manufacturing operation that went on below the aerial photos the city used to make its determination of the right site to clear away for an insurance company. It would have challenged the blight findings. Instead, the company found out about the project in the newspaper, after it was too late to object.

The company could do nothing but argue for a better valuation, which was an interesting and frustrating process in and of itself. Essentially, the company was stuck waiting for the city to come up with its valuation, using appraisers unskilled at determining the value of specialized companies. Even the city eventually recognized the problem, and flew in a specialized appraiser from Wisconsin.

The appraisal game is strange. Most people figure that what the appraiser says is a fair approximation of what a property is worth. In fact, there are appraisers who specialize in working for cities, and those who specialize in working for business owners. The city's appraisers can always be counted on to come in with a low appraisal. They know what to do if they want to continue to get lucrative work from the city. Strooh said his attorney's goal was to assure that the city chose the worst-possible appraiser and they chose the best, out of the field of many appraisers who worked in Des Moines. This way, it would be easiest to prove the city's numbers were wrong and to secure a better settlement in the end. The attorneys interviewed all the best appraisers and provided them with their numbers, which then made them ineligible to work for the city. The city ended up with the staid, longtime appraiser, who ultimately was unable to give a proper valuation without outside help, according to Strooh.

Eventually the city offered $1,082,500 million for the business, plus, under state law, the city had to pay for relocation costs. Des Moines Blue Print asked for $1.75 million. In Iowa, if the two sides can't come to terms, the matter goes before a board made up mostly of retired real estate agents. "The whole point is not to put your company's fate in the hands of some blithering idiot, seventy-five-year-old retired Realtor on the board," Strooh said. "Especially here in Iowa, where they mostly appraise farms, and there's no hope that these board members would understand what we do."

It was a dicey situation. The city's offer was far too low—Des Moines Blue Print would never be able to get up and running on that offer. Part of the problem was that the company overpaid for the next-door building. It wasn't an overpayment given their business needs, but the specialness of the location was not included in the formula. In

Iowa, which follows federal guidelines, business good will—the intangible value of the business and its clientele—was not reimbursed either. If the board comes up with an offer that is too low and the business owner decides to appeal, the city goes ahead and takes the business, then deposits the offer in an escrow account until the matter is resolved. That puts the business owner out of business essentially for about two years, since he cannot touch any of the money. The system is designed to avoid appeals, and only a wealthy business owner can afford to float the entire worth of the company while the matter is battled in court. "You better be a wealthy business to appeal," Strooh said. "If you are a little guy and you hope to stay in business, you can't do it."

After tense negotiations, the city offered $1.275 million and Des Moines Blue Print decided to take it. Legal expenses generally are not reimbursed in such matters. Attorneys received about one-quarter of the difference between the city's original offer and the final, accepted offer. So about $48,000 went to the law firm, which comes right out of the business' final payment. As Strooh said, it's not cheap to get "just" compensation.

Through happenstance, the company found another building just outside the city's downtown. "We came out okay," said Strooh. "Len lost money initially, but the location has been good." The move did make it tough for the company to weather the tough economic times following the September 11 terrorist attacks and the slumping economy, but business eventually picked up at the new location. The key word is "despite." The business survived despite the many efforts by the city to drive it into the ground.

"The frustrations and stress were incredible," Strooh said. "We had to buy a building without knowing what we were going to get. Plus, we had to deal with all the meetings. There were meetings with the city, meetings with appraisers, meetings with attorneys on a regular basis, meetings with Realtors. You'd meet with an appraiser, and then the city's appraiser, maybe four, five, six times. We had to talk to all of the vendors of our equipment to get it ready to move. We had to work with a rigging company. We had early morning meetings before work, after-hours meetings. We had to find contractors and start construction from scratch again, get all the new city permits. We were in negotiations all the time, plus we were trying to keep the old business going. This is a small company. Len and I are the only executives. Eminent domain says you must be made whole. But you don't have a leg to stand on. We did as well as we could, but it was the most difficult time in our lives."

It would be bad enough to put individuals through such stress and financial loss to make way for a highway or other public use. But this was done to make it easier for an insurance company to build a new building. And, remember, Des Moines Blue Print was treated much better than most victims, because it had the time, talent and resources to fight.

YOUR BUSINESS IS WORTH NOTHING

It's not atypical for cities, especially those most zealous about invoking eminent domain on behalf of developers, to treat their victims shabbily, especially when it comes time to make a fair-market offer. As discussed earlier, the city of Garden Grove, California, tried to drive hundreds of homeowners out of their neighborhood to build a theme park. But the city's treatment of many small-business owners was even worse than its treatment of the residents it wanted to remove so it could build that theme park.

Korean immigrants Joseph and Yae Hong built a thriving, $2 million-a-year car brokerage and rental agency along the city's main drag, Garden Grove Boulevard, near a collection of other Korean businesses. The Hongs leased their business, so when the city came along to offer "just compensation" it offered $16,000. That's right, sixteen thousand dollars—far less than the cost of a new car, and a pittance in the Southern California real estate market.

California is one of only a handful of states in which the government is required to offer businesses what is known as "good will." That's the intangible value of the business. Here's how California law describes good will: "The benefits that accrue to a business as a result of its location, reputation for dependability, skill or quality, and any other circumstances resulting in the probable retention of old or acquisition of new patronage."[62]

In other words, if someone owns a business in a particular town and is forced by eminent domain to surrender a prime location and can only relocate in another town far from its clientele, it is losing a great deal of value beyond the worth of the property itself. But even in California, where such value must by law be reimbursed, the city of Garden Grove refused to offer any sort of compensation to that effect.

Basically, the city added up the value of the office supplies, furniture and other hard property the Hongs owned and affixed a price to it. For the Hongs, most of their assets—cars—could be moved. They had a ten-year lease in a prime location, but they did not own the property. For many businesses, it's the same story, even though a leasehold interest is a property right.

More often than not, when thriving businesses are forced to move, they lose much of their hard-earned clientele. City officials don't care about what they are doing to business owners, given that most of them have spent their lives in government agencies, never having had to meet a payroll or develop a happy clientele of customers themselves. Garden Grove officials showed the Hongs a couple of other locations that were available, and seemed unhappy that they were unwilling to consider these offers. So when it came time to offer them a cash settlement, the city decided it didn't need to pay any good will because it had offered them an alternative location.

When I talked to Yae Hong in the middle of her struggle with the city,[63] she was devastated. Her husband, who spoke little English, was depressed. They were doing remarkably well, and then were forced on short notice to liquidate about forty cars. They began running up debt to stay afloat. That's because the city forced them out of business, and they no longer had their income to not only make ends meet but also to pay for lawyers to battle Garden Grove's eminent domain action. Governments have endless resources—taxpayer dollars—to fight these types of cases. For people like the Hongs, their lives turn into a living hell. For city officials, it's just another day on the job. City officials have every reason to drag the compensation matter out as long as possible, thus wearing down the owners.

The Hongs' business was not blighted. It was in the middle of a thriving and interesting Korea Town. Finally, after one-and-one-half years, the Hongs got a better deal. Under pressure from a lawsuit, the city upped its offer by sixty times the original one, eventually providing $950,000 to the couple. The disparity shows the degree to which the city was trying to take advantage of that young, entrepreneurial immigrant couple.

Also in Garden Grove, a Romanian couple had its property taken by the city in 1997. Their business has struggled since being moved to a less desirable location.

Daniela and Dionisie Goia had paid $778,000 for the property in 1990 and $100,000 for their car rental and repair business, according to a 2001 article in the *Orange County Register*.[64] They bought at the height of the market, and values dipped somewhat in following years throughout Southern California. So the city offered the supposed market value of $640,000 for the property in 1997. The market goes up and down. Most of us would ride out a temporary drop in the value of our real property or most other investments, but with eminent domain, the owner is stuck. You must sell your property at the bottom of the market, take the loss, and keep paying on something you no longer own. To add to the outrage factor, the city refused to give the couple anything for the business itself, declaring it worthless. The court in 1998 handed the couple $1.07 million for the business and the property, which again shows how Garden Grove, like other cities, tries to steal property—not simply use eminent domain to take it. As the *Orange County Register* reported, Garden Grove had to cough up nearly $3 million in less than a year to property owners suing for fair-market value.[65]

When I talked to city officials, they insisted they were only being careful with public funds. That's an irony, given the millions of dollars they lavish on big corporations and their debt-spending spree. Not to mention the money they spend on projects that fail. Then, all of a sudden, when it comes to dealing with small-business owners and homeowners being driven out of their homes, they get fiscally conservative and try, literally, to take the properties for pennies on the dollar. Big companies often do well in the world of eminent domain. Those small companies that fight for their rights get put through the wringer.

"If you're going to take property, you have to pay for it," said John C. Murphy, an attorney with Nossaman Gunther Knox Elliott LLP in Irvine, California, who represented the Hongs and Goias, in the *Register* article. "Instead, Garden Grove runs up attorneys' fees, and then—and only then—will it pay. . . . This may be a good business-litigation strategy. But the city is not dealing with sophisticated litigants, but with small-business owners, who are out of business during the process."[66]

THE THEORY AND THE REALITY

As we've seen, in the real world of eminent domain, government routinely takes properties for non-public uses. Property owners are lucky to get any sort of notice of the action, let alone real due process. Cities rarely offer anything close to "just" compensation, at least in the initial offer. Many of the moving, legal and related expenses are not reimbursed. There's no "just" price that could be paid to cover the hassles and uncertainty that property owners must go through. And, of course, there's no way to compensate people who flat-out are not interested in moving or selling.

Even the legal definition of "just" compensation is rigged to favor the government over the individual property owners. According to the law, the fair-market value to be paid is "the highest price on the date of valuation that would be agreed to by the seller, being willing to sell but under no particular or urgent necessity for doing, nor obliged to sell, and a buyer, being ready, willing and able to buy but under no particular necessity for so doing, each dealing with the other with full knowledge of all the uses and purposes for which the property is reasonably adaptable and available."[67]

That sounds okay, but think of the matter in terms of your own home or business. You have the perfect home, fixed up in the perfect way. Your property has a beautiful view that can't easily be replaced, and you have gotten to know your neighbors over the years. Given financial pressures, or a busy schedule or health concerns, you do not have the time and energy to devote to finding a new home. So, if someone knocked on the door and offered you the going neighborhood price for your home, you would tell that person to take a hike. In this situation, the price it would take to convince you to sell your property would have to be far higher than what the law considers the fair-market rate. It's not a matter of profiteering, but of choice. Few of us would sell something that we don't want to sell unless the price was significantly higher than the market value. In the Garden Grove theme-park situation, the property owners and city officials agreed that the dislocated residents could never find what they had in such a prime location. Decent-sized tract homes on big lots are rarities in that urbanized area. The price the city would have paid would have been about what it costs to buy a condominium in a similar location. The residents figured if the deal went through they would have to move far away to a lower-cost desert region, starting all over and leaving neighbors, friends and family behind.

Why is that fair? What is just about paying an unwilling seller the market price for his home, when that market price wouldn't be anything near what it would cost to replicate his living situation? And that's assuming a city will offer a true market price, and that the relocation expenses offered actually cover the entire relocation, which are rarities in the current world of eminent domain.

So even in the best of worlds, the law doesn't make the seller whole. As attorney Gideon Kanner, with Berger and Norton in Los Angeles, and professor of law emeritus at Loyola University in Los Angeles, points out in an article,[68] even the U.S. Supreme Court admits that the victims of eminent domain do not get reimbursed for all of their costs. In a 1945 decision, *United States v. General Motors Co.*, the court explained: "No doubt, all these elements of [damages] would be considered by an owner in determining whether or not, and at what price, to sell. No doubt, therefore, if the owner is to be made whole for the loss consequent on the sovereign's seizure of his property, these elements should properly be considered. But the courts have generally held that they are not to be reckoned as part of the compensation for the fee taken by the government."

The only thing that has changed since 1945 is that eminent domain's victims must absorb significant financial losses—in addition to irreplaceable losses in freedom—not for the public good, but for private gain. Des Moines Blue Print had to absorb $200,000 or more in costs, not to mention the stress and aggravation, not so a school could be built, but so an insurance company could build a new office more conveniently and profitably.

"Why the government should thus get to enjoy a 'free lunch' at the condemnees' expense, and not have to reckon in the compensation formula the losses it consciously inflicts on citizens, the court has never explained," wrote Kanner.[69] "And so, on the one hand courts tell us that the award of 'just compensation' is to put the condemnees in the same pecuniary position they would have occupied had there been no condemnation, but on the other hand they assert that the condemnees must nonetheless suffer a variety of demonstrable losses which the courts deem noncompensable. These anomalies become particularly morally intolerable in the context of today's redevelopment condemnations which are often not for any real public use at all, but rather for the private enrichment of redevelopers, mass merchandisers, automobile dealerships, professional sport team owners and even gambling casinos."

GOOD-WILL HUNTING

The issue of business goodwill is significant, given the impact on businesses when they are forced to leave their locations. A great corner of a busy street is the key to success for many businesses, and after they are forced to move to a less desirable location, it's often too hard to regain the same clientele. Many businesses fail after being removed by eminent domain. Others struggle for a long time, and in essence have to rebuild from scratch.

The majority of states don't allow repayment for goodwill. Even in California, which since 1976 has mandated such payments when eminent domain is invoked under certain conditions, it's tough going for business owners. Cities, which lavish subsidies on the businesses they want to have in their midst, are notoriously stingy and even cruel toward the businesses they drive away. We saw this with the Goias, who were offered zero dollars for the value of the business and no good will. The city of Garden Grove also refused to pay the Hongs for anything more than the sum total of their office equipment.

How could they try that in a state that mandates the payment of good will? "California was very enlightened in the 1970s when it adopted the good will statute," said attorney John C. Murphy. "The problem is public agencies do their best to circumvent the statute."[70] In essence, a city will say that it only has to pay good will if a business has any good will in its location. Not surprisingly, cities always determine that the business could move without suffering any loss.

The good-will statute is limited. It only requires payment based on the business location, Murphy explains. So if a city can find a new location at another adequate site, then the business supposedly is made whole. We saw with the Des Moines Blue Print example what type of help cities provide in finding "adequate" sites. Same thing for the Hongs and Goias—city officials provided a list of sites, most of which were unusable. The business owners get the list, Murphy explains, and start making calls and find out that some of them are zoned improperly for their business, others are already sold, still others are off the beaten track and would be the business' death knell if it moved there. To the city, they are all adequate sites, which takes it off the hook, goodwill-wise.

"Cities think every business can relocate," Murphy said. "I've never seen a city offer any good will." Another problem: The businesses slated for redevelopment often are the least desirable businesses, from the government's point of view. They tend to be auto-related businesses, junkyards and, ironically, churches—the businesses that have a tough time getting permits. So they always lose an enormous amount of good will, yet no matter that fact, cities argue that they owe nothing in terms of good will.[71]

The federal guidelines for eminent domain, followed by most states, allow up to $20,000 in business good will if the business owner waives moving expenses. Such a deal! A business can be driven from Garden Grove to the desert, and lose all its clientele in the process, and officials shrug their shoulders and say, "Who cares?"

OTHER EXPENSES

Anyone who has ever moved a household or a business knows the high cost of such a process. Different locales offer different forms of reimbursement. In Des Moines, the city was responsible for paying for an entire professional move for Des Moines Blue Print. In California, municipalities must pay for moving expenses, but there is a lid of $10,000 on re-establishment expenses and a lid of $2,500 for search expenses for a new company. Essentially, the victims must eat many costs for a move they don't want to undertake.

"However, despite the availability of loss of business good will, business owners have historically been unable to recover for temporary business losses caused by construction of an eminent domain project," writes attorney Sean O'Connor, an eminent domain specialist with Sheppard Mullin Richer and Hampton in Costa Mesa, California.[72] "Depending on the scope and the type of the project, the impacts from the project can be devastating to the business owner. For example, during the construction of a typical street-widening or freeway-widening project, the condemning agency will tear up the land with an arsenal of heavy equipment. Traffic is often rerouted and access to the affected businesses is almost always temporarily impaired, if not entirely cut off. . . . Unfortunately, condemning agencies almost never offer anything to compensate the business owner for these temporary lost profits."

Of course, if the company cannot find another good site in time for the move—remember the short time frame in which Des Moines Blue Print had to move its complicated manufacturing operation—it's the business that has to eat the losses in income. If a booming business is moved to a lousy locale and loses its clientele, it's the business that eats the costs. And, when it comes to litigation, often owners have to eat the costs to assure a fair-market payment. Only Florida requires legal costs to be compensated by the condemning agency.

Attorney Sean O'Connor advises, "Property owners should never accept the agency's first offer. You will always leave money on the table."[73] Condemning agencies almost always try to get the properties at bargain prices, abusing the fact that they are not dealing with willing sellers. They have been known to offer below their own appraisals. In the Cottonwood Christian Center case, in which O'Conner represented the church against an effort to take its property to make way for a Costco retail center, O'Connor said in an interview that the city offered $14 million, which was several million dollars less than the actual value. All the properties around it had appreciated dramatically, yet the city decided that the one particular property it wanted had barely increased in value in a couple of years. How convenient for it! John Murphy points to cases even more egregious than those of the Hongs and Goias, in which the city tried to get million-dollar businesses for the price of a used car or less. In one case of a manufacturing facility, the condemning agency offered zero for the property, but the owner finally agreed to take $650,000.

"You get frequent corruption as people pressure city halls to seize land on the cheap," argues legal scholar Richard A. Epstein in a January 4, 2002, *Wall Street Journal* article.[74] In one case in Anaheim, California, the city wanted the company that would gain the properties through eminent domain to do the appraisals of the properties.[75] How would you like the chance to appraise a home or business you plan to buy?

Legal expenses are an absolute must for eminent domain proceedings. Without lawyers, property owners will get, quite literally, robbed. Attorneys generally receive contingency fees for the portion of the payment above the initial offer. That's fair enough, but that payment comes out of the take of the property owners. Governments ought to be the ones forced to pay the attorneys. Let's say an agency offers $100,000 for your property. You cannot ask for more than its real worth. So if it takes an attorney to get you the fair-market value of $500,000, you will receive far less than its fair value after you pay your attorney. This isn't fair.

APPRAISING APPRAISERS

Unfortunately, even eminent domain's victims don't always understand what is being done to them. They think that an unbiased appraiser will come along and give them a fair price for their property, but in reality the appraisal process is a game property owners will lose unless they have hired an attorney to help play it for them. "Many appraisers work mostly with government, and many work mostly with businesses," Murphy explains. "There is a big misconception about appraisals," he said. There is no right price, per se. "Appraisers assemble arguments about valuation. They present arguments about what their clients want."[76] In other words, the city's appraiser will do everything in his power to get your property for as close to nothing as he can, assembling arguments to support the low valuation. The appraiser, doing the bidding of those for whom he works and for whom he wants to continue to work, will find every negative factor about your home or business he can and make it seem that the city is doing you a favor by taking it off your hands. That's why victimized property owners need competent legal counsel who can hire the right appraisers to make the best possible case that the home, though modest-looking, is really similar to the Taj Mahal. Those property owners unwilling to play this game are going to get ripped off, plain and simple.

"The jury will listen," Murphy adds. "But it's a lot of work and a lot of expense. The agency doesn't have much incentive to pay better because most people don't fight. They don't have the will." Many of the homes and businesses slated for redevelopment by government agencies are family businesses. The owners are older and often are thinking about retirement. Often victims are ethnic minorities who don't speak much English or are unfamiliar with the American legal system. They sometimes are targeted because they are minorities. Even when that's not the case, they are disproportionately the victims of eminent domain abuse as cities try to rebuild older areas. Typically, Murphy explains, agencies won't move off of their first, unreasonable offer until a lawsuit is filed and they are close to an actual trial. Cities will usually lose in court, as juries usually are sympathetic to victims of government bullying, but one has to fight a long time and run up a lot of legal expenses just to get to the point where a reasonable offer is made. And, furthermore, cities usually hire high-powered law firms to handle cases for them. "These law firms love cities. It is steady work, even at discounted rates," Murphy said. "You can build a practice around work for cities. How do you sell yourself to them? By being aggressive toward the condemnee."[77]

That's why we see the heartless way that small-business owners and homeowners are treated. "Public-agency staffers don't have a clue," Murphy said. "They are not business people. They are just arrogant. They have the attitude that, 'we're the city and we can do what we want.'" Then, the small-property owners must fight against some of the toughest law firms around. Government agencies, like district attorneys' offices, have ethical obligations, Murphy adds. DA's are not ethically allowed to pursue a case against someone they know not to be guilty. They have an ethical, legal obligation to promote justice and serve the public. Likewise, public attorneys are supposed to uphold similar values, striving to put the best interest of the community ahead of their interest to serve the client's goals at all costs. "But they hire these firms and they do not strongly buy in to these ethical obligations. They are wired to be aggressive," Murphy said.[78] They are trying to save as much money as possible for the city or agency for which they work.

Gideon Kanner traces the unfairness in the system partially to the nineteenth century, and the "unwholesome relationship between railroads and judges who often enjoyed free railroad passes," he wrote in the article, "Making Just Compensation Just." "All this eventually produced a prevailing judicial culture that until this day views American condemnees with suspicion and at times with outright hostility. Nowhere is that better illustrated than in the area of business losses where most courts repeat at times absurd justifications for denying compensation to condemnees for the destruction of valuable businesses conducted on the condemned land. Adding insult to injury, when it comes to non-condemnation fields of law—such as business torts, divorce and taxation—the same courts that profess an inability to value businesses somehow manage to do so just fine."[79]

The current system rarely pays adequately for the losses and expenses involved in losing one's business or home, and allows victimized owners to be dragged through legal proceedings to get fair compensation. As such, it feeds on itself. The more cities get away with, the more blatant they get in bullying other property owners. They know that the courts allow them to get away with the most egregious and aggressive actions, and that property owners must be well-heeled and determined to fight the good fight. So they target more and more properties, hiring appraisers who are more and more creative in their theft-like offers. This is why the right to say no is the ultimate right when it comes to property ownership. But cities act like a mugger with a gun to the victim's head.

"What needs to be kept in mind clearly, but alas is too often overlooked, is that the people who find themselves in the path of a public project are not some sort of enemy to be treated with disdain," Kanner wrote in "Making Just Compensation Just." "They are Americans—good, ordinary people who have been minding their business, paying their taxes and generally putting their property to useful and lawful purposes. When by reason of true public necessity they have to be dragged into court so that their land can be taken from them, and they have to be moved, that should be done through a process that is fair to them. They are called to surrender their hard earned property for the good of society, so it is only fair that the true cost of the acquisition be fairly spread on the society that benefits from the creation of that public project, and is thus under a moral obligation to recompense them fairly.

"As for the takings that, though legally denominated for 'public use,' in reality are for the creation of private profit making enterprises, there is simply no excuse for denying compensation for all demonstrable losses suffered by the condemnee."[80]

One of the most astounding truths about eminent domain is the degree to which victims are treated as enemies, not by the condemning agencies but by the court system. Kanner, who has spent 40 years defending property owners against condemnation actions by government, points to only one of the many cases in which he has been involved in which the finding for the condemnee was anything but grudging. Repeatedly, victims of eminent domain—who, as Kanner points out, have done nothing wrong other than having the misfortune of having their property coveted by a government agency—are dramatically under-compensated and must spend a small fortune in legal costs getting their just desserts.

"When condemnees protest that this is unfair, they are told by judges that their plight is a part of 'common burdens of citizenship,' and that in order to gentle the 'harsh' law of eminent domain, they should take their complaints to the legislature and seek legal reform as an act of legislative grace rather than constitutional rights, in spite of the fact that the courts also hold that they, not the legislature, are supreme in shaping the law of 'just compensation,' " Kanner wrote in "Making Just Compensation Just."

Kanner tells of cases of severe abuse by condemning agencies, such as a Florida case known as *United States v. 320 Acres of Land, More or Less, Etc.*[81] Hundreds of recreational parcels were condemned by the government, which convinced a federal judge to enter judgments without a public hearing. The properties were taken, in other words, before their owners had a chance to be heard in court. In other cases, Kanner has seen government attorneys try to destroy the reputations of property owners simply to influence a jury against providing just compensation. Even in cases in which the condemning agency used fraud or abused its power to obtain a property, the courts have upheld the taking. The courts also allow the government to invoke the Declaration of Taking Act, "whereupon it can file a declaration of taking ex parte, depositing into court a sum of money that it alone determines to be adequate, whereupon it instantly obtains title to the condemnee's land, without notice or hearing, with determination of actual compensation deferred, sometimes for years," Kanner wrote in an article about eminent domain and ethics.[82]

As Kanner sees it, the courts believe that fair treatment of property owners will get in the way of needed projects. Property rights, which the courts are supposed to uphold, get cast aside in the name of "progress." Yet the courts don't explain why individuals must be forced to foot the bill for such progress, especially when progress means private gain by Costco and other private companies.

There are exceptions to unfair treatment, of course. As California attorney Sean O'Connor explains, "It's tough on the little guy. But big businesses are savvy. How just the compensation is depends on how big and aggressive you are."[83] For most people, the system is patently unfair, and the process is enough to sap the life out of some owners, and to cure them of any illusions they had about the nature of government.

Manny Ballestero, the activist who helped stave off the destruction of his Garden Grove neighborhood, said that the most stunning thing to his neighbors, upon reflection after the storm had cleared, was that city officials would look them in the eyes and lie to them.[84] They just couldn't believe they were told that nothing was going to happen to their properties, while all the time the city was planning to bulldoze them. Ballestero discussed the time Bob Dinsen, a plain-spoken past council member from Garden Grove who opposed eminent domain, approached a council member who supports it. Dinsen talked about the use of eminent domain to remove a well-kept neighborhood of trailer homes, where mostly elderly people lived. "How many of them died after that happened?" Dinsen demanded to know. They had lived there many years, were close to the hospital and to neighbors. When these elderly people were forced to leave, there was no place for most of them to go. Many of them lost the will to live, and some of them died soon after the neighborhood was bulldozed, he argued.[85] No amount of compensation can make up for that.

THE FUTURE IS ON HOLD

One of the cruelest aspects of the abuse of eminent domain is that it puts individual lives on hold indefinitely, until the city or agency finally gets around to taking the property and paying for it. Much value is lost in the process. Rarely do courts compensate owners for this type of loss, even though it is one of the severest types of losses eminent domain victims face.

Nearly ten years ago, the city of Huntington Beach, California, began buying property in its downtown to make way for a massive redevelopment project. The old downtown was typical of many older beach communities. It was filled with funky old bars, night-clubs, restaurants and surf shops. The city wanted to replace it with a modern area of luxury hotels, restaurants and stores. The city targeted Perqs, a brick tavern and nightclub that wasn't seedy, but was a bit rough around the edges. "They put it in a redevelopment area," said longtime employee Alan Lutz, "but they didn't have a specific plan for the site."[86]

"They put me on hold for ten years," said co-owner Gary Mulligan. He bought the bar in 1974, at the urging of city officials who thought a nice nightclub would be an improvement from the biker bars that were typical downtown. Mulligan renovated the bar and was planning to open a restaurant on the second floor. This is a prime location, on Main Street, just a block from Pacific Coast Highway, which runs along the beach. But once the redevelopment process started, city officials refused to grant him the permits he needed to open the restaurant. They offered instead for Mulligan to join in the redevelopment project, which would have meant leveling the bar to replace it with a nondescript stucco complex. He refused, and the city proceeded to make his life difficult by taking away parking spaces and threatening to use eminent domain. He wasn't allowed to do anything to improve the property, including the completion of earthquake upgrades, because the city wanted to take the land.[87]

The city went through three different developers, none of which ever got around to building on the Perqs site. It dragged on for years. The property's value plummeted, so Mulligan couldn't sell, and the city wasn't getting around to actually taking the property. Denied parking and permits and forced to endure nearby redevelopment-related construction inconveniences, the bar's take plummeted from $500–$1,000 a day to about $100 a day. So Mulligan and co-owner Loren Johnson sued.

"We were held hostage," Johnson told the *Orange County Register*.[88]

"The building department and redevelopment agency want their way, period," Mulligan said. "They didn't want any input from building owners. But it was the owners who had to suffer through the process with reduced revenue, reduced property values, and reduced options," he told me in an interview. Mulligan was battling cancer during the fight, which made the problems even more difficult to handle. While I was interviewing him in the bar, blues musician Walter Trout stopped in and told him: "Fight it [the cancer] the same way you fought the city." City officials just don't understand or care what they put people through, or the depth of emotions these cases engender.

"Each time the owners sought city permits to improve the building, they were told it was certain to be condemned," Johnson said, according to the *Register* report. "But the city never went ahead with condemnation proceedings."

So in a rare instance, the court agreed that the city had deprived the owners of their right to run their business. The jury granted them $1.2 million, and later added $800,000 in legal fees. But the city appealed, and rather than fight on, both sides agreed to a $1.5 million settlement, with attorney fees coming out of that amount. That sounds like a good sum, but it really isn't. A prime business in a prime location was denied the ability to operate beyond the most basic level for nearly a decade. Then take $800,000 out of the settlement, and Mulligan and Johnson had just enough to get the business back and running. The city is still hassling them, demanding that Perqs relinquish eleven feet of eating area—the prime front area of the business—in exchange for a permit to operate a second floor.[89] So the battle goes on. In many ways, a simple taking would have been more humane.

SPECIAL SITES

An appraiser can offer a value for a property, but properties are not like cash assets. They are unique. An old brick bar in the heart of an old beach city might be worth a certain dollar-and-cents figure to an appraiser, but it might be the life's work of its owner. In many ways, the property is irreplaceable. Des Moines Blue Print wasn't just a building, but the end result of years of hard work and investment to its owner. The modest houses in Garden Grove were beloved homes to their owners. For many of them, no financial amount could compensate the loss of their neighborhood.

Forbes magazine featured a short 2003 article titled: "Sell Cheap or Die."[90] "Using a strong-arm tactic that Vito Corleone would admire, the second-largest city in New Hampshire is trying to force a publicly traded company that owns the local water utility to sell its assets to the municipality. This in a state with the motto 'Live Free or Die.' " The buyout offer, backed by a threat of eminent domain, appears low, but how does one determine the price of a specialized utility outside of a free-market transaction? This company cannot be replicated, and although the owners are a far cry from the small-business owners depicted in much of this chapter, they too would be deprived of an irreplaceable asset—a business that can't start up across town.

"The people who suffer most for compensation," explains the Institute for Justice attorney Dana Berliner, are businesses that won't be offered any good will and "people who have property that is uniquely good for them."[91] Talking about the Lakewood, Ohio, situation, she pointed to one property owner who has eye troubles and can't drive. His house is near four bus lines and near his job. The thought of relocating somewhere unknown is horrifying to him. Another family there has a special view they could never get anywhere else.

"Compensation is based supposedly on what it would sell for, not what it would cost to have what you have now," Berliner added. "This is not part of the equation. Yet, there is a big group of people getting unique benefits from their property. They don't sell." It's unfair, then, that they are forced to sell. They are handed real, non-compensated losses. There's nothing "just" about the process, especially when eminent domain is used to benefit another private party rather than the public.

4. PROPERTY RIGHTS ARE HUMAN RIGHTS

The poorest man may in his cottage bid defiance to all the forces of the Crown—it may be frail. Its roof may shake, the wind may blow through it— the storm may enter, the rain may enter, but the King of England cannot enter; all his forces dare not cross the threshold of the ruined tenement.

> — William Pitt, 18th-century
> British Prime Minister,
> 1783–1801 and 1804–1806[92]

Think about that statement from William Pitt and the radical idea it represents. The lowliest individual, living in the humblest cottage, has the power to keep the King of England out of his household through the simple, legal power of property ownership. Traditionally, the king was eminent and all the land was his domain. He could take any piece of property he wanted at any time and for any use, and kick the poor tenants out on their behinds. Compensation was paid only if the king or his minions were in merciful moods.

Hence the significance of the U.S. Constitution's Third Amendment: "No soldier shall, in time of peace be quartered in any house, without the consent of the owner, nor in time of war, but in a manner to be prescribed by law." The leader of the government could not have his troops take quarters in an individual's home.

Equally radical was the Fourth Amendment: "The right of the people to be secure in their persons, houses, papers, and effects, against unreasonable searches and seizures, shall not be violated, and no warrants shall issue, but upon probable cause, supported by oath or affirmation, and particularly describing the place to be searched, and the persons or things to be seized."

The government cannot just pound down the door of one's abode and rifle through one's papers, seizing whatever it is the government wants to seize. An even more radical point enforced in the Bill of Rights comes in the Fifth Amendment: "No person shall . . . be deprived of life, liberty, or property, without due process of law; nor shall private property be taken for public use, without just compensation." No matter how modest or lowly.

Some might complain that the nation's founders allowed the government to take property from private owners for any reason. But the Constitution's requirements that due process be afforded the property owner, that the property can be taken only for public use and that—most important—just compensation be paid were radical departures from the traditional way things were done. They enumerated the natural rights of property ownership. Even the humblest soul could withstand the forces of the king, or of the democratically elected president, with the Constitution in his hand. In the past no compensation had to be paid. Now, under the Constitution, no individual would be forced to bear the costs of the public good. The king would have to pay up, and at a sum determined by a disinterested party. The founders never used the term eminent domain in the Constitution. They talked only about the taking of private property by government. The term eminent domain was discussed by courts and theorists later. Eminent domain came from the Dutch philosopher Grotius, who used the Latin term *dominium eminens*.[93]

In England, the king, by divine right, could take his land back as he chose, before the *Magna Carta*.

The 14th Amendment of the U.S. Constitution applied the Fifth Amendment to all the states, even though many state constitutions have their own property-rights protections. Section I of the 14th Amendment states: "All persons born or naturalized in the United States, and subject to the jurisdiction thereof, are citizens of the

United States and of the state wherein they reside. No state shall make or enforce any law which shall abridge the privileges or immunities of citizens of the United States; nor shall any state deprive any person of life, liberty, or property, without due process of law; nor deny to any person within its jurisdiction the equal protection of the laws."

The framers were influenced by earlier thinkers. "In 1215, King John of England agreed to the demands of his barons and authorized the Magna Carta," according to a Hoover Institution book, *Property Rights: A Practical Guide to Freedom and Prosperity.*[94] "This influential charter protected property owners against the powers of central government. . . . By the sixteenth century, it was clear that the crown's authority stopped where private property began. The ideas of individual sovereignty and individual proprietorship became entrenched in the common law of Britain and subsequently in the Constitution of the United States."

America's founders were greatly influenced by John Locke, who argued that property rights are natural human rights. From the creation, God granted mankind property that was meant to be used to meet his needs. Writes Locke in 1690 in *The Second Treatise of Civil Government:* "God, who hath given the world to men in common, hath also given them reason to make use of it to the best advantage of life, and convenience. The earth, and all that is therein, is given to men for the support and comfort of their being. And tho' all the fruits it naturally produces, and beasts it feeds, belong to mankind in common, as they are produced by the spontaneous hand of nature; and no body has originally a private dominion, exclusive of the rest of mankind, in any of them, as they are thus in their natural state: yet being given for the use of men, there must of necessity be a means to appropriate them some way or other, before they can be of any use, or at all beneficial to any particular man."[95]

This sets out the natural-law case for property rights. As Locke and America's founders understood, this right is a fundamental human right granted by God and nature, not by the monarch or even by the democratically elected government. It is no more just for a majority to vote to steal property from the minority than it would have been for the king to have decided to have taken it on his own. Individuals have the absolute right to own property. This idea is so significant because of what it meant for the average individual. The poorest man is a king in his own cottage. It is a protection that benefits the most those individuals without power against those with power.

There has been debate over Thomas Jefferson's views of property. Jefferson transformed John Locke's "life, liberty and property" to "life, liberty and the pursuit of happiness" when he wrote the Declaration of Independence. That has led some scholars, especially leftist and liberal scholars, to argue that Jefferson had a lesser view of property rights than Locke. Some even argue, based more on their own prejudices than on any evidence, that Jefferson did not believe in property rights at all—a point at odds with the Declaration, the founding principles of the nation and Jefferson's long record of upholding the pre-eminence of property rights in assuring individual freedom. Professor Gideon Kanner argues that Jefferson used the word "happiness" rather than "property" because he was a precise user of the English language. Property, which by its nature is alienable—i.e., it can be sold, leased, etc.—could not be inalienable.[96]

Nevertheless, undermining property rights is a key goal of certain ideologues, who understand that without property-rights protections, the individual has little standing to oppose the designs of the government. Because modern liberalism is mainly about expanding the power of the state, it is understandable that liberals would have a vested interest in arguing that Jefferson was not a friend of property rights. But their argument is untrue.

"Some authors argue that, even if Jefferson was indeed a Lockean, he did not believe in the natural right of property," wrote Marco Bassani, a scholar for the free-market Ludwig von Mises Institute.

"He thought that property was a conventional right, to be taken away or granted to people by majorities and so on. Now what kind of Lockean would believe this is hard to say, but that is how the story is told."[97]

Bassani points to many quotes from Jefferson affirming property rights. In fact, Jefferson appears to use "property" and "happiness" interchangeably. "Despite the gallons of ink wasted on the controversy, it does not seem possible to construe an opposition between property and happiness in revolutionary American rhetoric," Bassani added. "Life, liberty, property, security and happiness are the most recurrent terms in the American discourse on natural rights. Looking for a powerful trio, it is reasonable to believe that Jefferson preferred happiness to property mainly because of style (it was less legalistic and conveyed the same idea)."

"The founders regarded property rights as so basic they didn't think it needed such extensive protections," argues Tibor Machan, a professor of ethics at Chapman University in Orange, California. "They thought it was understood. They assumed the right to life, liberty and happiness was based on property."[98]

Jefferson and the founders knew that property was the basis for protecting the poor as well as the rich from excessive government. Yet in the dominant liberal view prevalent today, property rights are about protecting the rich and powerful. Those who stand up for property rights are exploiters of the poor, despoilers of the environment, corporate barons who want to avoid their communal responsibilities. But when property rights are undermined, it is the little guy who suffers most. The rich and powerful are rich and powerful. They have the ear of the king, the president or the mayor. They generally get their way, regardless of what the law might say. It's the small-property owner who gains the biggest advantage from the property-rights protections in the Constitution. He is the one who can stand up to all the king's men and kick them out of his decrepit cottage. So when eminent domain is abused, and the clear constitutional protections afforded property owners are no longer recognized, then the rich and powerful run roughshod over the poor and powerless. Yet the Left never learns.

Perhaps the most famous recent case of eminent domain abuse, reported widely in the national media, involved an elderly Atlantic City, N.J., homeowner named Vera Coking. As the Institute for Justice, which defended Coking, explained, billionaire Donald Trump asked the Atlantic City redevelopment agency in the mid-1990s to condemn the widow's property and give it to him for use as a limousine parking lot for his casino.[99] Coking eventually won the case, which is a stark example of how the Constitution's words can still protect the weak against the powerful. In a world without property rights, the powerful and well-connected would always win. The king would have entered Coking's property and given it to the courtier Trump. When the Constitution works, as it did in Atlantic City, Coking could stand inside her cottage and tell king and Trump to take a hike. In Coking's case, property rights protected her human rights. Unfortunately, it's a rare time when a property owner actually wins the right to remain in his or her property. Almost always, the court cases are about the amount of compensation, not the legality of the taking.

"When private clients consult an eminent domain lawyer, often their first question is, 'What can you do to stop this? I don't want my property (or my house or my business) taken by the government.'" explains Alice Beasley, an attorney writing in *Western City* magazine. "More than 99 times out of 100, the answer is 'Nothing.' The lawyer's role is generally limited to obtaining the best possible price for the client's property. Most citizens are shocked to learn that their rights of private-property ownership are subordinate to the government's needs."[100]

Or the government's wants. Or the greedy desires of another property owner, or a big corporation that dangles promises of sales-tax dollars before the eyes of government officials—if only they use the power of eminent domain to clear away properties that are in the way.

Chris Sutton, a Pasadena, California-based attorney who has represented many victims of eminent domain abuse, champions the phrase, "property rights are human rights."[101] He even had the words printed on a bumper sticker. An old-time liberal who recognizes the role of property in protecting the downtrodden, Sutton blames the current situation on a combination of thinking from both sides of the political spectrum: "The Left believes the government will perform beautiful things. Give it the power to take property and redevelop areas and everything will be wonderful. Some Republicans, however, believe that we will help the big boys and promote a pro-business agenda." The net effect: bipartisan support for taking advantage of small-property owners. That's something evident on many city councils, as pro-business Republicans join with big-government liberals to drive small-business owners off their land. Oftentimes, Republicans' main concern is that the taxpayers don't pay too much to compensate property owners. It's the worst of both worlds: The liberal defense of big government allows the property to be taken and the conservative defense of the taxpayer assures the property owner gets a low pay-out.[102]

"How do liberals square the idea of taking something from people with their view of the dignity of man?" Sutton asks. "How do conservatives square it with their belief in the freedom and independence of choice in economic decisions?"[103]

Good questions, but ones not asked frequently enough. Sutton talks about the innate importance of property to human aspirations, and relays stories of people who have literally died after their life's work, such as a business or the family homestead, is taken by the government.

The importance of constitutional protections in protecting the average person is not as widely understood as it should be. Steven Hill, West Coast director of the left-wing Center for Voting and Democracy, writes in the *Seattle Post-Intelligencer*: "The point is that the Bill of Rights and Constitution were really there to guarantee the property rights of the rich and the rich wannabes—to ensure the government stayed out of their business. . . ." The nation's economic and political inequalities, he added, "are a direct result of—not in spite of, but because of—the priority given by the Bill of Rights and U.S. Constitution to protect the private property of rich individuals and wealthy corporations over basic human rights."[104]

Leftists usually deny that the Constitution protects property rights, given that such arguments lead to their desire: giving government more power to redistribute income and affect economic outcomes. They usually make arguments similar to the ones referred to earlier that deny that Jefferson and the founders believed in property rights. Sutton refers to one professor he knows about who teaches his classes that there is no such thing as property rights.[105] So, in a sense, Hill's recognition of the preeminence of property rights in the U.S. Constitution is refreshing, no matter his ideologically-driven hostility to the concept.

Hill's directness, and his willingness to call for the "substantial revision" of the Constitution, is rare. But his thinking isn't. The Bill of Rights, many believe, is just a means for the rich and powerful to stay rich and powerful. Yet tell that to Vera Coking or to the other Americans who can live their lives in relative freedom because the government must respect their property. In a world without property rights, the powerful could do as they darn well please—the same nasty, brutish state of affairs in existence before the Enlightenment, and in every authoritarian and totalitarian nation across the globe.

"People whose property is not secure from government are extremely limited in their freedom, for, as Supreme Court Justice Felix Frankfurter noted, 'The free range of the human spirit becomes shriveled and constrained under economic dependence. The right to property therefore preserves other personal rights and maintains a separation between the state and the individual," writes Bernard Siegan in his book *Property and Freedom*. He is the University of San Diego law professor who was kept off the 9th Circuit Court of Appeal by Senator Ted Kennedy, D-Massachusetts, because of Siegan's constitutional view of property rights.[106] Siegan points to the pre-eminence of property rights in the Constitution, quoting James Madison: "Government is instituted to protect property of every sort; as well that which lies in the various rights of individuals, as that which the term particularly expresses. This being the end of government, that alone is a just government, which impartially secures to every man, whatever is his own."[107]

Clearly, the judges who have allowed eminent domain to be used to redistribute property to other private owners are ignorant of or have rejected Madison's view. They have embraced judicial activism—the twisting of the law to advance certain modern concepts in defiance of the Constitution's clear statements. They have rejected the classically American view of property rights and embraced the old, feudal way of thinking. "Eminent domain actually is a relic of feudalism," Professor Machan argues.[108] "In that system, sovereignty resides at the top, with the king having power over all of his subjects. The American revolution was fought so we could be sovereign citizens, not subjects."

In Machan's view, the founders set up a limited government, and that government needs space to operate in certain limited areas. So, yes, the government needs the ability to acquire land for courthouses, jails and other public uses. But eminent domain's rampant use for non-public uses is "basically reactionary," a return to the system in which the American citizen is not sovereign over his or her own life, but a serf subject to the whims of those who lead the government.[109]

So as property rights recede, the radical American experiment of liberty and self-government recedes with it. According to America's founders, the government could only avail itself of eminent domain if it gave due process to property owners, if it paid just compensation and if the use was for the good of the public, as opposed for a narrow purpose that would benefit politically well-connected private interests. Think back to the case in Garden Grove. The mayor and his allies wanted to take the properties owned by working-class people and give them to rich developers, some of whom potentially could be supporters of their political campaigns. Yet, as unconstitutional as the Garden Grove situation appears to be, that, not the idea set forth by Madison, is the standard in America.

THE EARLY DAYS

Throughout the early days of the Republic, the Constitution's words were more consistently accepted as meaning what they said, although there were many exceptions. In the mid-1800s, the railroad acts that funded the railroads' western expansion gave the companies the power of eminent domain. That led to some convoluted routes, as rail companies pressed ahead through valuable properties, taking what they could by force and expanding their domain.[110]

Often, farmers didn't even feel the need to ask for much financial compensation for easements across their property, given the abundance of land and the benefits the railroads provided.[111] Still, the abuses were real. The free land and power of eminent domain no doubt led to an over-abundance of railroads—something that happens anytime a good or service is subsidized. The power granted to railroads caused tensions with traditional constitutional protections. Court cases from the time document individuals trying to protect their property from the sometimes rapacious intentions of railroads, which often abused their power to grab as much land as possible, and which, in the process, looted the public treasury.

"In the case of the railroads, the state courts' use of eminent domain—also known as public-use doctrine—had a major impact on the traditional protections of private property, chiefly because railroads took so much more land than was required by other industrial improvements, and because even after taking it the railroads represented a continual danger to the communities through which they passed. For these reasons the objections to the taking of lands by railroads were correspondingly great and were usually raised by the owner of the property taken," wrote Sarah Gordon, in the book, *Passage to Union: How the Railroads Transformed American Life, 1829–1929.*[112]

In 1905, the U.S. Supreme Court even authorized the condemnation by private parties of their neighbors' land for farming purposes. But such abuses were the exception, not the rule. An early U.S. Supreme Court case that addressed the government's taking of private land and transferring it to other private users is *Missouri Pacific Railway Co. v. the State of Nebraska.* In the late 1800s, the railroad companies still owned the grain elevators, and although railroads were regulated by the newly formed Interstate Commerce Act, the grain elevators themselves were not regulated. Farmers began to complain about the excessive fees charged by the railroads for use of the elevators. In Nebraska, in the city of Elmwood, farmers asked the transportation board to take some of the land owned by railroads and give it to the farmers' cooperative for the construction of a competing grain elevator. Looking at the details of the case, it seems likely the railroads were gouging the farmers, perhaps making up in elevator fees for a loss in revenue in the newly regulated railroad business. They had a monopoly business, and the farmers were clearly at the owners' mercy.

Even though most modern Americans would view this as a hard case, the Supreme Court was wise enough to rule based on the simple words found in the Constitution:

"To require the railroad company to grant to the petitioners a location on its right of way for the erection of an elevator for the specified purpose of storing from time to time the grain of the petitioners and of neighboring farmers, is to compel the railroad company, against its will, to transfer an estate in part of the land which it owns and holds, under its charter, as its private property and for a public use, to an association of private individuals, for the purpose of erecting and maintaining a building thereon for storing grain for their own benefit, without reserving any control of the use of such land, or of the building to be erected thereon, to the railroad company, for the accommodation of its own business, or for the convenience of the public."[113]

By a unanimous opinion, the court ruled that, "The taking by a state of the private property of one person or corporation, without the owner's consent, for the private use of another, is not due process of law, and is a violation of the 14th article of amendment of the Constitution of the United States."[114]

No dice, even though Nebraska alleged that its use of eminent domain was for the benefit of the general public.

The traditional concept of public use continued to hold, according to Martin Anderson, in his 1964 book, *The Federal Bulldozer*. In 1913, he explained, the Massachusetts Supreme Court voided an effort by the state to use eminent domain to clear away properties for an urban-renewal project.[115] The court rejected the government's justification of "public use," explaining that although it is a public good to create nice, new housing, that doesn't mean the government should be the one providing it. Then the 6th Circuit Court of Appeals in 1935 rejected an effort by federal housing authorities to clear away four city blocks in Louisville, Kentucky: "If, however, such a result thus attained is to be considered a public use for which the government may condemn private property, there would seem to be no reason why it could not condemn any private property which it could employ to an advantage to the public."[116]

That's a compelling and important argument. Many good things are, generally speaking, in the public's interest. Turning a slum into a safe neighborhood, or improving tax revenue so that cities can fund public services, or putting a needed shopping center on a vacant lot, or . . . you name it. What the court said—upholding the traditional, constitutional view—is just because a plan might in some arguable way benefit the public does not make it a genuine public use and therefore give the government the right to take property by force to make that plan happen. If the government were free to do that, then no private property would be safe no matter how well-kept it might be. Surely, government officials can always find a more lucrative and publicly beneficial use for any property. If that's the standard, then property rights really don't exist in the United States. That's why the Constitution's crystal-clear standard is "public use," not the nebulous "public benefit."

Yet since that 1935 decision in Louisville, everything has changed. Today, a theme park is a public-enough use to justify the destruction of a neighborhood, or new condominiums or a Costco retail center, or a new housing development. If the government declares the proposed plan a public use, it almost always is held by the courts to be a public use. There are exceptions, but legislative bodies are usually granted the widest latitude in making public-use designations. The unfair, unconstitutional and un-American situation the court warned against in 1935 is the state of affairs in 2004.

THIS IS NO ABERRATION

Supporters of the government's use of eminent domain typically describe every outrageous taking, or attempted taking, as an aberration. Well, maybe that city got carried away, but without broad eminent domain powers it would be tough for older, blighted neighborhoods to revive. These are not aberrations, however. The use of eminent domain to take properties from one owner and give it to another is typical in America today. It happens in almost every state.

The Washington, D.C.-based Institute for Justice produced a comprehensive report on eminent domain across the country. It found 10,282 filed or threatened condemnations on behalf of private parties in the last five years, with more than 4,000 properties currently living under the threat of eminent domain in forty-one states. Only nine states had no such actions.[117]

The problem is not just the takings and the threat of takings. It is the number of properties included in redevelopment areas nationwide, in which condemnation is not pending, but in which condemnation hearings could begin at any time. As explained in the Garden Grove case, cities create redevelopment areas. In those areas, they are able to capture a larger share of property taxes. Typically, they gain the power of eminent domain within those areas. Some cities, such as Westminster and Stanton, California, are almost entirely within redevelopment areas. Even if the power of eminent domain is excluded from the areas—sometimes that's necessary to avoid public opposition to the redevelopment plan—it can fairly easily be placed back within the area. Owners of these properties within these areas have far fewer property-rights protections than those whose properties are not within such areas.

Here are short excerpts from media articles documenting what's happening repeatedly:

From the *Cincinnati Enquirer*, January 10, 2002: "For an upscale shopping center and pricey homes, Newport (Kentucky) officials are willing to sacrifice part of Wiedemann Hill, the working-class neighborhood that stands in the way. It's the latest example of an increasingly controversial trend. Nationwide, governments are using eminent domain to take private property not just for public roads or parks, but also for privately owned shopping malls, restaurants and hotels."[118]

From *Reader's Digest*, March 2001: "With its Norway spruce trees and old wooden farmhouse, the 140-acre property in Bristol, Connecticut, had long been home to Frank and John Bugryn. They'd grown up on the land their father purchased over sixty years ago, and hoped to spend the rest of their days there, surrounded by a lifetime of memories. That was before Yarde Metals, one of Bristol's fastest growing businesses, needed a new facility. In the summer of 1996, the city asked if the Bugryns' land would do. Company President Craig Yarde decided that it would—and, indeed, wrote to Bristol's mayor, suggesting that he might move his business to nearby Southington unless the city got him what he wanted—twenty-two acres, at about $35,000 each."[119]

From WorldNetDaily, June 24, 2000: "The most recent fight in Pittsburgh was provoked after Mayor Tom Murphy announced plans to condemn major portions of downtown under eminent domain and hand the property over to Chicago-based Urban Retail Properties for development of the site as a suburban-style shopping mall. . . . Pittsburgh residents are not alone in their fight against city hall. An inner-city church, City Chapel in South Bend, Ind., is engaged in a David versus Goliath struggle against their city to keep their church building from being plowed under to make room for a privately owned office complex."[120]

From the *Wichita Eagle*, April 29, 2003: "In 1998, the Kansas Supreme Court held that taking the homes of 150 families to make way for the privately owned Kansas Speedway in Wyandotte County was a 'public' purpose. Cities such as Independence and Topeka have followed suit, and Merriam condemned a used-car dealership for a higher-priced BMW dealership. This month, the Kansas Supreme

Court ruled that Shawnee County could use eminent domain to take private property for a Target distribution center."[121]

The examples go on and on. Anyone with Internet access can type "eminent domain" in a search engine and find one story after another. As eminent domain foe Doug Reed of the Allegheny Institute for Public Policy told WorldNetDaily in its coverage of the Pittsburgh abuses: "We have reached the point that 'public use' is defined to mean anything they think is better than what's there now. I find it hard to believe that James Madison had an eighteen-screen movie theater in mind when he wrote the takings clause of the Constitution."[122]

American citizens are supposed to live under a clearly defined rule of law, one based on the idea that individuals have natural rights that must be protected against the encroachment of government. Too many Americans today believe that government is the best way to achieve all manner of good things, having lost sight of the wisdom of the founders, who believed that government is necessary but dangerous, and must therefore be kept limited lest it abuse the natural rights of individuals. Part of the problem comes from a lack of understanding about the difference between "negative rights" and "positive rights." The founders created a system of negative rights, in which individuals have their natural rights—right to life, liberty, property—protected from the incursions of government. "Negative rights, it is said, amount to walls of protection from the kind of intrusive government that Thomas Jefferson and his contemporaries feared; positive rights, in contrast, require government intervention to satisfy needs or relieve burdens that citizens would have to endure if left to their own devices," explains Columbia University History Professor David Greenberg.[123] Positive rights— the right to health care, to a job, to a better tax base—must be taken from someone else. In other words, my "positive" right to health care means you have to provide it for me.

The difference between America and, say, China is a matter of law, and a political culture that upholds that law. We are raised in a world where checks and balances and constitutional limitations—despite certain erosions of key principles—still hold sway. But when eminent domain law developed in such a way that public use could be construed to mean anything that's better than what's there now, government officials throughout the country acted in the way the law allowed them to act. They decided that movie theaters are better than older neighborhoods, and condemned property to implement their plans. They decided that they can act in a "positive" way to fulfill the desires of certain people, rather than simply to protect the natural rights of individuals. It's worth noting that in China, eminent domain has become a hot issue as government officials and wealthy developers try to remake decrepit cities into modern metropolises. The Chinese government is adding new property-rights assurances at the same time that American officials are trampling on this nation's historic property protections.[124] It goes to show that nothing ever is static, that individual rights and liberties must always be defended in every country.

"Since there is no such entity as 'the public,' since the public is merely a number of individuals, the idea that 'the public interest' supersedes private interests and rights can have but one meaning: that the interests and rights of some individuals take precedence over the interests and rights of others," wrote Ayn Rand in *The Pull Peddlers*.[125] That's what's happening with property rights today. Despite the frequent use by government officials of the word "public," eminent domain has become a tool whereby some private interests are given things at the expense of other private interests. To minimize such abuses, the founders intended "public" use to be strictly limited to uses that could "affect the population as a whole," as the dictionary explains it. Anyone can benefit from a road. The community as a whole, at least arguably, benefits from schools and courthouses. The aqueduct that brings water from the Colorado River to Southern California benefits everyone in Southern California. But private parties are the main beneficiaries of shopping centers, hardware stores and condominiums. The founders never envisioned their Constitution would be twisted to justify the sort of eminent domain practices widely used today.

JUDICIAL ACTIVISM TRIUMPHS

Several federal cases, and a variety of state rulings, changed the nature of eminent domain in the United States. Here is a look at three cases that, many experts believe, have paved the slippery slope of eminent domain abuse.

1. IT'S A POLITICAL QUESTION, PERIOD

In the 1923 case *Rindge Co. vs. Los Angeles County*,[126] the United States Supreme Court dealt with two questions: Was the construction of a coastal highway through a private ranch that is now Malibu a public use, even though the road was designed to provide coastal views rather than to connect to another city or town? And were the property owners' due-process rights violated because the road was planned and approved without giving the owners a chance to argue their case?

The court ruled in favor of the government on both counts. "The ranch owners concede that a genuine highway, in fact adapted as a way of convenience or necessity for public use and travel, is a public use," according to the court.[127] "Their real contention is that these particular roads, while called highways are 'highways' in name merely, that is, that they are shams under the name of public improvements, which cannot, in fact, furnish ways of convenience or necessity to the traveling public. The argument is based upon the fact that they extend through the ranch alone, the main road terminating within its boundaries, and connect with no other public roads at their western and northern ends. These roads will, however, be open to the general public to such extent as it can and may use it." The ranch owners argued there was no public necessity for the road, just the desire by the government to give the public access to a privately owned scenic ranch.

The second point deals directly with the issue of due process: "In 1916 and 1917 the Board of Supervisors, the legislative body of Los Angeles County, without notice to the ranch owners, adopted, by the required vote, two resolutions declaring that the public interest and necessity required the construction of the two highways now in controversy 'for public highway purposes' and it was necessary for such 'public uses' that the lands included therein be acquired by the county; and directing that condemnation proceedings be instituted for such purposes." The owners argued that, had they been informed of the proposal, they would have argued for a different route through their property. The county decided to build the route right along the coast rather than a route along the hills above the coast.[128]

The court concluded that "public uses are not limited, in the modern view, to matters of mere business necessity and ordinary convenience, but may extend to matters of public health, recreation and enjoyment. . . . The necessity for appropriating private property for public use is not a judicial question. This power resides in the Legislature, and may either be exercised by the Legislature or delegated by it to public officers."[129] The court cited other federal cases that say a public use "is purely political, does not require a hearing, and is not the subject of judicial inquiry." In other words, if a legislative body—Congress, the state legislature, the board of supervisors, the city council—wants a property, then the property is by its nature a public use, and it owes the property owners no public hearing, no due process. It's a political question, and whoever has the political power wins. The term "public use" is so broad, in the court's view, that anything the public might enjoy qualifies as one.

And due process and providing proper notification don't matter. As attorney Chris Sutton explains, "Because the property owner receives an equivalent of property back in the form of money, they haven't lost anything. If they were paid, they have no right to notice. Only in eminent domain is there an assumption that real estate is not unique."[130]

2. THE GOVERNMENT CAN DO WHAT IT PLEASES

As Aesop wrote, "Any excuse will serve a tyrant."[131] So, with eminent domain, any excuse will do for covetous government officials. In *Rindge*, the U.S. Supreme Court gave governments fairly free rein to use eminent domain, but because the case dealt with a purpose that most observers believe to be public—i.e., a road—the decision didn't have an enormous effect. But in 1954, in *Berman v. Parker*, the U.S. Supreme Court paved the way for the abuses described in this book and elsewhere. The case was a tour de force of liberal judicial reasoning, a case that gave government carte blanche to do as it pleased with regard to eminent domain. As long as it was justified in the name of the public good, private owners could now directly benefit from the state's power of eminent domain on their behalf.

Berman set the stage for the heavy-handed use of eminent domain on behalf of the urban renewal programs that destroyed so many inner cities during the 1950s and early 1960s. It was issued by a liberal court in an era in which the government was viewed as the best means to clear away slums and uplift the inhabitants. Unfortunately, the main result of the programs seemed to be moving aside the inhabitants of settled neighborhoods and replacing them with housing blocks, government buildings and vacant lots.

No city or redevelopment agency, especially those that operate in affluent suburban communities, would dare to use the term "urban renewal." It conjures up bad memories of social-engineering schemes that scraped away thriving neighborhoods and replaced them with concrete. It brings back memories of the federal authorities putting high-rise housing projects—many of which have been dynamited in recent years after serving as incubators of crime, dependency and drug abuse—in the middle of urban ethnic neighborhoods. Yet the 1954 *Berman* decision remains the basis upon which modern urban and suburban redevelopment rests.

At issue was the District of Columbia's Redevelopment Act of 1945. As the court explained, the city (then run by a commission appointed by Congress) took privately owned land by eminent domain in keeping with a redevelopment plan meant to revitalize a poor section of the city. The goal was to eliminate slums and substandard housing conditions, and the taken property could be sold or leased to private parties for commercial and private uses.

"Congress made a 'legislative determination' that 'owing to technological and sociological changes, obsolete layout, and other factors, conditions existing in the District of Columbia with respect to substandard housing and blighted areas, including the use of buildings in alleys as dwellings for human habitation, are injurious to the public health, safety, morals and welfare; and it is hereby declared to be the policy of the United States to protect and promote the welfare of the inhabitants of the seat of the government by eliminating all such injurious conditions by employing all means necessary and appropriate for the purpose," the court ruled.[132]

The court deferred to Congress, which found that private enterprise alone would not fix these problems. Congress had created a redevelopment land agency to assemble developable tracts using eminent domain if necessary, and directed a planning commission to create a general plan to designate new uses in that area. The commission, the court wrote, conducted surveys revealing that large portions of the dwellings were substandard and that nearly all of the people affected were Negroes.

The owners of a department store filed suit against the taking, explaining that their property is not substandard, is not used for human habitation, and provides no threat to public health or safety. Pointing to the Fifth Amendment, the owners argued, according to the Supreme Court's summary, that "To take for the purpose of ridding the area of slums is one thing; it is quite another, the argument goes, to take a man's property merely to develop a better balanced, more attractive community." The appeals court ruled that the agency could only condemn property "for the reasonable necessities of slum clearance and prevention," but the Supreme Court ruled otherwise.

Writing for the majority, Justice William O. Douglas ruled:

"Public safety, public health, morality, peace and quiet, law and order—these are some of the more conspicuous examples of the traditional application of the police power to municipal affairs. Yet they merely illustrate the scope of the power and do not delimit it. . . . Miserable and disreputable housing conditions may do more than spread disease and crime and immorality. They may also suffocate the spirit by reducing the people who live there to the status of cattle. They may indeed make living an almost insufferable burden. They may also be an ugly sore, a blight on the community which robs it of charm . . . which makes it a place from which men turn. The misery of housing may despoil a community as an open sewer may ruin a river."[133]

Read that wording, filled with its modern conceptions of the public good, and its broad acceptance of the notion that government can fix any problem and uplift humanity through the exertion of police powers. *Berman* had plenty of talk about suffocating the spirit, and ugly sores, and communities as open sewers. But it lacked any serious discussion of the constitutional principles upon which this nation was founded. The U.S. Constitution was special, in that it made no promises of material equality or spiritual uplift. It simply protected individuals, their liberties and their property from incursions from the government. *Berman* was about positive rights, not the negative rights correctly enshrined in the Constitution. But in those heady days, who was worried about the musty old Constitution?

No doubt, conditions in inner-city Washington, D.C., were miserable, as they still are in so many parts of that and other cities. On a practical level, an increase in property rights and free enterprise is what's needed to improve material conditions for the individuals who live there. But as a matter of constitutional principle, the American government makes no promises about fixing up blight or providing healthy and happy neighborhoods. It is about protecting rights, nothing more.

Although the Washington, D.C., neighborhood that was the subject of *Berman* was poor and blighted, lacking proper utilities in many buildings, the targeted property was not blighted. Here is how Justice Douglas justified the taking of non-blighted property:

"The experts concluded that if the community were to be healthy, if it were not to revert again to a blighted or slum area, as though possessed of a congenital disease, the area must be planned as a whole. It was not enough, they believed, to remove existing buildings that were unsanitary or unsightly. It was important to redesign the whole area so as to eliminate the conditions that cause slums— the over-crowding of dwellings, the lack of parks, the lack of adequate streets and alleys, the absence of recreational areas, the lack of light and air, the presence of outmoded street patterns. It was believed that the piecemeal approach, the removal of individual structures that were offensive, would be only a palliative."[134]

The Constitution is about individual rights. The justice said that individual concerns—whether or not a particular property was blighted—don't matter as long as there is a justification for a community-wide redevelopment project. Ironically, this idea that piecemeal development is bad, that communities must be planned as a whole, is still a driving idea behind modern redevelopment, and the accompanying use of eminent domain to achieve it.

During city council meetings at which planning officials seek to scrape away scores of properties, taking with them beautifully kept ones along with crumbling structures, the government always rails against piecemeal developments. It is simply assumed that such things are bad, even though the nature of American freedom is one of piecemeal development. The whole concept of property rights is based on the idea that each individual owns a piece of the pie, rather than the central-planning model in which everything must be built by own developer, or controlled by one owner. We'll look at this planning philosophy in Chapter 5.

The *Berman* decision is filled with totalitarian-sounding pronouncements:

- "If those who govern the District of Columbia decide that the Nation's Capital should be beautiful as well as sanitary, there is nothing in the Fifth Amendment that stands in the way."[135]

- "If owner after owner were permitted to resist these redevelopment programs on the ground that his particular property was not being used against the public interest, integrated plans for redevelopment would suffer greatly."[136]

- "If the Agency considers it necessary in carrying out the redevelopment project to take full title to the real property involved, it may do so. It is not for the courts to determine whether it is necessary for successful consummation of the project that unsafe, unsightly, or unsanitary buildings alone be taken or whether title to the land be included, any more than it is the function of the courts to sort and choose among the various parcels selected for condemnation."[137]

The court concluded that as long as just compensation is paid for properties taken by eminent domain, the Fifth Amendment is satisfied. From there, of course, government agencies took the widest possible latitude, as guaranteed to them by a court more interested in social engineering than the specifics of the U.S. Constitution.

3. HARD CASES MAKE BAD LAW

Although *Berman* set the stage for the current situation of eminent domain abuses, many observers of the current situation blame a 1984 decision known as *Hawaii Housing Authority v. Midkiff* for compounding the problem.

Midkiff is an example of the saying, "Hard cases make bad law." In *Rindge*, *Berman* and *Missouri Railway*, the courts were dealing with straightforward questions: Is a scenic road a public use? Can eminent domain be used to rebuild an inner city neighborhood? Can this power be used to take land to build a grain elevator? The court's conclusions in these matters could easily be transferred from one locality to another, with the situation being relatively the same. But in *Midkiff*, the court was asked to evaluate an act of the Hawaiian Legislature designed to remedy a unique situation in the United States: the ownership of almost all of the state's land by a handful of owners outside of the federal government. The reality was a bit different from how the Hawaiian Legislature and the courts perceived it, however. Here is the description of the case, as made by the U.S. Supreme Court:

"To reduce the perceived social and economic evils of a land oligopoly traceable to the early high chiefs of the Hawaiian Islands, the Hawaii Legislature enacted the Land Reform Act of 1967 (Act), which created a land condemnation scheme whereby title in real property is taken from lessors and transferred to lessees in order to reduce the concentration of land ownership. Under the Act, lessees living on single-family residential lots within tracts at least five acres in size are entitled to ask appellant Hawaii Housing Authority (HHA) to condemn the property on which they live."[138]

It was a supposedly tough question. How to fix a land-ownership situation reminiscent of a Third World country? In reality, the federal and state governments owned nearly half of the land in the state of Hawaii, with an additional 47 percent owned by seventy-two private landowners.[139] The lack of available land resulted in the unusual situation in which people would build homes based on long-term leases, with the property reverting to the original owners at the end of the 50- or 75- or 100-year period.[140] The real cause for increasing prices was not the old oligopoly, but the control of the land by the government and excessive regulations that constrained the housing market. The state singled out one private owner, the Bishop estate, because it was the only trust that subdivided its land and leased it to residential tenants, explains Professor Kanner. The other trusts used their land for commercial and agricultural interests, and were thus left untouched.[141]

The Hawaii Legislature's fix was troubling. Tenants living in a condominium or neighborhood could petition the Hawaii Housing Authority to condemn the owners' property and sell it to them. The authority would hold hearings to determine if the use of eminent domain would "effectuate the public purposes," and then negotiations or a trial would determine the price.

Ironically, as the court explained, many of the state's landowners were ready and willing to sell their property, but didn't want to do so for federal tax reasons. "By condemning the land in question, the Hawaii Legislature intended to make the land sales involuntary, thereby making the federal tax consequences less severe. . . ."[142] Furthermore, as the court notes, nearly 49 percent of all of Hawaii's land was owned by the state and federal governments. It's unfortunate, then, that a problem exacerbated by the government couldn't be fixed with some tax exemptions and a sell-off of many parcels of government-owned land. Instead, the Hawaii Legislature created a system of massive land condemnations, in which many tenants could simply demand that their homes be sold to them, and with a government agency at the ready to take the land by force. One silver lining: The jury verdict came in exactly on the valuation figures provided by the Bishop estate, "the poshest part of Oahu, and probably all of Hawaii." according to Kanner. This wasn't about helping the poor.

Even though the reality was different from the depiction of the situation, the dynamics of the Hawaii real estate market were far removed from anything that could be contemplated in the 49 other states. But rather than think through the implications of its decision on the nation's long-established system of property rights, the court upheld the Hawaii Legislature's program. Writing for the unanimous court, Justice Sandra Day O'Connor argued:

"The mere fact that property taken outright by eminent domain is transferred in the first instance to private beneficiaries does not condemn that taking as having only a private purpose. The Court long ago rejected any literal requirement that condemned property be put into use for the general public."[143] In making that broad statement, Justice O'Connor referred to the *Rindge* decision.

And she referred also to *Berman*, quoting from it extensively. As attorney Chris Sutton points out, Justice O'Connor also wrote approvingly of the *Missouri Pacific Railway Co. v. Nebraska* case, upholding the idea that there must be a "justifying public purpose" to use eminent domain. Nevertheless, the result of the *Midkiff* decision was to reinforce the idea that governments could take property from anyone and give it to anyone else, provided it is justified as a public purpose. The Hawaii Legislature, Justice O'Connor said, enacted its land-reform law to undo "the perceived evils of concentrated property ownership in Hawaii—a legitimate public purpose."[144] In *Berman*, of course, Congress allowed the District of Columbia to take property for the supposedly legitimate public purpose of slum removal.

And in *Rindge*, the county of Los Angeles took valuable oceanfront property for the supposedly legitimate public purpose of building a road, even though the road connected to nothing and went nowhere beyond the Rindge Co.'s private property. It wasn't much of a leap, then, to the supposedly legitimate public purpose of bulldozing houses to build a theme park in order to prop up a city's revenue, or to the supposedly legitimate public purpose of taking any property if only a public agency could think of a "better" or higher tax-paying use for the land.

"It is one thing," argues Kanner, "to argue that policy decisions of Congress or a state legislature should be deferred to by the court. But what about the decisions of every rinky-dink, two-horse town where the city council people and the would-be redevelopers are political buddies, and where there are no diverse points of view, as in Congress?"[145]

It's a long slippery slope from John Locke and his views about the God-given right of property ownership, and from William Pitt, with his views on the power of the lowly cottage owner, to Justice O'Connor and her views of property rights. But this is the world in which American property owners live today. There has been some movement in the other direction, but by and large a homeowner or small-business owner in the United States has few protections if a government agency, acting on behalf of a big developer, decides that it has a better use for a property.

In America today, property rights no longer are human rights.

5. THE NEW URBAN RENEWAL:
AS BAD AS THE OLD URBAN RENEWAL

As in all utopias, the right to have plans of any significance belonged only to the planners in charge.

> — Jane Jacobs, author, *The Death and Life of Great American Cities*[146]

The term "urban renewal" conjures up plenty of memories, almost all of them bad. Started in 1949 to address the problem of dilapidated slum areas in America's major cities, this heavy-handed federal approach to blight removal cut a path of destruction through the nation, yet wasn't put to rest in that form until 1974.

The idea behind urban renewal was simple: Private enterprise, acting on its own, would not revive the nation's inner cities, so the federal government would lead the effort, although private companies would be contracted to build most of the new housing and commercial projects. Planners and architects, dreaming big visions, would create functioning, modern inner cities, but first government officials would need to clear away the "blight" that already existed. The tool to clear away the blight was eminent domain. In fact, it was an urban-renewal project that led to the groundbreaking *Berman* decision, which thus cleared the path for the widest possible definition of "public use" to justify the condemnation of privately owned properties.

Most of the areas targeted by urban renewal were indeed blighted by almost any definition of the term. But not all of them were, and too often the resulting projects led to conditions far worse than what had previously existed. In the process, individual rights and private property were treated so shabbily that it's hard to believe that such abuses could take place in a land noted for its constitutional liberties.

But after *Berman*, the floodgates opened nationwide.

The problem, of course, was that the "blight" was actually the homes, businesses, neighborhoods and schools of individual Americans. These Americans were promised, in the U.S. Constitution, the right to pursue life, liberty and happiness without the government's interference. But now the arbiters of the Constitution, the U.S. Supreme Court justices, found only one protection for property owners, the right to receive just compensation after their property was taken. If the government declared something blighted, through a legitimate legislative process, then who were the justices to argue?

Most Americans who lived through that era remember it well: Older urban neighborhoods bulldozed to make way for towering, bleak, unadorned public housing projects that quickly turned into dangerous, dehumanizing slums. Whereas some of the old slum neighborhoods were lively, full of street life and small businesses, the new high rise government-planned housing blocks were soulless and cold, more *Clockwork Orange* than *It's a Wonderful Life*. Many of the neighborhoods targeted for improvement were teeming slums, but the end result often was worse.

The projects triggered white flight, as middle-class residents began fleeing their once-settled neighborhoods for the suburbs. That wasn't the only cause, of course. The government subsidized the flight to the suburbs. But urban renewal played a role. In the heat of 1960s-era racial politics, some liberal big-city politicians viewed urban renewal as a way to break up older ethnic neighborhoods for blatantly political purposes.

The new projects would take years to complete, so after neighborhoods were bulldozed, large tracts of land would languish. This earned the projects mocking nicknames, such as "Hiroshima Flats" in St. Louis, "Bunker Hill" in Los Angeles and "Ragweed Acres" in Detroit, according to Purdue University History

Professor Jon C. Teaford, writing in a 2000 Fannie Mae Foundation policy paper.[147] Even the urban blacks who were the supposed beneficiaries of many of the projects had good reason to be afraid of federal renewal efforts. Urban renewal became known as "Negro Removal"[148] to civil-rights activists, given that the end result of so many of these projects was to clear away existing African-American residents to make room for downtown skyscrapers and luxury apartments.

"Congress launched the federal urban redevelopment program in Title I of the Housing Act of 1949, and during the next two decades, planners, mayors, journalists, and the public dreamed of grand schemes to revitalize the nation's cities," wrote Teaford. "Artists' renderings of slick glass and steel skyscrapers set in sunny plazas appeared in metropolitan newspapers and city planning reports, and nurtured hopes of a golden future. With the aid of Uncle Sam, cities were supposedly to be cleansed of their ugly past and re-clothed in the latest modern attire. By the early 1960s, however, skeptics were questioning the merits of federally subsidized urban renewal, and ten years later the program generally evoked images of destruction and delay rather than renaissance and reconstruction."[149]

Teaford explained that the basis of urban renewal thinking was the European modernist architects, such as Le Corbusier: "Ugly Victorian relics and pompous Beaux Arts edifices would give way to a city that conformed to the sleek functionalism favored by the greats of modern architecture." As a result, he wrote, Boston's old West End, a close-knit Italian community that bordered on the city's financial district, was cleared away to make room for "2,400 swank, high-rent apartments in soaring towers."[150] Such scenes were replayed time and again in cities throughout America, as the rich and powerful used federal government powers of eminent domain to grab hold of prime urban real estate.

Here we see urban renewal in its full horror: the destruction of the homes and livelihoods of people of modest means to benefit those of higher means. Yet many so-called advocates of the poor and down-trodden were—and remain—advocates of giving government vast powers to undertake social-engineering schemes. Academics, journalists, community activists, business leaders and urban planners celebrated and advocated for these programs in the 1950s and 1960s, and they continue to shill for their modern variations today.

Without eminent domain, very little of the destruction could have taken place. But once the government had the right to take whatever it pleased in the name of the "higher good," then the sky was the limit. Nothing stood in the way of what Martin Anderson, later to become a prominent Reagan administration official, called *The Federal Bulldozer,* in his prescient 1964 book.

Anderson's book—the first widely published conservative critique of the urban-renewal program—documents the destruction the policy caused to individual homeowners and neighborhoods and the government's misuse of eminent domain powers, but his case against the program is as much principled as pragmatic: "First, there is the important question of whether the federal urban renewal program is right in principle. Should government officials use taxpayers' money and the power of eminent domain to scatter residents of run-down areas of cities, demolish the buildings they once lived in, and then guide the reconstruction according to aesthetic, social and economic standards which they feel to be more suitable?"[151]

Ironically, although most observers now believe that the federal urban-renewal program was a disaster, few have learned the right lessons about it. Unlike Anderson, few observers recognize the problem is rooted in the principles behind it, not in the specific parameters of the program. By the way, Anderson realized in 1964 what some observers still refuse to realize forty years later: The beneficiaries of eminent domain are not the poor and the downtrodden, but the wealthy and influential:

"Who wants urban renewal?" he asked. "Certainly not the lower-income groups—they get displaced from their homes to make way for the modern apartments they cannot afford to rent. It is hard to know whether the middle class is much concerned with the changes that have occurred in the cities. . . . Then who is behind the tremendous push for urban renewal? Raymond Vernon, former Director of the New York Metropolitan Region Study, has speculated that the main stimulus for urban renewal comes from two elite groups—the wealthy elite and the intellectual elite. Both groups have strong economic and social attachments to the central city."[152]

Nothing much has changed today.

By the end of the federal urban-renewal program in 1974, cities that refused Title I funds and let the market hold sway over downtown redevelopment projects generally had more impressive downtown revitalizations than those that relied so heavily on federal power and that abused property rights so egregiously.[153] So it's hard to give credence to those who argue that without federal help, the nation's downtowns would not have revived themselves. Few people could have missed the demolition of St. Louis' Pruitt-Igoe and other hideous housing projects that came to epitomize what the urban-renewal program was all about: creating high-rise, crime-ridden slums that eventually had to be dynamited before any real urban progress could be made.[154]

Some of the "slums" and downtowns that urban renewal cleared away had many characteristics that today's urban planners are trying to re-create. This is an irony of government planning: It is driven by fads. In the 1950s and 1960s, international-style high-rise glass boxes, connected by big highways and plazas, were the in thing. It was the future, as taught in schools of architecture and urban planning. Buildings were to be devoid of character and fussy ornamentation. Streets were to be empty and bland. It was a brave new world, and old prejudices and preferences had to give way to modern times. This thinking was, in a way, totalitarian. The individual's preferences had to give way to what the central planners knew was best. Old prejudices and styles had to yield to a new, modern lifestyle. It's no surprise that the Nazis, fascists and Soviets embraced this type of planning and architecture.

One would have hoped that American planners and architects would have held different ideals, but this wasn't the case. The planners remade the cities according to a specific vision, using taxpayer dollars and eminent domain to achieve their goals. That is why double-decker freeways block views and access to rivers in many cities, and why downtowns often are cold and sterile, and why there's so little neighborhood life in so many places.

This approach seems so outdated and wrong today. But rather than reject central planning, modern planners have simply embraced a new type of central planning. This time, they are sure, they will get the formula right.

The new planning fashion is called New Urbanism. Its goals are to reinvigorate cities with many of the things stripped away by the last round of planning. Cities will be filled with street life, buildings covered in ornamentation. Planners a half-century ago hated the idea that people would live in small apartments above their stores, or that neighborhoods might have a crowded mix of homes, businesses and offices. That led to disorder, overcrowding, and a lack of public safety. But the New Urbanism is going to restore all those things. Instead of building freeways, today's planners want to boost the density of neighborhoods, and expect Americans to get around by light rail, the modern version of streetcars. Mixed-use is an important element of New Urbanism.[155]

The new plans, like the old plans, are based on some sound ideas. There was nothing wrong with the goal of clean, modern housing. The downtown ideal, with its shimmering skyscrapers and vast public areas, has its place. So does the New Urbanism. People like to walk around and shop in small stores. In many urban neighborhoods, streetcars are more efficient than automobiles. The problem with the new outlook, like with the old outlook, is that it doesn't respect individual choices or freedom. It doesn't accept that many types of neighborhoods and land uses can coexist in different parts of an urban region, or that different people will choose different neighborhoods at different stages in their lives. There's no acceptance of the classic American, founding ideal: Individuals are sovereign and make their own housing and work choices, not the planners.

Most important, the new plans, like the old ones, are based on the idea of force. Those who live and work in areas targeted for reform by the planners must leave their properties and their dreams behind. By the time things go wrong, and the faults of the New Urbanism become as obvious as the faults of the old urban renewal, it will be too late for the individuals whose lives have been disrupted. By then, the planners will be on to some other perfect new planning idea. They will sharpen the "tool" of eminent domain and start the whole process rolling again.

Just like the old planners, who created the urban-renewal mess and destroyed so many central cities, the new planners want to impose their vision on the rest of us from the top down, whether we like it or not. And the same legal theories of eminent domain that allowed the old urban-renewal projects to move forward are still in place, in service to a modernized version of the same centrally planned vision. For individuals, it's the same thing, whether their business is being bulldozed to make way for a housing project or an auto mall or a faux downtown: The king is no longer barred from the humble man's cottage.

FORGET THE POOR; SHOW US THE MONEY

For as bad as the old urban renewal was—and almost everyone from every political perspective has criticized the outcome of this massive federal program—at least it was done to remedy what its proponents saw as genuine urban problems of substandard housing and rundown neighborhoods. Since at least the early 1980s, urban renewal has morphed into something known mainly as redevelopment. Advocates of modern redevelopment projects often use the same language of blight to justify their efforts, but the purpose has changed dramatically.

Whereas the old urban renewal was designed largely to wipe away areas that unquestionably were down on their heels, the new urban renewal is basically about filling city coffers with money. It's about building tax bases. It's about luring new commercial retailers into older areas to bring in additional property and sales taxes. Just because these financial motives are sometimes (but not always) dressed up in the language of New Urbanism or downtown revitalization or blight removal should not fool one into thinking that the new urban renewal is about anything more than money.

"At the time of *Berman*, there was this feeling that there were terrible slums," explains Dana Berliner of the Institute for Justice. "A great new future was ahead of us if only we can clear away these slums. It was perceived as a huge national problem, and the court fell for it. The language of *Berman* was out of a 1950s-era sociology textbook. Since then, everyone knows those waves of urban renewal were total disasters. These days everyone is talking about lifestyle centers. There's always some kind of planning thing that will improve everyone's life. But first we must wipe out what's already there. . . . [156]

"In the 1950s and 1960s, at least [advocates of urban renewal] were claiming they were getting rid of substandard housing," says Berliner. "Now, government is nakedly using eminent domain to remove lower-income people and replace them with higher-income people. They are replacing property owners with higher-paying taxpayers."[157]

One of the best examples of this process is the situation in Lakewood, Ohio.

"As there were no structural problems with the houses, the city relied on terms like 'economic and functional obsolescence' to find blight," wrote Berliner, in her book, *Public Power, Private Gain.* "Translation: The houses lack two-car attached garages and second bathtubs and their yards are a little too small. No modern family could possibly want a historic, well-maintained house without a two-car attached garage."[158]

It's just as Berliner argued: City officials are using the power of eminent domain, not for a public use, but for the private advantage of wealthy people who want to live in areas now dominated by less-wealthy people. In Lakewood, there was the pretense of blight, but that blight definition is so ridiculous it is meaningless. In the 1950s, despite the destruction wrought by central planners backed by court-sanctioned eminent domain, at least officials were trying to deal with a real problem of slums. Now, the same power and program is used to remove lovely, middle-class homes in an area devoid of anything that could realistically be called blight, simply to put in their place the types of homes favored by the government officials.

In the Lake Elsinore, California, situation described more thoroughly in Chapters 1 and 9, attorney Bob Ferguson explained that, in creating a redevelopment area that encompassed hundreds of low- to moderate-income homes and trailers near a lake, the county's obvious intent was to wipe away the older structures and build an upscale, lake-oriented development. Ferguson saved the homes, but he did not get a published court decision.

He wishes the case was on record, to show that restrictions on eminent domain abuse should apply to areas that are not wealthy.[159] The county's Environmental Impact Report, he noted, said the area had a "resort-like quality" about it. The targeted neighborhood had lower crime rates than wealthier nearby areas, and was what Ferguson calls "an oasis for lower- and middle-income people, a lower- and middle-income Shangri-La." The purpose of the government was, pure and simple, to replace less wealthy residents with wealthier ones.

Even where planners blather about remaking urban areas and ridding blight, their goals increasingly are economic. They mainly want to replace older stores and businesses that pay modest amounts of taxes with big stores that pay oodles of taxes. In Brea, California, the city used the redevelopment process to bulldoze its old downtown and create a new downtown. Officials in that expensive Orange County city thirty-four miles from Los Angeles like to throw around New Urbanism as a justification. The new downtown has many elements of this planning fad: A promenade designed for walking rather than driving, densely packed houses within walking distance of the downtown, small loft apartments above the stores, hip signage and restaurants and nightclubs designed to lure people after dark. Everything is brand, spanking new, and every store and restaurant conforms to the same design theme.[160]

But Brea is not, and has never been, a blighted area. It is one of the wealthier communities one will find in the country. The previous downtown was old, but not seedy. And the new downtown, although attractive, is by no means a real downtown. It is more of an outdoor entertainment mall. Two mega-plex movie theaters are the anchor, along with a comedy club, several restaurants, a major-chain book and music store, and various boutiques designed to lure shoppers and moviegoers. The nearby housing is expensive, and most residents have no reason to walk downtown from their homes except, perhaps, to eat dinner or catch a movie.

So what is Downtown Brea all about? Despite its pretense, it is about gaining general-fund revenue for the city. It is about money, and about doing what the planners and officials want, rather than what individuals, operating in a free market, want. The small businesses and family-owned restaurants that were cleared out of the old downtown had to give up their futures because the city—which has turned itself into that area's main retail center—wanted the highest-possible tax return on such prime real estate.

It's a long way from inner-city Cleveland to Lakewood, from Watts to Brea. It's hard to understand how a program designed to clean up old slums could morph into a program to make wealthy communities even wealthier. *Berman*, of course, created the legal precedent for this process. But a Michigan Supreme Court decision really got this process rolling.

DESTROYING POLETOWN

During the 1950s and 1960s, government officials were worried about the expansion of slums, so property rights were sacrificed on behalf of the noble objective of renovating rundown urban neighborhoods. In the 1980s, officials in older, rust-belt cities were worried about the loss of jobs to other regions and other nations, and again property rights were sacrificed to the Issue Du Jour.

The starkest example of this took place in Detroit, along the border of the city of Hamtramck. Jobs were fleeing, crime was rising, and Detroit was perceived as a city without much of a future. Books could be written about the decline of this once mighty industrial powerhouse, but suffice it to say that high taxes, excessive unionization, liberal welfare policies and an incompetent city government that failed to adequately tend to traditional city services deserved much blame for the problems.

Instead of dealing with the root causes of the city's decline, Detroit officials decided to stop the decline on the backs of working-class homeowners who lived in a neighborhood known as Poletown. The residents there were unfortunate enough to live in a neighborhood coveted by General Motors for the construction of a new Cadillac plant. City officials were eager to land the new facility, one that would be built in the South, GM officials said, if Detroit didn't use eminent domain to clear away the 1,300 homes, 4,200 residents, 140 businesses, six churches and a hospital that were in the way, according to a *Detroit News* account.[161] Despite two Catholic churches that would be bulldozed, the archdiocese strongly supported the deal.

"The neighborhood adjacent to Hamtramck's southern border was, like Hamtramck, home to Poles as well as Albanians, Yugoslavs, Blacks, Yemenis and Filipinos," according to the *Detroit News* article.[162] "But some families had been there for generations, since the influx of Polish workers to the auto plants in the 1920s and '30s, and even before. Some of the first Polish settlements in the city in the 1870s had been in this area. It was the home of the original St. Mary's College and Polish Seminary at the corner of St. Aubin and Forest. It was the original location for the International Institute. St. John the Evangelist Catholic Parish had been founded there in the 1890s, Immaculate Conception Parish in 1918."

Although some of the homes were rough around the edges, Poletown was a settled, historic neighborhood, and most of the residents had no interest in moving. It was a clear case of city officials sacrificing the interests of individuals in the name of the "greater good," but in reality it was nothing more than the transfer of property from poorer residents to wealthy special interests. Perhaps because the villain here was General Motors, the fight against the use of eminent domain gained support from liberal activists who typically are uninterested in property rights. Ralph Nader helped lead a campaign against the taking from the basement of a soon-to-be-demolished Catholic church. Ironically, as Detroit was becoming known mainly for its decrepit neighborhoods and frightening slums, the city conspired to bulldoze one of the few vibrant communities left within its borders.

The case ultimately went to the Michigan Supreme Court, which in 1981 upheld the project in a 5–2 decision, *Poletown v. City of Detroit*. Although the decision applied only in Michigan, the ruling clearly was a signal to redevelopment agencies elsewhere that not just individual properties but entire neighborhoods can be bull-dozed to benefit private interests, provided some broad economic benefit can be argued. In *Poletown*, the city of Detroit did not even make an argument about blight or renovating the old area. It made a pure regional economic argument. The neighbors must sacrifice to keep jobs and the tax base in the Detroit area.

Here are the words of the majority:

"This case raises a question of paramount importance to the future welfare of this state and its residents: Can a municipality use the power of eminent domain granted to it by the Economic Development Corporations Act . . . to condemn property for transfer to a private corporation to build a plant to promote industry and commerce, thereby adding jobs and taxes to the economic base of the municipality and state?"[163]

As the court explained, the property owners argued that the tak-ing was mainly to benefit a private corporation, whereas the government argued that whatever private benefit occurred was inci-dental to the broad, public good. The court then agreed with the city of Detroit and General Motors:

"The power of eminent domain is to be used in this instance pri-marily to accomplish the essential public purposes of alleviating unemployment and revitalizing the economic base of the commu-nity. The benefit to a private interest is merely incidental. . . . If the public benefit was not so clear and significant, we would hesitate to sanction approval of such a project."[164]

In a dissenting opinion, Justice James L. Ryan made sensible arguments, but ones that increasingly have been ignored:

"With regard to highways, railroads, canals, and other instru-mentalities of commerce, it takes little imagination to recognize that without eminent domain these essential improvements, all of which require particular configurations of property—narrow and generally straight ribbons of land—would be 'otherwise impracticable'; they would not exist at all. . . . [I]t could hardly be contended that the existence of the automotive industry or the construction of a new General Motors assembly plant requires the use of eminent domain. . . .

"One of the reasons advanced by the defendants as justification of the taking in this case, and adopted by the majority, is the claim of alleviation of unemployment. . . . But the fact of the matter is that once [the Central Industrial Park or CIP] is sold to General Motors, there will be no public control whatsoever over the management, or operation, or conduct of the plant to be built there. . . . The level of employment at the new GM plant will be determined by private corporate managers primarily with reference, not to the rate of regional unemployment, but to profit."[165]

Justice Ryan was right. The number of jobs created was far less than promised. As the book, *Poletown: A Community Destroyed*, by Jeanie Wylie, explained in 1989, GM's promises largely were broken, but nearly a decade later it was too late to do anything about it.[166] The beauty of property rights is that they provide a bulwark to protect individuals from the state, regardless of the noble intentions of the state's actions. Officials always have some high-falutin reason for wanting to condemn property, whether it is slum removal or economic development. But as the courts give the government more leeway, the government continues to define its public uses down, to reinvent a phrase from Daniel Patrick Moynihan, who coined the term "defining deviancy down."[167] We're now at a stage where the mere promise of additional tax revenue is enough of a public purpose to justify the broad use of eminent domain's police powers. It's a downward spiral.

AN INCREMENT HERE, AN INCREMENT THERE

Every state has its own redevelopment laws and taxation system that determine exactly how redevelopment and eminent domain will be used in each locality. But this much is certain: It is widely used throughout the country these days and, in the wake of

Poletown, officials increasingly use financial justifications to argue for their proposals. It's all about the tax base.

The main financial mechanism is known as Tax Increment Financing. Don't let your eyes glaze over because of the technical nature of the concept. One of the reasons redevelopment agencies have been able to get away with as much as they have gotten away with, is their portrayal of the system as one that is unknowable to mere mortals. Only the experts, they say, are knowledgeable enough to understand it. Their message to the public: "This is complicated stuff. Trust us to do the right thing." But the public needs to understand what motivates the blatant abuse of eminent domain as the first step toward battling such abuses.

Tax Increment Financing, or TIF, simply means that once a government redevelopment agency declares an area blighted, and it becomes part of a redevelopment area, the agency gains all the additional property-tax revenue generated in that area, instead of the additional money going to other parts of government. Let's say the homes and businesses in a five-block area pay $500,000 a year in property taxes. The redevelopment agency decides that it wants to build something else on those blocks. So it declares the area blighted, based on a wide range of factors, and makes that five-block area a redevelopment area (or adds it to an existing area).

Now all the property taxes paid in excess of that $500,000 will go to the redevelopment agency. The idea is the agency came in and cleaned up the blight and turned it into a tax-generating area, so it should be rewarded with the new tax dollars. Those new property-tax dollars are called tax increment, and they continue to flow to the agency until—at least in theory—the bond that funded the project is repaid, and the area reverts to its previous tax status. In reality, once an area is a redevelopment area, it almost always remains one in perpetuity. It's like a "temporary" tax increase. We know they can exist in theory, but it's hard to find a government agency willing to sunset a steady stream of taxpayer income.

This tax mechanism might be justifiable if, say, that five-block area were a vacant lot collecting weeds and trash rather than tax revenue. All of a sudden the redevelopment agency revives the area and puts a tax-generating shopping mall on the site. Sometimes that's the case. But in a real-estate market that's on the upswing, property values are going up anyway. After the area is declared a redevelopment area, the agency gets all the tax-revenue increases, even if it had nothing to do with those increases. Critics complain that redevelopment agencies purposefully choose areas that already are improving, and then simply benefit by the natural increases in the area's tax base.

"While inflation naturally forces up expenses for public services such as education and police, their property tax revenues within a redevelopment area are thus frozen. All new revenues beyond the base year can be spent only for redevelopment purposes," according to *Redevelopment: The Unknown Government*.[168]

The end result: Tax increments divert money from traditional public services, such as police, fire, schools and courthouses. When entire cities declare themselves redevelopment areas, what they in fact are doing is stealing tax revenue that would typically go to the county or state and redirecting them into the city. So, in addition to seeking new property-tax revenue by sparking the development of new retail centers, redevelopment agencies want to create new redevelopment areas to divert existing property-tax revenue from other government agencies. Some of the more entertaining lawsuits related to redevelopment pit one government agency against another, especially as school districts fight to maintain revenue through what are known as pass-throughs, which compensate the districts for money lost through redevelopment. In Garden Grove, California, for instance, the redevelopment agency has tried to shortchange the school district on such payments.[169]

The broader the agency's redevelopment footprint, the larger its tax base. So the system gives agencies incentive to create as many redevelopment areas as possible. Although officials can specifically exempt redevelopment areas from eminent domain power, this is rare. Even where such powers are exempted, it always is possible to add them back. Typically, a supermajority vote of a city council is what is needed. While cities and their agencies convince the public to accept these redevelopment plans as a way merely to bolster revenue that funds city services, they really are convincing the public to give officials greater power over private property. They are allowing officials to clear away whatever properties get in the way of any new development officials prefer.

Property tax is a main lure. Tax increment is the lifeblood of the redevelopment agency. It can subsidize projects, pay for infrastructure within the project area and service the bond debt. Part and parcel of this property-tax mechanism is debt. Redevelopment agencies must incur debt by floating bonds. It's part of the law. "By law, for a redevelopment agency to begin receiving property taxes, it must first incur debt. In fact, property tax increment revenues may only be used to pay off outstanding debt. Pay-as-you-go is not part of redevelopment law or philosophy," according to *Redevelopment: The Unknown Government.* The bonds can be floated without a public vote. As a result, the small city of Brea, 36,000 population, has total redevelopment indebtedness of nearly $435 million.[170]

Another lure is sales tax. States divvy up their sales tax differently, but in some states local communities get a portion of the sales-tax revenue. In California, arguably the state with one of the largest numbers of redevelopment and eminent domain abuses, property-tax revenue is capped because of Proposition 13, the statewide initiative passed in 1978 limiting property-tax valuation increases to 2 percent a year and capping property tax bills at 1 percent of the valuation. The goal was to keep people from being taxed out of their homes as property values soared in the late 1970s. It remains a popular initiative, and one of the most important checks on excessive taxation in a state where officials are addicted to taxing and spending.[171]

But for all its good, Proposition 13, and subsequent legislation divvying up property-tax revenue, gave the state control over property-tax dollars. Instead of property taxes going to fund local services, they went directly into the state coffers, and cities became dependent on the state for their funding. Big cities with political clout were well taken care of, but smaller cities got shortchanged. They no longer gained much benefit from property-tax increases. Small cities—and even the most urbanized areas of California are primarily collections of smaller, adjacent cities—came to view sales tax as manna from heaven. In California, 1 cent of every dollar in taxable sales in a city's boundary goes into the city's general fund, as income that can be spent in any way that cities choose.

So redevelopment areas became the hottest thing. Once an area was formed, debt would be created in the form of bond issuance. The bonds would be sold to guarantee revenue to pay for the project and provide "incentives" to retailers to locate in the area. The tax increment would repay the bond. And—here's the key point—the sales-tax revenue generated by the new stores would fill the city's general fund with discretionary dollars. The stores most preferred are the big-box stores—Costco, Wal-Mart and Home Depot—as well as auto malls and shopping malls. These types of stores provide the maximum sales-tax payout per square foot of property, so anything that paid less than the optimum amount would be a prime target for eminent domain. And that's a best-case scenario. "In reality, as the negotiators get down to final details of the deal, there is much horse trading, so that often the municipality will trade away (or diminish) its share of the sales tax (i.e., let the redeveloper have it), and lose its shirt on the deal," explains Gideon Kanner.[172]

Like with everything, whether it is good or bad, California is on the cutting edge. But the same process was taking place in cities across the country.

In downtown Pittsburgh, Mayor Tom Murphy had been trying to redevelop an area around Fifth and Forbes. The original plan would have condemned 62 privately owned buildings and eliminated more than 100 store owners[173] and handed the land over to a developer that would bring in national chain stores. The project eventually failed, after Nordstrom pulled out of the development following a year of contention, and the city pressed on with a plan that would not use eminent domain.[174] Although the city would not have gained sales tax directly, as would be the case with a similar project in, say, downtown San Francisco, the tax lure was still the main reason for the project.

"In Pennsylvania, property tax is the major source of revenue at the local level," explained Eric Montarti, policy analyst with the Allegheny Institute for Public Policy in Pittsburgh. "They wanted to get something built there to get an increase in the property-tax base. That would create economic activity in center city, and would provide revenue in the form of a parking tax and wage tax."[175]

However states divvy up the tax dollar, redevelopment is a means to provide more money to the cities that use it. As Montarti said, Pittsburgh officials have used broad blight designations to use redevelopment, but increasingly suburbs are using it to build on "greenfield" sites. In one policy paper for the institute, he writes that "The new owners of the upscale Galleria Mall in Mt. Lebanon are seeking a blight designation of the area in order to qualify for tax increment financing. These funds will be used to redevelop the mall's parking garage and redesign an intersection leading to the mall."[176]

In another policy paper, he makes this important point: "A seemingly neutral development tool, TIF can be bent to the will of its proponents. In Pittsburgh, for example, TIF has largely been used to build retail developments and commercial establishments not in blighted areas, but on some of the most valuable real estate in the region."[177]

How's that for a switch from renewing slums?

Tax-increment financing is common throughout the country, and various redevelopment agencies use different rationales to justify its use. For instance, the Rapid City, South Dakota, redevelopment agency explains that TIF is used "to encourage the redevelopment of deteriorated or otherwise blighted real property in Rapid City through the investment of public funds; to stimulate economic development in the community by assisting projects that promote the long term economic vitality of the community; to stimulate increased private investment in areas that would have otherwise remained undeveloped or underdeveloped and which will, in the long term, provide a significant source of additional tax revenues to all taxing entities . . . "[178]

That's a broad charge, and although it makes at least some nodding reference to improving blighted areas, it's easy to see TIF's main purpose of providing additional tax revenue to taxing entities.

Each state differs in the legal standards by which blight can be declared. Although California has been particularly abusive of TIF, state courts have required tougher standards for declaring an area blighted. That's probably because California localities have become so abusive of the redevelopment process that the courts were pressed to rein it in a bit. In Pennsylvania, blight determinations are nebulous. It's hard to know what the standards are, Montarti explains.[179]

The state of Nebraska, through its Community and Rural Development Division, argues that TIF "is primarily designed to finance the public costs associated with a private development project." Nebraska limits TIF to "redeveloping substandard and blighted areas within a community." In Nebraska, the state details five blight standards:[180]

1. Unemployment must be 120 percent of the state or national average;
2. The average age of buildings is at least forty years old;
3. More than half of the property in the area is unimproved and has remained unimproved for at least forty years;
4. The per capita income in the area is below the area average;
5. The population is stable or decreasing according to the last two censuses.

On the surface, Nebraska looks like it is imposing a tough standard on the use of tax-increment financing. The area must be blighted. But take a quick look at those standards for determining blight, and one realizes that blight is broadly defined. Unemployment being slightly above the state or national average? At any given time, the entire state of Nebraska might have an unemployment rate above the national average. Beautiful, upscale historic neighborhoods—of the type prevalent in Omaha and Lincoln—could be blighted simply because of their age. Nebraska has a population that is more stable than most parts of the country, and a slightly lower per capita income in one neighborhood could justify the use of eminent domain and tax-increment financing. Consider also that redevelopment areas can be gerrymandered as easily as congressional districts. If an agency wants to redevelop a fancy downtown area, it need only draw the boundaries to include a nearby poorer neighborhood to get a free hand with regard to TIF and eminent domain.

In South Carolina, the law limits TIF not only to areas that are "predominantly slum or blighted," but also to those which "threaten to become" that way.[181] That's fairly broad. So is the law's justification of TIF to control "sprawl conditions." The city of Spokane, Washington, requires that tax-increment financing be used in blighted areas or "for business ventures that would otherwise have upfront costs that can become expensive."[182] Doesn't every project have expensive upfront costs? In Arkansas, tax-increment financing can be used in an area that is not merely deteriorated, but "under-developed,"[183] which is a standard typical in almost every state. That is what paves the way for the development of normal, empty suburban and rural lots that should be developed under normal market circumstances.

Advocates of government-subsidized development often argue a case of "market failure"—i.e. the market wouldn't provide a supposedly needed project without the taxpayer-funded enticement. But as we saw in the *Midkiff* decision, many Hawaii property owners would not have been hesitant to sell their land were it not for a punitive element of the federal tax system. Often, the underdeveloped areas would develop on their own were it not for regulatory barriers to building on old sites. Often the regulatory cleanup requirements for old industrial sites (as well as the liability for owning polluted sites) are so severe that developers stay away. In many older cities, buildings cannot be redeveloped unless the new owners bring the old buildings up to modern code standards. In cities where property values are low, it isn't financially feasible to convert the old structures to new uses under those standards. Too bad that the League of Cities, the American Planning Association and other advocates for government agencies don't focus more attention on promoting solutions to these problems rather than defending eminent domain's use for economic development.

In Chicago, the *Bond Buyer* reported in 2002[184] on a plan to use a TIF-like process to redevelop a prime downtown piece of real estate—an old golf course that is surrounded by some of the prime real estate in the city. To get around the requirement that a TIF area be blighted, city leaders pushed ahead a special assessment district that, in all intents and purposes, was the same thing as a redevelopment area sans the blight findings. The goal was to build a large development that included condominiums and office buildings. When one looks closely at the situation, however, the special district seemed unnecessary. The reason developers ignored the site, the newspaper reported, was because of a city law requiring new developments to include parks and a public school. Developers had balked at developing the site because of those costly requirements.

That case didn't involve eminent domain. But this point is crucial: Cities use redevelopment, corporate subsidies and eminent domain to encourage development to either fix blight or bring in new tax revenue, or both. Usually, development would happen anyway. Often, if cities looked at fixing their own regulatory barriers to new development, they would get the tax revenue they need without destroying the property rights and aspirations of their citizens.

In a January 2000 issue brief from the Presidential Initiative Task Force on Economic Development, C. Vernon Gray argued: "Most experts agree that although tax increment financing can be used to great advantage under the right circumstances, it should never be used where it isn't needed."[185] The problem, of course, is that cities will use it anytime they want to expand their tax base or pilfer tax revenue from other agencies. They will use eminent domain to clear away the sites so they can bring in tax increment, and the sales taxes and other taxes that come from the new businesses. Without solid property-rights protections, that means the government calls the shots, and individuals must live at the mercy of those who rule them. Tax-increment-financing—and eminent domain—will be used where it is not needed as long as the courts allow the current situation to continue.

THE LIFE OF CITIES

To recap: In the Constitution, the government's right to seize property was limited to public uses. That was expanded from basic, government uses such as building a courthouse or a school to the construction of the first interstate transportation system—the railroads. Until the *Berman* decision, public uses remained fairly limited, despite some exceptions. But *Berman* unleashed the use of eminent domain for massive urban-renewal projects. Cities then pushed the envelope, and, after *Poletown*, used broader and broader rationales to justify the use of eminent domain. Now, government can call almost anything a "public" use or "blight" and is free to use eminent domain. The simple goal of expanding tax revenue often is enough, in the courts' view, to justify robbing Peter and paying Paul.

The consultants and planners who justify the land grabs base their new plans on the latest planning dogmas. At many a city council meeting, one hears development directors complain about "piecemeal development." In their view, development must be centrally planned, built all at once by a single developer. The existing "blighted" conditions are developed piecemeal, with different developers and different owners doing different things with their properties. Even the New Urbanists, who supposedly want to restore variety to urban settings, only want that variety if it fits in with their centrally planned theme. One doesn't want old mixed with new, shabby next to gleaming, or an ethnic store next to a national chain.

The new "downtowns" built under such thinking, such as Brea's, look like they are something Disney might have created. Actually, Disney has created such a project in Anaheim, California, called Downtown Disney, although it did not entail the use of eminent domain, and it doesn't pretend to be much more than an extension of resort-area theme parks. Such downtowns might be attractive and fun places to shop, but they have little to do with real blight removal. They have everything to do with tax revenue, and they should be built using market forces, not government powers.

For as much as things have changed, and for as different as the economic incentives are between the 1950s and the current day, thinking hasn't changed as much as one might suspect. Government officials still want to impose their vision on the governed. Central plans are preferred to the natural development that springs up in a free society. Big corporations are eager to work in partnership with government agents to take what isn't theirs and build profitable, subsidized projects.

Back in 1961, not long after *Berman* and while urban planners were still pushing ahead their disastrous urban-renewal projects, urban planner Jane Jacobs wrote her Jeremiad against the planning mentality of her day. It is called *The Death and Life of Great American Cities.*[186] Most of her critique could be directed against the planning mentality prevalent today.

Jacobs' main point is that cities need to evolve naturally. They need to reflect the hopes, aspirations and entrepreneurship of those who live in them. The planners, using eminent domain and government subsidies, ruined thriving communities, she explained, and imposed plans that often had the opposite effect of their good intentions. In *Death and Life,* Jacobs articulated the value of freedom. Regardless of the plans, and how good they look on paper and what they mean to, say, downtown business interests, they were no good because they ignored what she called "the intricate social and economic order under the seeming disorder of cities."[187] The planners come in, whether they are the old-school, big-government planners with their housing blocks or the new-school ones with their faux downtown shopping centers, and pretend that the life and vitality that already exist are worth nothing. They believe the properties are worth nothing more than what an appraiser says they are worth. They believe that business good will is worthless and that the friendships and memories created by those who live in the neighborhood can be scraped away and easily replaced. They believe the freedom to chart one's own destiny is worth absolutely nothing.

Wrote Jacobs:

"In New York's East Harlem there is a housing project with a conspicuous rectangular lawn which became an object of hatred to the project tenants. A social worker frequently at the project was astonished by how often the subject of the lawn came up, usually gratuitously as far as she could see, and how much the tenants despised it and urged that it be done away with. When she asked why, the usual answer was, 'What good is it?' or 'Who wants it?' Finally one day a tenant more articulate than the others made this pronouncement: 'Nobody cared what we wanted when they built this place. They threw our houses down and pushed us here and pushed our friends somewhere else. We don't have a place around here to get a cup of coffee or a newspaper even, or borrow fifty cents. Nobody cared what we need. But the big men come and look at that grass and say, 'Isn't it wonderful! Now the poor have everything!' "[188]

In America, the big men aren't supposed to be able to come in and take our rightly owned property, no matter how well-intentioned their purpose. They shouldn't be able to force people to live in ways they don't want to live. And, as Jacobs noted, the plans are almost always failures, because the big men don't understand individual lives and how they are affected by planning decisions:

"There is a quality even meaner than outright ugliness or disorder, and this meaner quality is the dishonest mask of pretended order, achieved by ignoring or suppressing the real order that is struggling to exist and to be served," she wrote.[189] That's why this nation eschews central planning in favor of individual freedom and local decision-making. It's what makes America what it is, yet that quality is evaporating as city managers and town councils bulldoze anything that, in their eyes, doesn't live up to their financial or aesthetic considerations.

Jacobs tells the story of Boston's North End, "an old, low-rent area merging into the heavy industry of the waterfront, and it is officially considered Boston's worst slum and civic shame. It embodies attributes which all enlightened people know are evil because so many wise men have said they are evil. Not only is the North End bumped right up against industry, but worse still it has all kinds of working places and commerce mingled in the greatest complexity with its residences. It has the highest concentration of dwelling units, of any part of Boston. . . . It has little parkland. Children play in the streets. Instead of super-blocks, or even decently large blocks, it has very small blocks. . . . Its buildings are old. Everything conceivable is presumably wrong with the North End."[190]

Yet, it was one of the most vibrant, interesting, safe, stable parts of the city. People flocked to the neighborhood to imbibe its ethnic culture and to shop in its grocery stores and eat in its restaurants. Yet, at the time, Boston's bankers and government officials were consumed with ideas of "doing something" about this supposed slum. Twenty years after she first visited the neighborhood, Jacobs was "amazed at the change." On their own, residents fixed up buildings and so forth. That was 1959, when she visited the area a second time. Today, the North End is one of Boston's prime historic neighborhoods, where crowds of tourists love meandering around the winding streets.

Fortunately, the North End survived the wiles of the planners. Look what Boston would have lost—not to mention what the tens of thousands of individuals who have lived, worked and played there over that time would have lost—had the city come in, used eminent domain to acquire the properties, and done to it what, say, Detroit did to its *Poletown*. In Orange County, California, the cities of Anaheim and Fullerton were two of the larger cities in the county as it boomed in the 1960s and 1970s. Fullerton did very little in the way of redevelopment and rarely misused eminent domain. It left its old downtown alone even during a dark period when few businesses occupied its old brick storefronts. Anaheim used eminent domain to acquire most of its downtown, and bulldozed it.

Now, downtown Anaheim is a virtual ghost town. There are some uninteresting office buildings, a few public buildings and little else, except for parking lots. Many of the glorious plans proposed by planners never came to pass. Some of those plans that did work, such as a Disney ice-skating rink, are nice enough, but do little to energize a downtown area. Oh, yes, in Spring 2004, city officials announced the latest new downtown plan that is sure to revive the area.[191] Don't hold your breath. By contrast, downtown Fullerton is one of this suburban county's historic highlights—an area filled with nightclubs, restaurants, interesting stores and a fairly vibrant life day and night.

Now think about what the planners said about Boston's North End. It's not much different from what they said about downtown Fullerton back when the city was thinking of "redeveloping" it. To the planners, piecemeal development is bad, but that's exactly what we have in those two places. To the planners, a lack of parks and small blocks are bad. But Anaheim has big blocks. That's not what makes an urban area attractive. Today's planners would complain that the North End and Fullerton don't bring in enough sales tax or property tax revenue. But that's no way to evaluate a city, or to determine who gets to stay and who must go.

Chris Norby is an Orange County supervisor, a former Fullerton city councilman, and a longtime statewide activist against eminent domain abuses. His organization, MORR (Municipal Officials for Redevelopment Reform), might not have the catchiest name, but it has helped put the issue of eminent domain abuse before the California Legislature. Norby has been complaining about eminent domain abuses by city governments since long before the issue made national headlines, and his efforts over the years have helped keep heavy-handed redevelopment plans out of Fullerton. He traces much of "this insidious thing back to planning dogma. Big is always better than small. It's a fascist mindset of forced conformity."[192]

"From an international standpoint, we pride ourselves as a country that respects human rights and honors property rights and economic freedom," he said in an interview. "There are cases throughout the world where legal decisions are far more protective of property rights than they are here. . . . In Japan, for example, eminent domain can only be used after the person who owns the property has died. Here's a country which has a highly collectivist sort of teamwork mentality in the best sense, yet there are farmers still out there (after fifteen or sixteen years) protesting land that was seized for Narida airport. . . . And an airport clearly is a public use. A similar thing happened in Mexico City when they were going to build a new Mexico City airport. They were going to use eminent domain to take the land of these peasants. They got rifles, they got tractors, they said you are not going to take our land. That's a public use, uses I wouldn't object to. And yet the concept of land ownership, of being tied to certain pieces of land is much deeper than it is here.[193]

"You go to Tokyo and you'll see tiny little houses and little sushi stores next to huge skyscrapers," Norby added. "It's the very thing that gives the street life in Japan such fascination. If you see these buildings, some old, some new, some high-rise modern, some single-story, almost right next to each other, it gives their street scene a really interesting vitality. Japanese cities from a distance are somewhat drab, but close at a street level they are very diverse and interesting, even within a neighborhood. Part of it is they didn't have the homogenization of urban renewal. . . . They weren't all built on this Stalinesque, grand, uniform scale. And yet these are the very uses which redevelopment condemns as being incompatible, small-property owners, irregularly shaped lots. They have to be all developed according to one plan, not just one land-use plan . . . but actually one owner."[194]

Norby's last descriptions—irregularly shaped lots, small-property owners, piecemeal development—are all justifications for blight designations, not just in California but throughout the country. And eliminating blight, the courts repeatedly rule, is a legitimate public use. So is replacing those small buildings with bigger ones that pay more in taxes.

Frank Hotchkiss, a former associate of Jane Jacobs who spent the bulk of his career in the belly of the planning beast as the head planner for the Southern California Association of Governments, insists that most of the planners he has known throughout his life are good and decent people who really want to make other people's lives better through well-thought-out development. But a recent brainstorming session among top planners and influential Los Angeles-area officials about what the region should look like in the next several decades epitomized the problem, as he, Jacobs, Norby and others would clearly see it.

"They talked about their concern for the environment, and about doing good for people and preserving history," Hotchkiss said in an interview. "But nobody talked about freedom. There was no excitement about entrepreneurship, or about letting the market work, and no belief in people making their own choices in a free society. When I brought up the missing value of individualism, I was told that 'individualism' epitomizes everything that is wrong with modern society."[195]

Hotchkiss wasn't stunned by the response, although he found it quite revealing. He noted that no planner that he knows is willing to live in the high-density, car-free communities planned for others. No planner, I assume, would like to have his home removed to make way for something else.

In a marketplace, planners are free to offer their ideas and projects. If the public wants to live in high rises, there will be a market for high rises. The problem is, planners have the force of government to take private property and make us live the way they want us to live. It all comes down to eminent domain. Without it, these men and women who want to improve our lives, but don't respect us enough to allow us to make our own decisions, could not come in, bulldoze a lively old urban area and try to force the residents into a high-rise housing project. Without the use of eminent domain in its current form, they could not bulldoze our entire neighborhood of single-family homes to build some theme-park or a faux downtown—whatever their pleasure may be, based on ideas as high-minded as the New Urbanism or as base as improving a city's tax revenue. The main problem is the abuse of the "tool" of eminent domain.

6. THE EMINENT DOMAIN MENTALITY

The greatest evil is not done now in those sordid 'dens of crime' that
Dickens loved to paint. . . . It is conceived and ordered (moved, seconded,
carried and minuted) in clean, carpeted, warmed and well-lighted offices, by
quiet men with white collars and cut fingernails and smooth-shaven cheeks
who do not need to raise their voice.

— C.S. Lewis[196]

Victims of eminent domain abuse cannot understand how something so utterly unfair can take place legally. Don't city officials, and the consultants and developers who benefit from the transfer of properties, have even a tinge of bad conscience from their efforts? Don't judges see the obvious violation of the U.S. Constitution?

In my experience, the answer is no. Those who are part of the eminent domain game have plenty of rationales for their behavior. They are promoting the public good, after all. Sure, there may be some discomfort by some people, they reason, but that's the price of progress. Others are so immersed in their bureaucratic regimens that it doesn't even dawn on them what they are inflicting on their fellow citizens. Americans no longer are taught to fear the power of government. Increasingly, the American public sees the government as an unquestioned good that is always working in the public interest. If the process is legal, then it must be okay. Ironically, the victims of eminent domain often are viewed as recalcitrant and ill-mannered people who are getting in the way of promised increases in sales taxes. Often, members of the public think that that old apartment building or working-class neighborhood or small strip mall isn't very attractive, and the new businesses or homes officials and developers are promising will be better for property values and for their own lives. Who doesn't want great new shopping? Who doesn't want a spiffier city? Often, no one bothers to think about constitutional principles and legal niceties like property rights.

And so, as the quotation from C.S. Lewis describes, a great evil takes place—not by men and women who are diabolical. But by individuals, with nice suits, good jobs and clean fingernails. Their motivations and justifications are complex. But, in knowing and interviewing many of the people who have advocated grievous eminent domain abuses, I've concluded that they mostly sleep well at night. They often are utterly convinced that they are the good guys in the process. Many of these people are our family members, friends and neighbors.

There is an ethical concept known as "administrative evil,"[197] which explains how people immersed in large bureaucracies can do things that are hard to understand in hindsight. The concept is usually discussed in terms of individuals who participated in, say, the Nazi concentration camp system, or in the Soviet gulag system. Historians and ethicists still wonder how good, decent German or Russian people could have earnestly worked in bureaucracies that sent innocent men, women and children to their deaths. It's talked about also in terms of the military, and how generally honorable officers and soldiers can participate in the killing of civilians. These aren't cases of evil men with evil intent, but of average people who go along with barbaric acts.

The concept applies to other evils, even if those evils are a far cry from concentration camps and mass killings. The use of eminent domain against people for private gain is certainly immoral if not evil. When used to transfer a family homestead to another private owner for simple economic gain, it is hard to justify on ethical grounds. Yet people do it, thousands of times a year. Many good, decent, hard-working Americans are involved in this industry, by working for either agencies that take properties or the many consultants and developers that also are part of this unseemly process.

This is what C.S. Lewis was writing about.

Consider the types of things eminent domain advocates say, and you'll understand a whole lot about this dreadful process. The head of the New London Development Corporation, the lead organization in a massive New London, Connecticut, redevelopment project that condemned an entire working-class waterfront neighborhood, has made statements that show the grandiose pretensions of some of redevelopment's true believers. As the Institute for Justice pointed out, the former president of Connecticut College, NLDC President Claire Gaudiani, told a Baptist church on Martin Luther King Jr. Day that her efforts to redevelop the city were like King's efforts. "You and I are called to be transforming interveners, like the Messiah, like Martin Luther King."[198]

Of course, I don't think Jesus or Martin Luther King Jr. drove people out of their homes to benefit the wealthy. Jesus was the friend of the poor and lowly. Martin Luther King Jr. sought to uplift the downtrodden. Gaudiani and powerful redevelopment people like her are trying to uplift the already uplifted on the backs of the poor and middle class. Gaudiani, the Institute for Justice points out, once said: "Anything that's working in our great nation is working because somebody left skin on the sidewalk." The obvious question: Whose skin? In New London, it was the property owners' skin, not Gaudiani's. The NLDC's Web site explains that "economic prosperity and social justice are two sides of the same coin."[199] That may be so, but not when that prosperity is created by driving people out of their homes and abusing their rights.

As outrageous as those statements are, they are revealing of how many redevelopment advocates think.

A May 9, 2003, article in the *Portsmouth (New Hampshire) Herald* captures the unfairness of the New London project: "The first time the city of New London, Connecticut, seized Pasquale Cristofaro's home, it was to make way for a sea wall that never materialized.

Instead, private medical offices sprouted over the backyard plot where Cristofaro once grew tomatoes, squash and grapes.

"Three decades later, when the city wanted to raze another Cristofaro family home to clear the way for a riverfront hotel, health club and offices, the seventy-seven-year-old Italian immigrant dug in and fought back in court."[200]

The city coveted the neighborhood of well-kept Victorian-era homes near the waterfront. As in many older cities, city planners had big dreams of revival, so they looked for prime areas of real estate— waterfronts, park views, etc.—that would be appealing to big developers, rather than to blighted areas that needed help. That's the scam about eminent domain: Cities "take areas that are in pretty good shape that a developer would want—good, solid, safe areas near the highway or with a beautiful view," said Institute for Justice attorney Dana Berliner.[201] The institute represented the homeowners in a lawsuit.

New London officials, acting through the private New London Development Corporation, sought to redo a ninety-acre area along the waterfront. On one end was Pfizer Inc.'s new research facility. In many ways Pfizer was the driving force behind the eminent domain plan. The *Wall Street Journal* reported in a September 2002 article how Pfizer came to the town with a plan: "In return for millions of dollars in tax breaks and other incentives, Pfizer would build a $300 million global research center next to Fort Trumbull and bring 2,000 jobs to New London. Scientists and other employees would move into spiffy new housing, spend their paychecks in the city, throng to a new hotel, conference center and health club nearby. And all of it would layer fresh tax dollars on the city's thin budget."[202]

By now this all sounds familiar. An influential corporation uses its economic leverage to secure subsidies and the use of eminent domain on its behalf. City officials trip all over themselves, salivat- ing over the new revenue. The ultimate goal is to remove middle-class and poor residents and make way for wealthier ones, of the type who live in expensive houses and visit the health club. The project is private, benefiting private parties, but then the city argues that it is really for the "public good" because of the promised new revenue. As the *Journal* explained, "What sets the New London case apart is that many longtime residents say the NLDC [New London Development Corporation] was merely a cover for Pfizer, giving a big corporation free rein to remake an area well beyond the boundaries of its own property."

This is the essence of how redevelopment officials think: What is good for General Motors (or Pfizer or Wal-Mart or Costco) is good for America (or their particular community).

In New London, the property owners who fought back achieved only mixed success. In a 249-page decision, a Superior Court judge ruled that economic development is a genuine public use, but spared some of the houses because city officials did not say how they were going to use the land. On March 3, 2004, the Connecticut Supreme Court ruled, in a 4–3 decision, against the remaining homeowners battling to save their properties.

"The New London Development Corp. (NLDC) has spent the last several years razing property in Fort Trumball," according to a statement from the Institute for Justice.[203] "Left standing amid the rubble are the homes of a group of committed property owners, including a family who has lived in Fort Trumball for more than 100 years and in the same house since 1905."

No doubt, there's plenty of skin left on the sidewalks.

The city of Garden Grove, California, explains its redevelopment programs this way: "As a declining area is improved and the causes of blight eliminated the entire community benefits through the creation of new or restored homes, prospering businesses, more attractive public areas and parks, and renewal of civic pride. Because you do not live in a blighted area, or because you avoid such areas, does not mean that you are safe from the effects of deterioration and decay in the community. The California Community Redevelopment Law was passed in recognition of the fact that the problems and adverse impact of deteriorating areas cannot be confined and ignored. . . . "[204]

The process sounds so good and so clinical. Garden Grove officials leave out all the information about targeting properties for theme parks, or about low-balling property owners when it comes time for just compensation, or about all the failed projects and corporate subsidies. But the sterile description above is the way many officials—and many residents who don't think too carefully about redevelopment—see the world. Somehow they accept the civic textbook explanation and tune out the voices of despair.

As the American Planning Association, an advocate for government prerogatives and eminent domain, explains in a 1995 policy guide on takings: "As our society has become more populous, with more people living relatively close together, the police power has become more important. It is a sort of civilizing agreement among humans living in a community that allows them to live in peace."[205] The APA views efforts to restrict the police power of eminent domain with alarm. Groups such as APA rarely express concern about police agencies abusing their powers. In its view, police powers—even the harsh power of taking property and giving it to other private owners—are a "civilizing" force that helps everyone get along.

That viewpoint is hard for most people to grasp. How can it be a civilizing force when government can take property from individuals to give to other individuals? Perhaps APA, like other advocates of government, finds it so uncivilized when people fight for their constitutional rights in court. It's far more civilized when government can simply exert whatever power it wants to make a project happen!

"The fact is that in the average community in the typical state, the system is working well," APA also explains, according to a Reason online article by Sam Staley.[206] "Property rights advocates are waging a guerrilla war of sound-bites, misleading 'spin doctoring' and power politics which characterizes government at every level as evil empires of bad intent." Perhaps that view would be justified if critics of eminent domain abuse were trumpeting one or two cases nationwide and making them appear as the norm. But we're talking about thousands of cases nationwide, in which government officials are taking property based on the slimmest "public use" rationales. It's not just property-rights advocates who are complaining, but a handful of judges, also. The real spin doctoring is coming from the planning community, which cannot bear the thought of anyone raining on their eminent domain parade.

This is how governments now routinely operate, taking property from small owners and giving them to big ones, and treating the victimized owners shabbily. It's no aberration. Yet we see that the clear immorality of the policy isn't clear to everyone, especially to those who gain personally and professionally from the current process. Mostly, I suppose, advocates of eminent domain and redevelopment aren't thinking at all about the impact on individual lives. Mostly, they are just trying to push forward projects that promote economic development. The rules are the rules, and that's as far as many people think about it.

In cases I've covered, government officials will talk about the community's stakeholders rather than the private land owners. In their view, everyone with an interest in a property's development should have the same amount of say as everyone else. A city official is a stakeholder, as is a neighbor, as are members of the community who are eager to see a new discount store in their community. The property owner has no special rights, and often seems to have fewer rights than everyone else. Those who complain are viewed as selfish or greedy. In one case discussed later in this book, the city referred to the property owner as a narrow "special interest," as if there is something ignoble about wanting to protect your own interest in your own property. I always wondered how city managers, city attorneys and developers who stood to benefit from the taking would act if the same principles applied to their property. I suspect they would be up in arms—and rightly so.

I'm not suggesting that redevelopment officials are purposely immoral. Sometimes they are, of course. But mostly they see the world in a way that is far removed from the world most of us live in. For instance, the National League of Cities, at its Leadership Training Institute, featured a speaker at an August 2001 conference who addressed the issue of Ethics and Credibility. It was designed to reinforce the idea that officials must use their power in an ethical and responsible way so they can have widespread community support for their redevelopment and other policies. The speaker, Vera Vogelsang-Coombs, explains:

"You can control your credibility by justifying, not excusing, your choices. Justification means that you publicly explain how your decisions reflect shared values or widespread norms. Four perspectives that reflect shared norms are: (1) consequentialism; (2) deontology; (3) natural rights; and (4) communitarianism.

"A consequential perspective says that an official is ethically obligated to make decisions that promote good consequences for the greatest number. Deontology says that an official has unbreakable obligations. The rights approach says that an official must make the protection of stakeholders a priority in decision making. Communitarianism obligates an official to involve families and neighborhood residents in designing solutions to community problems."[207]

Vogelsang-Coombs uses the example of a project that requires the use of eminent domain. Wrestling with the issue from each perspective yields different results. As an official, you might take the consequential approach and argue that the plan is a good one because it benefits more people than it harms. Or you might take the deontology approach, and argue that you are supporting the plan because you made a campaign promise to support it. Or you might take the natural-rights approach and oppose eminent domain, or you might use the communitarian approach and negotiate with the homeowners the conditions under which they will be forced to leave. "Which approach is the right one? All are ethically legitimate," Vogelsang-Coombs argues, "but they assume different things. Therefore, each has its advantages and disadvantages."[208]

If that's what passes for ethical decision-making with regards to private-property ownership, then all of us are in very deep doo-doo. For starters, this ethicist makes the four different perspectives morally equivalent. It's like saying that socialism, fascism, communism and republicanism are four types of governments that we can choose. Each one is legitimate, you see. As long as you pick one and stick to it, a country will develop an ethical and moral social and political structure. But there's a huge difference between selecting a free society that vests its power in individual choices and a totalitarian society that vests power in a central state. Likewise, there is an enormous difference between government officials basing their decision-making on the ideas of the founders (natural rights) rather than the other ideas. I thought that all government officials were sworn to uphold the constitutional ideals that are the foundation of our nation's legal system, rather than uphold other ideologies that have a different view of fundamental rights.

Notice also that the natural-rights approach, the third choice in the list of options, is not even spelled out accurately. It's about "stakeholders," Vogelsang-Coombs said, rather than property owners. Imagine if this approach was applied to, say, free-speech rights. Yet this is the way the League of Cities trains its members to think about ethical issues. Fortunately, the courts are still designed to assure that individual property rights are upheld, even if city officials don't give them much credence.

The California Redevelopment Association represents 342 of the state's 408 redevelopment agencies, and 262 associate members that are mostly private companies that benefit from redevelopment projects. Much of CRA's justification for redevelopment is based on mundane-sounding economic development lingo: "For over 50 years, redevelopment agencies in California have effectively provided the economic stimulus to rebuild declining communities,"[209] according to the California Redevelopment Association's Web site. CRA explains that redevelopment must step in where private enterprise has failed to do its job. This reflects a shoddy understanding of the market system, but is boilerplate stuff. Such descriptions are what one would expect from a redevelopment association. But there is a creepy element to CRA's worldview also. "Redevelopment has been successful in those communities that exercise foresight and effective administration by conscientious officials representing the citizens of their community," CRA further explains. "It has become a means to reduce urban sprawl by investing in existing urban areas and removing barriers to smart growth." In other words, it is about government having the power to do what government wants to do. Don't worry, though, as long as those officials are conscientious.

After the *Wall Street Journal* published a 1998 article on eminent domain for private uses,[210] two officials with the Washington, D.C.-based Community Rights Counsel penned this revealing response:

"Local governments rely heavily on eminent domain to achieve their land use planning objectives. It allows communities to acquire land necessary for schools, roads, parks and urban renewal projects. It also allows communities to preserve historic sites and purchase conservation easements to protect open space, habitat, scenic views and farmland. Even more importantly, eminent domain protects taxpayers from being held hostage by what economists call 'holdouts.' Without it, property owners could extort windfall profits from the taxpayers when they happen to hold key property necessary to complete a proposed road, park or project.

"Advocates of extreme theories of property rights have long clamored for the government to use eminent domain and pay compensation whenever it regulates permissible land uses. It is ironic that these same advocates, (Gideon Kanner, who is quoted in your article, is a notable example) are now attacking communities for using this critical power.

"Judges should not use anachronistic notions of absolute property rights to thwart critical land use planning, economic growth, jobs and the communities' best interests."[211]

That's a telling insight into the way redevelopment officials think. At least the authors admit that governments "rely heavily on eminent domain." And at least they admit that they believe the power to apply to just about anything "communities" (i.e., government officials) want to use it for, from conservation easements to land-use planning to economic growth to whatever they think is in the community's best interests. Typical of eminent domain supporters, the authors mush the distinctions between using eminent domain for bona fide public uses and for private ones. They talk in the letter about the Constitution allowing this power, but they do not deal with the founders' belief that eminent domain should only be used for public uses, not for helping Costcos and sports stadiums. They don't deal with important issues, such as the way governments treat property owners and often deny them due process and just compensation. The authors try to depict supporters of traditional constitutional concepts of property rights as extremists. And, in the authors' view, the worst possible thing is for someone to be a "holdout." Of course, the essence of a free society is that individuals always can be holdouts. We get to hold out against the plans government agents are hatching with our properties and lives.

Kanner, described in the letter as the supporter of an "extreme" form of property rights, shot back in a January 11, 1999, letter: "The U.S. Supreme Court has held that there must be some justifying reason before eminent domain can be used to take land from one private owner and transfer it to another. Forcibly taking the land of one business, merely to facilitate the growth of another, gives the 'public use' constitutional limitation an Orwellian spin, and gives the 'trickle down' theory a bad name. Finally, municipal behavior in these cases is often motivated by simple greed. New, high volume, high-ticket merchandisers (notably automobile and other large malls), generate large amounts of sales taxes that cities share. Thus, the high falutin talk about 'public benefits' all too often camouflages an old fashioned pursuit of the elusive free lunch: municipal officials want the added revenues but lack the backbone to impose the necessary property taxes on the benefited community. James Buchanan received the Nobel prize in economics for demonstrating that public officials act in pursuit of their self-interest, the same as everyone else. Here is the proverbial 'Exhibit A' supporting his thesis."[212]

In a sense, I admire the Community Rights Counsel letter's frankness. At least property owners know where they stand with eminent domain's advocates. Unfortunately, the courts often display thinking based more on the muddy and authoritarian concepts of redevelopment officials than on the clear, rights-based approach that is supposed to be the foundation of American law.

A good example is the Kansas Supreme Court's 2003 decision in the case of *General Building Contractors and Robert Tolbert v. Board of Shawnee County Commissioners*. The justices not only affirm the county's right to take virtually any property they choose in the name of economic development, but they also show open disdain for the property owners who are challenging the taking of their properties. Throughout the ruling, one sees an emphasis on process rather than on rights. As long as the government followed the letter of the law and the proper redevelopment process, then the court couldn't see what the controversy was about. Yet, courts are supposed to serve as a check on the government's edicts, holding them up to timeless constitutional principles rather than the planning ideologies of the day.

The question, the court explained, is "whether a Kansas county has the power under home rule to exercise eminent domain rights and condemn land for purposes of industrial or economic development."[213] Four specific matters were considered. First, whether counties have eminent domain power for economic uses. Second, whether the county must invoke eminent domain by resolution or motion. Third, whether taking private property for such uses is a valid public purpose. Fourth, whether there were any grounds to grant an injunction to stop the taking of the land at issue. On all counts, the court ruled in favor of the government and slapped down the property owners.

Reading through the decision, one will find precious little discussion about property rights or the state Constitution, or any of the natural-rights protections promised by the founders. The justices appeared to treat natural rights in a way that is similar to how that League of Cities speaker views them—one arcane way of looking at the world, nothing more.

As the court explained, Shawnee County voters had approved in 2000 a one-cent sales tax for use in economic development. The county hired an economic-development specialist to run a nonprofit economic-development corporation known as GO Topeka (Growth Organization of Topeka/Shawnee County Inc.). That was all good and proper, it said. Then GO Topeka went on the lookout for development sites and decided on some prime land near a major highway. The group selected several parcels, and the county commissioners approved the use of eminent domain to begin acquiring the properties.

The justices seemed surprised that anyone would question whether taking property was legitimate for economic-development

purposes. The county followed the rules and, after all, it hired consultants who testified that "the types of public benefits created by
the kind of industrial park included 'thousands of jobs, increased
payroll, increased standard of living, opportunities for many people
in the community, plus [a] greatly enhanced tax [base].' " The counties have statutory authority to take property by force, so who are
the justices to argue?

What's amazing, of course, is that the court never questioned the
validity of the claims or demanded detailed information.
Governments are notorious for making grand promises, yet so often
those promises fall short. Like in the *Berman* case, the justices in this
case accepted at face value that the stated goals of the government
officials would be accomplished. In *Berman*, the U.S. Supreme Court
justices accepted whole cloth the idea that government should be
free to take property to remove urban blight. The Kansas Supreme
Court was equally credulous, believing that taking private property
to make room for a Target distribution center and other industrial
and economic uses would be a public use beyond questioning. The
case has created a dangerous precedent in Kansas because the
Supreme Court has granted counties the widest latitude in making
such determinations.

The court relies heavily on previous legal cases. Here's one case the
Kansas Supreme Court quotes from: "'[T]he board of county commissioners may transact all county business and perform all powers of
local legislation and administration it deems appropriate . . . ' While
there is no express grant of home rule power to counties to acquire
property through eminent domain, none of the thirty-two subpara-
graphs . . . expressly prohibits or restricts a county's use of the power
of eminent domain."[214]

Americans in the other forty-nine states should be glad they
aren't dependent on the Kansas Supreme Court's understanding of
individual liberty. In the American founding experiment, the idea is

simple: The government is granted certain limited powers. Otherwise, individuals are left to their own devices. If something is not specifically denied an individual, it is assumed that he is free to do it. In Kansas, this is turned on its head. Government might not expressly be granted the right to abuse property rights, but if it isn't specifically denied that right it can do what it wants. The founders wanted to give citizens wide latitude to pursue their freedom. They created a system that protected individuals from government. The Kansas Supreme Court, by contrast, seems to view itself as the guardian of government power and prerogatives.

"We are to liberally construe home rule powers to give counties the largest measure of self-government," the court explained. "To adopt the landowners' arguments would be directly contrary to this direction." The justice's disregard for individual rights is breathtaking. The court goes statute by statute, pointing out that the Legislature allows governments to subsidize economic development and acquire property on behalf of private owners promising economic developments. But the court is supposed to be a check on the Legislature, assuring that laws passed do not conflict with essential constitutional protections. This was a sad ruling for property rights, but the decision gave much insight into the way many courts have viewed the matter, at least since *Berman*.

CONDEMNATION WITHOUT REPRESENTATION

The Pennsylvania Supreme Court hasn't been any more sympathetic to individual property rights than the Kansas Supreme Court, as it rejected in December 2003 a Coatesville family's efforts to protect the family farm from a government plan to create a private recreation center on the site, and on much acreage around it.[215] The city of Coatesville is a rundown steel town not far from Philadelphia. City leaders decided that the way to revive the town was to build a 210-acre resort with golf courses, bowling alleys, parks and a conference center to attract wealthy people from throughout the East Coast. Even the *Philadelphia Inquirer*, a newspaper with a liberal editorial page, thought the idea to be absurd. A newspaper editorial on May 22, 2002, argued that, "From the start the idea had an almost surreal quality about it. Coatesville is a poor, gritty ghost of a faded steel town with many residents living below the poverty line. It doesn't have a movie theater. Heck, it doesn't even have a supermarket. It is served by a school district so troubled the school board is attempting to close a $12.7 million budget hole by tossing out dozens of teachers, principals and aides."[216]

The county already has thirteen golf courses, the newspaper added. And if the foundation for the project wasn't bad enough, the city of Coatesville "either condemned or threatened to condemn privately owned properties right and left." One couple, Dick and Nancy Saha, however, decided to fight. The newspaper pointed to an oddity in Pennsylvania condemnation law. Smaller cities are allowed to condemn property in neighboring townships. The Sahas property is outside the city limits but subject to the city's condemnation efforts. That's a thoroughly unfair situation. The Sahas had to live under the rules of Coatesville officials even though they cannot even vote for those officials. It's worse than taxation without representation. It is condemnation without representation.

The Coatesville situation shows how absurd these eminent domain proceedings can become. When the courts allow eminent domain powers to be used for economic development, and not for standard public uses, then anything at all can justify these takings. In June 2002, after three years of wrangling, the city voted 6–1 to authorize taking the Sahas' forty-eight-acre farm, although as of March 2004 the battle was still going on. Here's the justification of one council member who supported the taking: "Eminent domain is something that is necessary in this scenario. What eminent domain does is treat everyone fairly. It locks the property into a fair market price."[217]

How's that for an example of how eminent domain advocates think? But it's hard to see how eminent domain can even plausibly be described as the best process to make sure everyone is treated fairly. The Sahas don't want to sell, and they will have to fight in court to get just compensation or a fair judgment. That's fair to no one except the government and the developer on whose behalf the government is acting.

Between 1999 and 2002, the city and the Sahas fought over whether the city needed to get what is called "subdivision approval" from the surrounding township to take the Saha property. A judge ruled that it needed such township approval, which is significant because it determines how much land the city could buy based on township zoning. Eventually, that ruling was overturned, and in April 2003 the Commonwealth Court cleared the way for Coatesville to take the Saha property and develop its resort.

Supporters of the Sahas gathered petitions in August 2003 to put three referenda before city voters that would stop the use of eminent domain for the project. The city battled those petitions in court. The petitions were upheld later that month. "The petitions seek changes to the city's home rule charter," according to an August 27, 2003, report in the *West Chester (Pennsylvania) Daily Local News*. "The changes, if passed, would require the city to put in place referendum votes for any efforts to engage in a golf course, to engage in a business enterprise that would compete with the privately owned business sector or transfer property outside the city's borders."[218]

After months of unveiling development plans and promotional videos and the like, city officials were stunned by a November 2003 vote approving all three of the charter amendments. Three of the council members who supported the project lost their re-election bids. Once again, the public showed itself to have a different view about eminent domain, corporate subsidies and the grandiose redevelopment plans favored by city officials. At the council meeting after the election, a large crowd of residents urged officials to drop their plans to condemn the Saha property. Council members insisted that they thought the votes were unconstitutional and debated ways to proceed with the project. Dick Saha spoke at the meeting. He emphasized that his property is not for sale but that an adjacent sixty acres are for sale. Why doesn't the city just buy those acres? he asked.[219]

But in December, the Supreme Court rejected the review of the case, thus leaving the property owners to twist in the wind. Meanwhile, the city challenged the three referenda, and owners of a golf course, bowling alley and ice rink "filed suit against the city in September seeking to halt the regional recreation center," according to the *Daily Local News*.[220] "Citing the city's home rule charter, attorneys for the business owners said Coatesville is prohibited from engaging in proprietary activities." According to the latest news reports, Saha supporters feared that the city would move forward with the project anyway, and planned to simply ignore the referenda.

"They won't pay any attention to them [the referenda]," Dick Saha said in an interview.[221] "They ignore them completely. The court completely upheld them. We won. It doesn't seem to mean anything to them."

Saha has been battling the city for five years, and in his frustration told the council to "Go to hell." He compared the council to Nazis, pointing out the way the Nazi government confiscated property in the 1930s. The council members accused him of being anti-Semitic, and the Anti-Defamation League sent Saha a letter expressing its displeasure, according to a March 12, 2004, article in the *West Chester (Pennsylvania) Daily Local News*.[222]

The letter "explained that the organization takes no stance on the land use issue, but has 'very strong feelings about matters where expressions of such great insensitivity occur,' " according to the news article. In my view, organizations such as the ADL ought to be more concerned about the abuse of rights than about the frustrated remarks of the victims of such abuses. It's unconscionable, really, that the ADL would step in, and bizarre that it would, in essence, side with a council that so clearly is abusing the liberties of a local family. It's another example of how Leaders Of Our Town rarely jump into the fray on behalf of the victims of official abuse.

Saha explained in an interview how the local Democratic Party got involved in local Coatesville elections to defeat one of the council members who was sympathetic to the Sahas. But Coatesville voters tended to sympathize with the Sahas' plight. Not only did they approve all three referenda, restricting the abuse of eminent domain, but they voted to replace two advocates of the plan with two opponents. Meanwhile, the city moves forward in its efforts to take possession of the Saha property, despite the injustice of it all.

This is what happens when the courts lose sight of their role of protecting individual rights and instead choose to protect the interests of government agencies. This is what happens when people who believe in "the greater good" rather than in constitutional individual-rights protections have the chance to flex their political power.

Malia Zimmerman, editor of the *Hawaii Reporter,* shares the sad story of what eminent domain did to a small-business owner in her state. Rick Ralston was a young artist who started a company called Crazy Shirts in 1964. In 1970 he opened his first store. The business took off, and Ralston eventually opened sixty stores, with 1,100 employees and $90 million in annual sales. He bought a beachfront home that he allowed his employees to use with their families. It was a great story of generosity and success.

"Little did Ralston know that eventually the government of Hawaii—the state he loved and contributed so much to—would three times bestow blows on him financially, with the final blow being so severe that it drove his company into bankruptcy," according to a September 6, 2002, *Hawaii Reporter* article. The blows came in the form of eminent domain. First, the city of Honolulu decided to take his North Shore property. "Ralston made the mistake of putting a shower on the beach for anyone who wanted to use it." That gave the city the idea of putting a park where his house was located.[223]

"Ralston was paid just a small percent of what the home and property were worth, so he was unable to buy another property near that location for even close to the price he was paid by the city," Zimmerman wrote. As Crazy Shirts began to expand in the 1980s, the company bought thirteen acres and invested millions into the expansion. Once again Ralston's property was condemned by the city so that it could use the property for its transportation head-quarters. Ralston said he lost about $10 million in that transaction. Finally, in the 1990s, the city seized the company's last location, agreeing to pay $9 million on a property that Ralston believed to be worth $30 million. Ralston agreed, rather than fight City Hall. "Only trouble is the city never kept its word. It never paid Ralston a dime by September 2000 or ever for that matter. And soon after, his company declared bankruptcy and the property was turned over to the lender, the Bank of Hawaii,"[224] the *Hawaii Reporter* explained.

Ironically, the city didn't just want to use eminent domain to take the land from the bank, but insisted that the bank, as the owner, clean up all the toxins it has found in the land, according to Zimmerman. The city used eminent domain to take property for pennies on the dollar—then declared that the land wasn't good enough. The owner had to spend millions to hand the city a pristine piece of property on the cheap.[225] This gives invaluable insight into the thinking of government authorities. As Zimmerman wrote, Ralston doesn't blame the city for the problems of his business, which he eventually sold. But he does believe its future might have been different had the city not imposed such a large economic hard-ship on him. That's safe to say.

This is just another day in America, where officials take what they want and don't care about what it does to individual property owners.

Don't expect the officials to care a whit about what they are doing. In Alabaster, Alabama, city officials threatened to take private property to make way for a development that included a Wal-Mart. Here's what one councilman thinks about the victimized property owners: "Sometimes the good of the many has to outweigh the greed of the few."[226]

Is it really greed when a person doesn't want to sell something that is his? Is it greed when he insists on a fair-market price when a gun is put to his head and he is forced to sell? Yet, that's the attitude. In January 2004, eight out of the ten targeted owners agreed to a settlement with the city and Shelby Land Partners to sell their property for the project, according to a *Shelby County Reporter* article on January 8.[227] "Regardless of public perception, our goal was to make this as much of a win-win for everybody possible," Councilman Tommy Ryals told the newspaper. "I think we accomplished that."

Yet it's difficult to have a win-win situation when one party in the negotiations has the power to take the property by force, and when those who try to get the fair-market value for their property are perceived by officials as being greedy and unworthy of decent treatment.

By this reasoning, property owners, such as a couple who are being forced to sell a motel to a Washington state housing authority for $800,000 less than its appraised value, must just be greedy also.[228] I wonder if those people doing the condemning would part with their homes for one-third less than they are worth. It's a nightmare, a form of administrative evil. But coveting and taking a neighbor's property isn't anything new, of course, as we learn from the Old Testament story of King Ahab—a story Gideon Kanner likes to point to in his discussions of eminent domain.[229]

As 1 Kings: 21 explains: "Now Naboth the Hezreelite had a vineyard in Nezreel, beside the palace of Ahab king of Samaria. And after this Ahab said to Naboth, 'Give me your vineyard, that I may have it for a vegetable garden, because it is near my house; and I will give you a better vineyard for it; or, if it seems good to you, I will give you its value in money. But Naboth said to Ahab, 'The Lord forbid that I give you the inheritance of my fathers.' "

Ahab was sullen and vexed. He told his wife, Jezebel, about the incident.

"And Jezebel his wife said to him, 'Do you now govern Israel? Arise, and eat bread, and let your heart be cheerful; I will give you the vineyard of Naboth the Jezreelite.' So she wrote letters in Ahab's name and sealed them with his seal, and she sent the letters to the elders and the nobles who dwelt with Naboth in his city. And she wrote in the letters, 'Proclaim a fast, and set Naboth on high among the people; and set two base fellows opposite him, and let them bring a charge against him, saying, 'You have cursed God and the king.' Then take him out and stone him to death.'"

Then the men did as Jezebel told them to do. When Naboth was dead, Ahab and Jezebel went down to the vineyard to take possession of it. But the Lord sent a man named Elijah the Tishbite to give a message to Ahab:

"Behold I will bring evil upon you; I will utterly sweep you away, and will cut off from Ahab every male, bond or free, in Israel; and I will make your house like the house of Jerobo'am the son of Nebat, and like the house of Ba'asha the son of Ahi'jah, for the anger to which you have provoked me, and because you have made Israel to sin."

Unfortunately, those who abuse others' property rights don't always face the same level of divine justice.

7. GOD DOESN'T PAY TAXES

It is hubris for the city of Cypress to decide a church isn't the best use of land owned by the church. In the Soviet Union, Stalin seized churches and turned them into museums. Cypress seizes a church and wants to turn it into a Costco. At least Stalin looked for something with artistic merit.

— Assemblyman Ken Maddox of
California[230]

At first blush, comparing the city of Cypress, California, a middle-class Orange County city with a population of about 40,000, with Stalinist Russia might strike most observers as a tad extreme. But upon close examination, city officials there—emboldened by a string of legal cases giving them carte blanche use of eminent domain—showed a mentality that was strikingly totalitarian in its expression. They did not want the members of Cottonwood Christian Center to build a worship center on their own, properly zoned land. They thought Cypress had enough churches, and were upset that a prime piece of private real estate would be used for religious rather than commercial purposes. Churches don't pay many taxes, and retail centers do. So city officials set about using public dollars to first malign the reputation of the church through a public relations campaign, then to use eminent domain to take the church's property and sell it at below-market rates to the $30-billion-a-year corporate retailer Costco.

City officials did not dress up what they were doing in legalistic language. They were brazen in their goals. They ridiculed church members at public meetings. They bragged about their ability to use eminent domain for whatever reason they chose, and they made it clear that the government's desires should take precedence over the desires of "a narrow special interest," which is how city officials repeatedly referred to the church. They mocked the idea that property owners had any special claim to their own land, especially when that land is an area coveted by government for a new development.[231]

It was, in the city's view, a clash between a narrow, selfish group of religious people against the broad-minded city officials who were trying to pursue the greater good. Many Cypress citizens, fearing an influx of members of a large religious organization and themselves coveting a new popular retailer, and worried about a lack of future tax revenue in the city, often backed the city's efforts.

Officials acted like despots. They could only do so, of course, because of the Supreme Court decisions documented in earlier chapters. The court, in *Berman* and *Midkiff*, waxed poetic about the public uses and the great things that government could accomplish. But the justices turned a blind eye to the abuses they were allowing by giving government officials such power over private property. Here's what happens when activist courts think they know more than the founders. The founders, in their simplicity, realized that everyone is protected when government is kept on a short leash. By contrast, the justices in those two modern cases believed that government must be given a lot of rope so that it can perform uplifting tasks such as removing blight and encouraging economic development. They forgot that property rights protect individuals—even and especially when the larger community doesn't want them there. When I wrote columns for the *Orange County Register* defending the church, I was shocked by the level of prejudice directed toward the church members by some residents of Cypress. They made it clear they didn't want these religious people in their midst. Religious organizations, ranging from Mormons to Buddhists to Muslims to Jews, have faced similar discrimination in seeking approvals to build religious buildings in various cities. It was a reminder that property rights, when upheld in the way the founders intended, are the best means to combat such prejudices.

The Cypress case gained national attention for three reasons: First, the matter was about a blatant attempt by a government to transfer property from one owner to another for the simple reason that the preferred owner would pay more taxes to the city. That was one of the more aggressive interpretations of "public" use one would find. Second, and most important to those who rallied to the church's side, was that city officials were targeting a religious institution. Unfortunately, some of the church's supporters insisted on viewing the matter as a purely religious one, and therefore downplayed the importance of property rights. Third, lawyers and commentators understood that this was a potentially precedent-setting case regarding a federal law designed to protect religious organizations against land-use discrimination.

What ensued was a contentious and at times circus-like battle that resulted in a compromise, following a federal judge's intervention in the form of a preliminary injunction. One troubling lesson from the ordeal is that small churches—indeed, small-property owners of any type—that cannot wage the costly legal and public-relations battle waged by Cottonwood have no choice but to follow a city's edicts, even when they are blatantly unfair.

Here's the story of Cottonwood and Cypress and what it says about property rights and eminent domain abuse in America.

A NEW ERA OF SOME SORT

After turning to the official Web site for the city of Cypress, California, today,[232] one would never know that the two major development projects championed by the city's Redevelopment and Economic Development department were proceeding only after more than two years of legal wrangling and a federal legal battle that was followed throughout the country.

"A new economic era begins for community," boasts the city headline. Project one is a 150,000-square-foot Costco wholesale store and the other is the construction of the Cottonwood Christian Center, with its seven buildings that will "compliment the city's business park." The only hint of the battle that came before it is this language:

"Cypress provides basic services (police, fire, parks) to its citizens with a very small and limited tax base. Further this tax base is not diversified. As an example, fewer than ten companies generate more than half of the city's sales tax revenues. Therefore, the city suffers from sales tax leakage in that our residents must go outside the city limits to shop for many of the items they desire. The establishment of the Costco store will begin the diversification of both the property and sales tax base and provide more revenues to the city to provide the services our residents demand and deserve."[233]

The city was explaining something explained in an earlier chapter of this book. Tax generation increasingly drives development decisions. What the city doesn't say is that the promise of taxes not only encouraged city officials to use tax dollars to subsidize Costco, but to try to keep out of its city limits the Cottonwood Christian Center project it now boasts about. The compromise that accommodates both projects is laudable, but the effort by the city was one of the most heinous municipal land-use abuses witnessed in recent years.

The Cottonwood Christian Center is a booming nondenominational congregation that meets in cramped facilities in Los Alamitos, just west of Cypress. About five years ago, church leaders realized they needed to build their own facility, given that they already were holding several services each Sunday to accommodate the waves of new church members. They wanted to stay within a few miles of their current location because most of their congregation lived in the communities bordering Los Angeles and Orange counties, so moving to the less-developed areas of the metropolitan area (twenty-five miles or more away) was out of the question. Los Alamitos and Cypress are older suburban communities with high real estate values and limited open space, so there was not an abundance of choices available to the expanding church.

Church leaders found an eighteen-acre property adjacent to the Los Alamitos Race Track, in the city of Cypress. The property was a parking lot that was owned by the track and three other owners. It had sat vacant for decades, and had been put into a redevelopment area by the city in 1990, but then languished there. By its own admission, the city had taken a laissez-faire approach to the property, not showing any great concern about who would purchase it until Cottonwood moved forward with its plan.

The redevelopment area was designed to promote business-park uses, and indeed the property had a valid permit for an office facility. The commercial zoning in that location specifically allowed church uses, and another large church was located nearby. So, after doing its due diligence, the church assembled the four separate parcels into one property and moved forward to purchase it. According to the church's pastor, the city affirmed that the church would be a proper use for the property, although a letter from the development director suggested city officials would "prefer"

Had the city simply allowed Cottonwood to build this facility, there would be no blight.

another use.[234] That was a sign of potential trouble, of course, but the church went forward with the purchase, figuring that property rights would trump a city bureaucrat's preferences. It was a nice, level property, the right size for the church at the right price, it had sat vacant for decades with little interest from the city, and the property already had an approved permit for office uses. Since church uses were specifically allowed in the same zone, and there was little difference between office and a church use, they didn't see a serious problem getting the required conditional-use permit.

In fairness, a consultant's study warned that the city might object to allowing a large worship center.[235] But even if the city would object, church leaders believed that they would face similar objections in any nearby city where they could assemble a large enough tract. That in itself speaks volumes about property rights in metropolitan areas today: If cities don't like a particular use—i.e., non-tax-paying churches—they will find a reason to deny a permit, even if the proposed use is proper under the current zoning. That's exactly what happened with Cottonwood and Cypress.

The church had bought the property shortly after the city had a change in staff. Officials had brought in an aggressive new city manager from North Las Vegas, Pat Importuna. He had gained a reputation for being aggressive as he pushed more development in his previous city. He, in many ways, represented the new era of city managers—ones who are eager to use government power to create the kind of tax base and development they want for their cities. He epitomized the techniques taught and discussed at conferences of the League of Cities, the association representing city officials.

"'Prior to Pat Importuna and (Planning Director) David Belmer, we had a very laissez faire attitude toward developing the vacant land around the racecourse," council member Tim Keenan, a strong supporter of taking the church by eminent domain, told the *Orange*

County Register in September 2002.[236] "Importuna . . . quickly changed that.

"'I drove him to the Towne Center (in Long Beach) and he said, 'We should have done that,' Keenan said. Soon, the city was drawing up plans for its own shopping center on the church's corner lot and talking to Costco, which could generate as much as $1 million a year in tax revenue.

"Church officials said they learned how serious the city was when their worship center application was returned unopened, and Costco took out real-estate advertisements touting restaurant sites in a planned shopping center on the church's land," according to the *Register* article. Costco later tried to distance itself from the project, but there was no doubt Costco officials were there working with the city. We'll deal with Costco, other retailers that take advantage of the current redevelopment system, and corporate welfare in the next chapter.

The church was determined to move forward, still believing that legal property protections rather than the particular desires of new city leadership, were ultimately what counted. The church had a religious mission, and viewed the battle in a David vs. Goliath sort of way. The city refused to process the church's permit, and found every reason to delay any consideration of the project. City officials claimed the application was incomplete, but that apparently was just another one of their delaying tactics. The City Council, which was following the lead of Importuna and the city staff, imposed a forty-five-day moratorium on development entitlements within that particular redevelopment area. The council then expanded the moratorium for ten months and then a year. Officials claimed they simply wanted to re-evaluate development possibilities within the city, but clearly officials were only trying to delay that one particular project as a way to give the city time to come up with an alternative development plan. City staff even forbade council members from meeting with church officials until late in the negotiating game as a way to avoid a settlement.

As the church fought fruitlessly to force the city to process its plan for its own properly zoned property, the city was marketing the property to other private owners. The city was hiring engineers and consultants to complete environmental and development studies on the land, even though the church didn't want to sell it. The city even sent the church a letter inviting it to "participate" in an exciting new retail project on the site.[237] Again, consider how you would feel if a city official sent you a letter inviting you to participate in an exciting new development slated for the current site of your own house!

The city hired a PR firm to produce a poll, filled with slanted questions designed to achieve the desired result, showing that the public wanted a Costco, not another church. Even the PR firm that handled that account, Waters & Faubel, of Lake Forest, California, eventually withdrew from the project. Roger Faubel said: "We advised the city to settle with the church. It wouldn't do it, so we dropped the client."[238] City officials sent out letters urging the public to support the city's plan. City officials suggested to Cypress' many elderly residents that their services would be imperiled if Costco wasn't allowed to build on the site owned by Cottonwood Christian Center. The city's crude rhetoric about the church was having the desired effect. An effort by an out-of-state religious organization to bolster support for the church with a crude mailer filled with religious references backfired and helped the city. Things didn't look good for the church, despite the outrageous unfairness of the situation.

"Why should the church be the best and highest use for land facing two arterial highways in the last undeveloped property in north county?" asked city attorney Bill Wynder at an April 2002 City Council meeting that pushed forward the eminent domain plan.[239]

An obvious answer is that the church happened to *own* the property. Owners of particular parcels of property are supposed to decide the highest and best use, not government officials or influential companies (Costco) that covet the land. Yet Wynder's words are a reflection of what happens when property rights are repeatedly undermined and dismissed. Everyone has an equal claim to everyone's property. A city official, not the owner, gets to decide the highest and best use of a property. Other stakeholders—neighbors, city residents, businesses, competitors—get to tell other people what they must do on their own land.

After the negotiated settlement eventually was reached, one *Orange County Register* article depicted the battle in a typical way: "The land-swap deal approved Thursday between Cottonwood Christian Center and the city of Cypress ends a bitter, much-publicized fight that threatened the city's reputation, cast the church's future in doubt and fueled a nationwide debate over what matters more: religious freedom or the public's right to determine how land in their city is used."[240]

Actually, the dispute was never about "religious freedom" or "the public's right to determine how land in their city is used." Religious freedom was certainly involved. If a church cannot build a church building it cannot properly exercise its religious freedom, just like a newspaper cannot practice its free-speech rights if the government takes away its printing presses. But "the public" has no collective right to "determine how land in their city is used." Individuals have rights. The public, in this context, means the government, and governments have power, not rights.

The Cottonwood case is about the government's ability to take privately owned land and give it to another private owner, an owner that the current officials prefer for various reasons. It is a battle about unjust government coercion and about whether "public use" has degenerated to the point that any use is public provided that the new uses pays more in taxes than the old use. If that's the case, then Katy better bar the doors.

With Cottonwood and Cypress, things had to get worse before they got better.

In late May 2002, the city moved forward on its plans for the site and at a council meeting invoked eminent domain to take the property. The meeting was a circus, as church members and even a handful of supporters of the taking were on hand, using bullhorns and making exhortations. Opponents of the church made the most of the fact that a handful of church supporters were a bit unsophisticated, pounding their Bibles and arguing that council members would end up in hell if they took the church's land. But most church supporters were intelligent and well-spoken, making simple property-rights and religious-rights arguments that anyone should be able to understand. They waited in line and gave their heartfelt testimonies about the value of the church before a mocking council. Other politicians and well-known attorneys from throughout Southern California also stood before the imperious council and explained why the taking would be an affront to property rights and individual liberties.

Nevertheless, the council members publicly attacked the church as a "very narrow special interest" that was trying to "bully" the city into giving it a conditional use permit to build a church. They told the other politicians it was none of their affair. Planning Director David Belmer expressed dismay that the church "was non-responsive to the invitation" the city offered to purchase the property. Imagine being non-responsive to an invitation to a theft. Council member Keenan demanded to know whether the church was coercing its members to mortgage their houses to pay for the new building—an unsubstantiated accusation critics say was designed to fan the flames of religious bigotry. Another council member captured the disturbing sentiment behind the eminent domain action:

The city, Anna Piercy said, is like a big family. The council members are the parents. The church members are like the kids, who "only want what they see." But the parents are the ones who have to make the tough and wise decisions. And their decision is that the kids don't need a new church. It was an almost unbelievable statement, and those in the audience couldn't believe what they were hearing.[241]

COURTING DISASTER

Fortunately, Cottonwood—a 4,500-member church with a TV program and an international audience—had the resources to fight the matter in court. It also received support from the Becket Fund, a Washington, D.C.-based religious-rights organization. At first, church officials appeared reluctant to fight. They also gave the benefit of the doubt to city officials, who repeatedly promised that they would work with the church to resolve the matter, even though it became obvious the city was interested in nothing more than taking the property by eminent domain and sending the church packing. But after the council meeting and the eminent domain vote, church leaders toughened their stance and filed papers seeking a preliminary injunction to stop the city from actually taking possession of the property. The gauntlet finally was thrown down.

The church filed its case in federal court, believing that constitutional issues were at stake. The church wanted to stop the taking and based its complaint on federal constitutional issues, arguing that taking the land and giving it to Costco was not a "public" use. The church also based its complaint on the Religious Land Use and Institutionalized Persons Act of 2000 (RLUIPA), a federal law passed with wide bipartisan support that banned the government from discriminating in its land-use decisions against religious institutions.

So, convinced that officials could do anything they wanted with regard to the property, the city mocked the lawsuit. "It's extraordinary that Cottonwood would ask a federal judge to issue an order to a state court," fumed city attorney Bill Wynder.[242] In fact, even many supporters of the church were preparing for the worst, given previous court decisions on eminent domain.

In its response, the city accused the church of forum shopping—i.e., going to the federal courts, where it thought it would get a more favorable decision, rather than the state court, which the city insisted was the appropriate forum for the dispute. The city claimed the transfer of property to a retailer was a public use, citing some of the cases cited in a previous chapter in this book. Cypress claimed RLUIPA applies only to zoning, not condemnation proceedings, that taking the church property did not infringe on the constitutional right to freely worship, and made some other technical arguments.

In August 2002, Judge David O. Carter, a Clinton appointee, surprised the city and granted the preliminary injunction. The trial judge in the case, Carter did more than temporarily stop eminent domain proceedings based on the legal requirement that the property owner had a fair chance of prevailing in court. He wrote a 36-page ruling that demolished every one of the city's arguments, and made it clear how he would eventually rule.[243]

"The administrative rejection of the CUP [Conditional Use Permit] application was significant because while Cottonwood was making plans and seeking approvals to build a church on its property the city had other designs for the land," the judge explained.[244] The city, in other words, refused to allow the church to build what it was allowed to build in order to pave the way for eminent domain. The potential, he wrote, that the city illegally prevented the church from being built was high enough to justify the injunction, and to therefore put matters on hold until the court decided.

As the judge explained, RLUIPA restricts a government from imposing "a land use regulation in a manner that imposes a substantial burden on the religious exercise of a person, including a religious assembly or institution, unless the government demonstrates that imposition of the burden on that person, assembly or institution—(A) is in furtherance of a compelling governmental interest; and (B) is the least restrictive means of furthering that compelling governmental interest."[245]

Judge Carter explained that the city's action appeared to impose a substantial burden on the church, and that the city used highly restrictive means to achieve its desired ends.

Through its CUP process, the city could wantonly discriminate against church uses, the judge ruled. Here are some other key points in the ruling:

- "The city could consistently grant secular uses that are practically no different from rejected uses. Judicial review must be in place to protect against this type of abuse any time a government agency is making individual assessments that might infringe on a fundamental right."[246]

- "Strict scrutiny is also appropriate because there is strong evidence that defendants' actions are not neutral, but instead specifically aimed at discriminating against Cottonwood's religious uses. . . . "[247]

- "Here, there is significant circumstantial evidence of a discriminatory intent. For nearly a decade, the Cottonwood property sat vacant. Despite having been declared blight . . . no improvements were made. . . . Once Cottonwood purchased the land, however, the city became a bundle of activity and developed the Town Center and the Walker/Katella Retail Project . . . "[248]

- "At first blush, the city's concern about blighting rings hollow. Why had the city, so complacent before Cottonwood purchased the Cottonwood property, suddenly burst into action? Although some innocent explanations are feasible—such as new leadership or robust economic growth—the activity suggests that the city was simply trying to keep Cottonwood out of the city, or at least from the use of its own land. This suspicion is heightened by the nature of the projects. The LART plan (the original redevelopment plan for the location) called for the Cottonwood property to be used as business offices. Yet, while the city has been insistent that a church would be inconsistent with this plan, it has proceeded to plan a shopping/entertainment center (the Town Center project) and a strip mall anchored by Costco (the Walker/Katella Retail Project), neither of which are consistent with a business park."[249]

It seemed clear to the judge that the city was doing exactly what officials at one time or another had said they were doing: Keeping Cottonwood out of the city because the church doesn't pay as much in taxes as retail centers.

Even the blight argument (i.e., the Cottonwood property was blighted and the city's plan would fix the blight), advanced at times by the city, was bogus. If, as the judge later pointed out, the city simply allowed the church to build its architect-designed $50 million campus on the blighted lot, the lot obviously would no longer be blighted. And furthermore, the judge noted that the city's own plans for the property were in clear violation of the existing redevelopment plans and zoning, whereas the church's planned use was consistent with them.

That's an amazing truth. The church was following the standards established by the city. But the city didn't want the church there, and it was proposing plans that conflicted with its own rules. The city officials play by their own rules. They can do anything they want, even plan something in direct and obvious violation of the city's zoning. But if a private party, in this case a church, decides to build something, it is refused an approval even though it is in compliance with every aspect of the law. This is rule by individuals, not by law, and we're fortunate a federal judge recognized what was happening and was disgusted by it.

What about the city's claim that a lack of revenue justifies the taking? The judge mocked that argument, noting that the city's mayor had recently boasted about its 25 percent budget surplus and its continuing ability to meet all its services and needs without a utility tax.

"Cottonwood is, as are most churches, a tax-exempt non-profit group. If revenue generation were a compelling state interest, municipalities could exclude all religious institutions from their cities."[250]

The city claimed it was imposing no burden on Cottonwood's exercise of religion. But Judge Carter disagreed: "Preventing a church from building a worship site fundamentally inhibits its ability to practice its religion. Churches are central to the religious exercise of most religions. If Cottonwood could not build a church, it could not exist."

RLUIPA requires that the government use the least restrictive means to advance its interests at a property owner's expense. Given that the city refused to work with the church to find another site, or to adjust the plan on the church's site to accommodate everyone's needs, the judge declared that "the city has done the equivalent of using a sledgehammer to kill an ant."[251]

Finally, and most important from this book's perspective, was the question of whether taking a church's land and giving it to a Costco could conceivably be called a public purpose.

"If defendants' taking decision was made in order to 'appease Costco,' the exercise of eminent domain is not for a 'public use.' . . . Eminent domain is commonly used to acquire land to build highways and railways. Public utility facilities such as power plants, water treatment facilities also have the traditional public use character, as does the construction of government buildings," the judge ruled. "Eminent domain can even be an effective tool against free-riders who hold out for exorbitant prices when private developers are attempting to assemble parcels for public places such as an arena or sports stadium. The framers of the Constitution, however, might be surprised to learn that the power of eminent domain was being used to turn the property over to a private discount retail corporation."[252]

The city, blinded by what had become almost rage against the church and its audacity to challenge the city's authority, issued a press release following this astounding decision declaring that the ruling did nothing more than maintain the "status quo." "The granting of a preliminary [injunction] in no way decides the outcome of the matter," said Wynder. "This simply preserves the status quo until the federal court hears all arguments and evidence."[253]

Yet the same judge who offered a stinging rebuke of the city on every point is the judge who would rule in the case. In reality, the sands shifted dramatically, and city officials eventually faced the reality that they must negotiate a settlement rather than risk a final court ruling that would uphold Cottonwood on every point and leave the city with no place to put the much-coveted Costco.

Ironically, the pastor of the conservative congregation, Bayless Conley, befriended an abortion doctor who owns the adjacent racetrack and golf course, Ed Allred.[254] Allred wasn't fond of the city's tactics, either. The parties agreed to a deal. The city would buy Cottonwood's acreage for $19 million, and then Cottonwood would buy 28 acres of the golf course from Allred for $17 million. Costco would get its subsidized store and the city its revenue. Cottonwood would get its church, and Allred would get some sort of satisfaction in helping fix the problem faced by his newfound friend, the pastor, along with a decent price for his acreage.

Even the wider public would get something. Although a preliminary injunction is not as powerful as a final appeals court or Supreme Court ruling, it is a published decision that influences other cases. Certainly, any city eyeing a similar policy will have to wrestle with the Cottonwood case.

LOOKING BACK

When I met with pastors Bayless Conley and Mike Wilson in January 2004, they were good-humored about the long battle they had fought. Things had turned out okay, although they later faced road-related concerns from a neighboring city. They knew not to trust the city officials, and had arranged a deal in which they would not turn over their property to the city until their new property on the old golf course was fully permitted and approved by city planners. That perhaps was the most striking lesson they had learned through the ordeal: That city officials would lie, cheat and connive to strip them of their property. City officials would do anything at all to get what they wanted. Cottonwood tried to act in good faith, but was challenged throughout the process by city officials who were not acting honorably. They were stunned also by the shabby way city officials treated any property owner who got in their way.

At one point in negotiations, after the city realized that Cottonwood was putting up a formidable fight, City Manager Importuna asked Conley whether the church would consider moving next door. Conley said that he would, and negotiations proceeded. Then it dawned on him that the city, which was acting like it controlled the property, might be planning to acquire it in the same way it was trying to acquire the Cottonwood parcel: through eminent domain. "I said, 'Do you own that property?' " Conley explained. "They said, 'no, we'll use eminent domain.' I stopped and said, 'That will never happen. I will never do it.' City attorney Bill Wynder then said, 'This is as American as apple pie.' "[255]

As he fought the battle, Conley heard from churches throughout the country that were fighting similar fights. They were in Long Beach, in Anaheim, in Arizona, in Oklahoma City. One case involved a church that had been established for 80 years. It was always a similar story: cities looking to remove churches with uses that paid more taxes. "People were coming out of the woodwork. I was surprised by how prolific this had become. I got a crash-course education in the whole property-rights issue," Conley said. Conley said it didn't matter whether it was church or a family-owned carpentry shop or a home. The process is immoral, and it undermines a fundamental aspect of American freedoms. Conley did some reading and was inspired by Booker T. Washington's book, *Up From Slavery*. Conley was struck by how much stock Washington put in property rights rather than the political process for uplifting former slaves. Washington knew that the only way people who are poor and mistreated could get a fair shake from those who were hostile to the aspirations of former slaves was for them to have secure constitutional property protections.

Conley pulled out the book and pointed to the section in which Washington offers this advice: "Besides, the general political agitation drew the attention of our people away from the more fundamental matters of perfecting themselves in the industries at their doors and in securing property."[256] Indeed, as Conley pointed out, Washington's book is infused with references to the importance of property. Conley was also reminded of the central role of property rights in the correspondence he received from the church's supporters throughout the world. His church has relationships with churches around the world, and when news of the city's actions was broadcast, "Almost without fail, their comments were, 'We didn't think this was possible in America.' Everyone was stunned," Conley said.

Cottonwood attorney Andrew Guilford of Sheppard and Mullin in Costa Mesa pins the victory on Judge Carter's ruling, a ruling that was based as much on concepts of religious freedom as property rights. "The city thought we were going to lose," Guilford said.[257] "They were very confident they would prevail." That's why the city was so unwilling to cooperate, and why it was so shocked by the hard-hitting nature of the decision. That clearly changed things, and a key role in the victory goes to RLUIPA.

RLUIPA'S BENEFITS

Perhaps the best lesson from Cottonwood is that if a city over-reaches so dramatically against a church that has the resources, it might get knocked back a step or two. It's similar to the lesson from Garden Grove, California. If a city goes too far, it might not get away

with the most egregious abuses of eminent domain. But equally hor-
rific takings happen every day, and if the parties are not powerful
enough or sympathetic enough or well-funded enough, then their
property rights are abused.

The church issue is glaring, because cities increasingly don't want
to permit churches anywhere in their midst largely for reasons based
on taxation. Most of the time the abuses in property rights don't
require the use of eminent domain, but the principle is often the
same: government intervening to stop the free use of property
because the officials prefer uses on the locations that pay higher
rates of tax revenue to the city.

Churches almost always need to gain conditional-use permits.
Those permits grant specific operating conditions, not only to
churches but for most business uses. For instance, a restaurant will
want to locate in a commercial area zoned for restaurants, and then
city officials will grant a CUP that includes specific parking and seating requirements. If the restaurant refuses to go along with these
specific and oftentimes subjective conditions, no permit. If the
restaurant ever violates its permit, by, say, seating more people than
stipulated, the city can come in and shut down the operation. The
same goes for churches.

Typically, churches are no longer allowed to locate in residential
areas, for parking and noise reasons, although many churches are
"grandfathered" in existing residential areas. But in older cities,
especially, officials don't want prime commercial land used for non-
taxpaying purposes either, so they routinely deny churches permits.
This is an abuse of property rights and a form of a taking, but one
that doesn't require the use of eminent domain. The unfair treatment
churches received from cities, and the declining number of places
where they can legally locate, was the driving force behind RLUIPA.
The law, authored by the political odd couple of Republican Orrin
Hatch of Utah and Democrat Ted Kennedy of Massachusetts, passed

Congress unanimously and was signed into law by Bill Clinton in 2000 with much fanfare.

In North Las Vegas, Nevada, Rev. Betty Smith and her congregation of about 100 people located in one of the few places that accommodate a church: a small commercial building surrounded by small businesses including a Gold's Gym. But the city didn't want a church operating in a commercial zone, so it used a technicality to force the church to leave. Although RLUIPA was not invoked, this is the type of case that sparked its overwhelming support in Congress.

The church fought City Hall and won the battle to allow churches to operate in commercial areas. Then lo and behold, the city discovered that the church had to leave anyway because of other newly discovered zoning violations.

"On July 3, City Council members decided the church still didn't conform to conditions for buildings on the north end of the plaza," according to the July 18, 2002, *Las Vegas Review-Journal*.[258] "Those buildings must be occupied by medical or professional offices. Also, the church is about 10 feet away from homes abutting the plaza's north end, in violation of zoning rules that say churches can't be within fifty feet of residential areas. . . .

"City officials said only one area resident complained about the church, but they did not disclose the resident's name. None of the businesses that share the building, parking lot or plaza space has objected."

How is that for due process? One unnamed person complained. That unnamed person could have been a city official. And what was the complaint about? It's a mystery. This is standard operating procedure for cities, which twist and contort the law, or miraculously find technicalities, in service to whatever their goal may be. Here, they didn't want the church, so even though the church won the battle over commercial zoning—a case that could have been litigated under RLUIPA—it still lost for other reasons.

The church leased the building, so the city blamed the property's owner for not informing the church of these arcane conditions. The property owner claimed it was the church's responsibility to understand the zoning and required the church to continue paying on the lease. Of course, the city never told the church about the problems when it was doing its due diligence.

This isn't eminent domain, of course. But real property—a three-year leasehold interest in a property—was taken from the church by the government with no compensation paid. It's yet another example of the lengths to which city officials will go to keep churches out of tax-generating areas, and the unfair way officials will treat those property owners and leaseholders without the resources to hire attorneys and fight back.

Given these situations, I cannot help but applaud RLUIPA. At least it is a tool available to defend against these cruel actions.

Granted, conservative critics have questioned whether RLUIPA is constitutional, in that it imposes a federal standard on local land-use decisions. Liberal critics have decried the impact of the federal law on land-use regulation. "Critics say RLUIPA goes too far," Martin Lasden wrote in *California Lawyer* in July 2002.[259] "They note that this is the first federal law to specifically target local land-use ordinances and that in the name of religious freedom the law radically impinges on the prerogatives of local government."

As I see it, the law forces local governments to live by the terms of the U.S. Constitution. Yes, of course, it imposes a federal standard on local land-use prerogatives. But often those prerogatives—as we see from the Cottonwood case—tread on the nation's tradition of property rights. The law has provided a new means for religious organizations to stand up to local land-use bullies, and has given many churches better footing to negotiate a deal with cities that don't want them, even for the most outrageously discriminatory reasons. The problem, however, is that RLUIPA only applies to churches and religious groups, and is based on religious freedom rather than property rights. It is a useful tool, but a far better tool would be the upholding of the Constitution. Nevertheless, it's refreshing to see some federal law actually advance liberty rather than advance government power and the welfare state. Supporters of RLUIPA argue that *Berman* and *Midkiff* eroded constitutional rights, but RLUIPA simply restored them a bit.

Another useful idea, proposed by U.S. Rep. Ron Paul, the Texas Republican who is the most consistent supporter of constitutional principles in Congress, would bar the use of federal funds to take churches. His measure passed in 2000, but the bill it was attached to failed, according to a Libertarian Party explanation.[260] He then reintroduced language that would "amend the Housing and Community Development Act of 1974 to prohibit the use of community development block grant funds for activities involving acquisition of church property, unless the consent of the church is obtained."

LIKE *ALICE IN WONDERLAND*

Rep. Paul's proposal comes at the urging of the Libertarian Party of Nassau County, New York, which has been pushing for reforms in the wake of an egregious church taking for a federally funded redevelopment project.

Like Cypress officials, officials in North Hempstead, New York, didn't want a church in an area known as New Cassel, so it denied the church permits to operate, misled the church about what was going on and about the process it needed to follow to get its permit, then eventually used eminent domain to take the church to use the land for a private development. Unlike Cypress, this story of greed and public bullying had an unhappy ending, and it revealed just how little due process is afforded any property owners—churches or otherwise—when dealing with public agencies bent on taking their property.

The story has a distinct *Alice in Wonderland* quality about it, given the nonsensical and deliberately incomprehensible way the city proceeded. (As one memorable passage from Alice's adventures go: "Fury said to a mouse, That he met in the house, 'Let us both go to law: I will prosecute YOU.—Come, I'll take no denial; We must have a trial: For really this morning I've nothing to do.' Said the mouse to the cur, 'Such a trial, dear Sir, With no jury or judge, would be wasting our breath.' 'I'll be judge, I'll be jury,' Said cunning old Fury: 'I'll try the whole cause, and condemn you to death' "[261])

The *Westbury (New York) Times* in January 2000 captured the gist of the eminent domain abuse:

"In 1997, Reverend Fred Jenkins purchased property . . . with plans to restore a building that had lain dormant and dilapidated since the early 1980s. The new building was to house Jenkins' congregation, St. Luke's Pentecostal Church, which, for twenty-one years, had been renting space at various local churches, while saving up to buy a church building of their own."[262]

Rev. Jenkins had come before the city to get the proper permits to turn this blighted building into a nice facility. In fact, the previous church owners had obtained all necessary permits, and Jenkins' plan would deviate from it only slightly.

"It was only after the property changed hands, Jenkins claims, that the Zoning Board of the Town of North Hempstead informed him he did not have a suitable number of parking spaces," wrote the *Times*. The church hired a lawyer and fought to gain its permits, which it succeeded in doing. Throughout the permit fight, however, city officials never told the reverend that all along it had planned on taking the property by eminent domain and using it for a private business development.

"When St. Luke's tried to object to the condemnation, the NHCDA (North Hempstead Community Development Agency) successfully argued that St. Luke's opportunity to object had been lost in 1994, before the church had even bought the property," wrote the Institute for Justice's Dana Berliner, in her book, *Public Power, Private Gain.*[263] "New York has a thirty-day window for objecting to condemnations, and the window happens right after the agency approves a redevelopment plan, often long before the condemnation actually takes place. . . . In August 2002, the New York state court denied St. Luke's motion to reopen. The court held not only that state eminent domain laws do not require the NHCDA to provide actual notice to the owners when a property is designated for condemnation, but also that inadvertent failure to provide a condemnee with actual notice does not invalidate the taking."

The court found nothing wrong with the fact that the church was legally required to have appealed the eminent domain proceeding several years before it actually bought the property. The court found nothing wrong with the fact that the city of North Hempstead did not inform the church about its plans. By the way, the city gave the church $50,000 less than it paid for it. This was a first-class mugging, completed by officials intent on keep a poor church out of their community so that the land could be used as a shopping center.

In addition to treating the church unfairly in its "just" compensation offer, town officials revoked the church's property-tax exemption without informing church officials about it. The church was not a functioning church, so it shouldn't be tax-exempt, the city said.[264] But the church was not a functioning church because the city would not grant it the permits needed to be a functioning church. Welcome to the world of *Alice in Wonderland*.

"We have enough churches here in New Cassel," a member of the town zoning board told the *Westbury Times*.[265] "I would like to see done with the property what it was earmarked for . . . business."

North Hempstead officials, similar to officials in Cypress and elsewhere, claimed that the property was blighted, as a justification for taking it and rebuilding it as part of a federal renewal project. But the rundown church would not have remained blighted for long had the city simply allowed St. Luke's to follow through with its plans. Jim Lesczynski, media-relations director of the Manhattan Libertarian Party, calls the North Hempstead case his "favorite recent eminent domain case—for sheer audacity and meanness."[266] Hard to argue with that observation. Hard to argue with columnist Jacob Sullum's depiction of the case as one in which "the owners did not have a clear sense of what was going on until it was too late."[267]

WITHOUT NOTICE

Although the taking of a church is particularly galling, especially because town officials prefer business to worship, the St. Luke situation raises another outrageous aspect of eminent domain and the wide latitude the courts give the government in exercising it. Even though the church did not get proper notice and a chance to appeal the decision, the courts said it was okay to move forward with the condemnation. Redevelopment laws vary by state, but every law gives some sort of deadline for appealing a blight designation and other aspects of the taking. Usually, the time frame is short, which gives cities the incentive to be as deceitful as possible in alerting property owners of their intentions. With cases such as North Hempstead, the courts have said, in effect, that cities can lie, cheat and steal. They can forget about proper warnings and due process, and there will be no penalty to pay. Under such a line of legal reasoning, why shouldn't officials do everything they can to keep property owners in the dark? The more notice they give, the more chance owners will have to find lawyers and fight the proceedings.

Even supporters of redevelopment and eminent domain use should be able to see the importance of assuring that the targeted owners get their day in court. Yet, that is expecting too much. In response to bad publicity about the North Hempstead case and other recent eminent domain abuses in the state, the New York

Legislature, on a unanimous and bipartisan basis, passed a bill that would have righted this particular wrong by requiring a proper notice be given to targeted property owners. Governor George Pataki, a Republican, on the advice of Attorney General Elliott Spitzer, a Democrat, vetoed the bill, arguing that it would impose too many costs on government and would hold up important public works projects.[268]

"Under current regulations, municipal agencies may announce their intent to condemn someone's property for a 'public use' merely by posting legal ads in the classified sections of newspapers," explained *Journal News* (New York) columnist Phil Reisman on October 5, 2003.[269] "Those ads are not scanned regularly by the average reader, who may not discover the pending loss of his or her property until it is too late and the chance to fight the seizure in court is lost.

"In other words, the game is rigged. . . .

"Your rights and mine, the governor seems to be saying, aren't worth the price of a postage stamp."

And as Reisman correctly explained, the governor is holding to an outdated view of eminent domain. He used the example of slowed-down transportation projects, but these days eminent domain is used for transferring property ownership from the little guy to the big corporate developer.

The New York vote showed the interesting political dynamics of eminent domain. Liberals and conservatives in the Legislature were able to see the injustice of the current system. Conservatives can see how the process destroys property rights, and liberals can see how it allows big developers to take advantage of small-property owners. But it cuts the other way, also. A Republican such as Pataki, whose apparent concern is business interests, and a Democrat such as Spitzer, whose apparent concern is protecting government power, can be blind to the injustice taking place in their own midst.

New York isn't the only state to have fought—and eventually lost—a battle over the proper notification of eminent domain victims. In 1991, in the case of the *City of Los Angeles v. Chadwick*,[270] the state court of appeal sided with a property owner who had not been given sufficient notice that his building would be removed to make way for a fire station. There was no question that the use of eminent domain was for a public project, but the owner argued that he had no chance to argue against the action.

As the court ruled, "*Chadwick* was deprived of due process by the inadequate notice and opportunity to reasonably challenge the irrevocable earlier decision in effect to condemn his property."[271] As the court earlier explained, there are several standards governments must meet before taking property by eminent domain, and proper notice is one of them. Ultimately, Spencer Chadwick was granted a new trial to determine the value of his property, given that his business had long since been relocated and the fire station built on his old property.

The state Supreme Court, however, voted not to publish the opinion, meaning that it applies only to the parties in the case and cannot be used as case law in deciding other cases. Cities had become frantic at the appeals court's ruling, given that it would have allowed eminent domain actions to have been overturned if proper notice was not given. So *Chadwick* was a good decision, but no one else in California has benefited from it.[272]

Of course, the issue of notification is of concern to churches and non-churches alike. It's a reminder that, ultimately, eminent domain is about property rights, first and foremost. When property rights are obliterated, everyone suffers, including churches.

LEVELING ST. MARY'S

When talking to victims of eminent domain, this much comes through: Despite what the courts and government officials say, property means more than the dollars and cents offered to replace it, even in the cases when the government offers a truly fair-market value.

Attorney Chris Sutton, with his "property rights are human rights" saying, is acknowledging that point. People invest their lives and their whole beings in their businesses and homes. This feeling comes through repeatedly when we're dealing with churches that have been targeted by the government for eminent domain. It's unconscionable to rob individuals of their own freely obtained properties to give to another private party who covets the property for another use. But even when eminent domain is legally justified, as in the cases of projects that are clearly public uses, this power should be used sparingly. Often governments are so emboldened by this power that they use it when they don't have to. Some creativity might yield an alternate route for the road, or an alternate site for the school. But why bother, when agencies can use police powers to take whatever suits them the best?

Chronicles magazine Executive Editor Scott Richert explains the loving care in which St. Mary's Catholic Church—which had been targeted by the county for eminent domain to make room for a massive prison expansion—was restored in downtown Rockford, Illinois: "Between the first Sunday of Advent, 1997, and Christmas 2002, Father Bovee oversaw a massive renovation of the church. The altar rail was restored; two side altars were constructed, honoring the Blessed Virgin and St. Joseph; the steep roof was replaced and the steeple repaired; and, at a cost of over $400,000, the stained-glass windows ('some of the finest in the Midwest,' according to stained-glass expert Frank Houtkamp) were removed, cleaned, repaired and reinstalled. Organist and choir director Mark Dahlgren, at great personal expense, replaced St. Mary's aging organ."[273]

The historic church, built in 1885, and lovingly rebuilt after a fire, is an anchor in the city's downtown, and drew members of a committed Catholic community from an hour or more from the city. This is no mere building that can be replaced with money, based on an appraiser's estimate. Yet Winnebago County wanted to level it in order to complete its nine-acre jail expansion project. The final chapter has not yet been written, but it appears that in the face of massive public resistance, the county will spare the church.

Still, questions are raised—questions that apply across the country and not just to this one place. Why can governments continue to discriminate so wantonly against church and religious uses? Why do they have so much power to destroy communities, such as the community that revolves around St. Mary's, without having to pursue other alternatives first? Why can officials decide that a Costco or an office building or even a prison is so much more valuable than a church that they can bulldoze the church and offer its congregants a pittance of what the facility meant to their lives?

8. CORPORATE WELFARE QUEENS

These men, in point of fact, are seldom if ever moved by anything rationally describable as public spirit; there is actually no more public spirit among them than among so many burglars or street-walkers. Their purpose, first, last and all the time, is to promote their private advantage, and to that end, and that end alone, they exercise all the vast powers that are in their hands. . . .
— H.L. Mencken[274]

With all the talk about the "public" good that surrounds the use of eminent domain to transfer property from one private owner to another, it's easy to forget what the whole process is about: private gain. Mencken, though writing about government bureaucrats in the quotation above, could just as easily have been writing about the retailers, professional sports franchisees, casino owners, lawyers, consultants and bond dealers who stand behind the officials, urging them to use their powers to give them the property and subsidies they are coveting.

There's some debate over whether the abuse of eminent domain is driven by government officials seeking new tax revenue and new powers to remake their communities in their own vision, or by profit-seeking "looters"—to borrow Ayn Rand's description of businesses that rely on government rather than on the entrepreneurial spirit—whispering promises into the ears of officials. Each project has its own dynamic, no doubt.

"It's a chicken and an egg thing," explains Scott Bullock, an attorney with the Institute for Justice. "Even though we're critical of businesses or developers who take advantage of this, the ultimate responsibility lies with government. Costco, IKEA and wealthy developers don't have the power to take your property."[275] Bullock is right. It is the law that is most responsible for the abuses. It is the government that is mainly to blame. Your neighbor might like to have your car, but probably won't steal it. Now, if the government allowed him to use a legal process to take it, he might do so. The law that allows legal theft is ultimately the problem.

Nevertheless, the process still is immoral. It still is destructive of individual rights and freedom. It is still a form of theft and abuse, and those companies that benefit from the process, and especially those that zealously take advantage of the benefits it offers them, are co-conspirators. They deserve public outrage and scrutiny. At the very least, they ought to know better. "I'm discouraged by the willingness of so many businesses and developers, who should know about the principles of free markets, to set these principles aside," Bullock added. "They run to the government, or are willing accomplices of the government, to take other people's property. Looters? They really are. This is not just an aberration. It is blatantly unconstitutional and just plain wrong from any philosophy or morality you critique it from."[276]

"The retailers take the system as they find it," explains California attorney Eric Norby. "If I were a retailer, why wouldn't I want free land?"[277] Norby, who has represented clients battling eminent domain abuse and is active in the fight against corporate subsidies, wasn't defending the abuses, only explaining why they have become so prevalent.

Ironically, most of these private beneficiaries of eminent domain get testy when anyone criticizes them for it. In their view, as long as it is legal, it is okay. There's a big problem with that kind of morality. Just think of any despotic regime in which awful things are legal. Does the mere legality of a theft negate the moral implications of the action?

Perhaps it is unreasonable to expect profit-seeking corporate leaders, any more than tax- and power-hungry government officials, to act in anything but their own self-interest. But consumers routinely buy products that conform to their standards of good stewardship.

Automakers are routinely implored to build more environmentally friendly cars, and they often are quite sensitive to criticisms regarding any number of social values, from the percentage of minority employees they hire to the quality of the company's overseas factories. Why, then, shouldn't companies be criticized when they participate in projects that abuse the rights of American citizens by bulldozing their property rights? Why shouldn't they be willing to act responsibly when the spotlight is pointed toward their abuses? Why do these corporate executives act so sheepishly when confronted by minority activists and eco-activists, yet so belligerently when confronted with the critics of their land-clearing policies?

COSTCO: CORPORATE DARTH VADER

When it comes to eminent domain, there are plenty of corporate abusers who don't think twice about accepting ill-gotten gains. Retail stores, especially big-box retailers that bring in enormous sales-tax revenue to local governments, are among the main beneficiaries of eminent domain. Many well-known retailers, including IKEA, Home Depot, Wal-Mart, Target, Walgreens and Nordstrom, have been involved in redevelopment projects built on property taken by force from other private owners. Big corporations, such as the *New York Times* and Pfizer, have been involved in such projects as they have built new corporate offices.[278]

Car dealerships are notorious corporate raiders, also. In one interesting 2004 case, the city of Santa Ana, California, is condemning an office building on behalf of Crevier BMW, one of the car dealers in the Santa Ana Auto Mall. The building is occupied by county restaurant inspectors, which is creating a novel twist on redevelopment: A clearly public use (whether one believes in restaurant inspections or not) is being removed by eminent domain for the clearly private use of a car dealer.[279]

Even small businesses that could just as easily be victims of eminent domain sometimes get in on the act as villains. In the *60 Minutes* special on eminent domain abuse, an Ace hardware store owner in Mesa, Arizona, admits that he went directly to the city rather than to an auto-repair shop owner to gain the shop owner's property at a prime commercial intersection.[280] In that case, one small business was using the government to get a prime location owned by another small business, and the hardware store owner couldn't understand why the victim was so upset about this eminent domain process. Why even bother with free-market negotiations in the current world, when cities will do the dirty work for you? Listen to the statements made by companies that take advantage of current eminent domain laws and unscrupulous city governments. They can't understand why they shouldn't be able to have what they want, or why some little guy can stand in the way of progress. They use the law to do what they would never try on their own.

Among all the many corporate villains, large and small, one national retailer in particular, Issaquah, Washington-based Costco, has earned a reputation as the nation's Corporate Darth Vader of Eminent Domain. Most of the other companies mentioned above have been involved in one or two eminent domain cases, but Costco and eminent domain have become virtually synonymous. Not only has Costco been involved in a large number of controversial projects, but its officials are unusually aggressive in defending this practice. Based on conversations with Costco representatives, court rulings and newspaper accounts, it is clear that Costco has decided as a corporation to take full advantage of these eminent domain takings. When caught in the act, its officials act shocked at the controversy.

I wonder if Costco would be so supportive of eminent domain if it were being used by a competitor, say Wal-Mart, against Costco. But as Mencken understood, we're not dealing with consistency or principle here, just some executives who are no better than thieves or streetwalkers, looking for nothing more than private enrichment. Given this reality, it was almost funny observing the company's president, $6-million-a-year executive Jim Sinegal, act like a wounded puppy after Costco received a media black eye for its role in the Cottonwood debacle.

In the Cottonwood Christian Center situation, Costco was always there in the background as the city of Cypress tried to deny the church its permits to build its campus on its own properly zoned property. After the church rejected Costco's offer to buy the eighteen acres, Costco began negotiating with the city directly, cutting the property owner out of the process. Costco knew what it was doing. Its officials had to be aware of all the bad publicity surrounding the deal.[281]

Eventually, after the criticism got to be too much, Costco officially terminated its interest in the Cottonwood project, although it jumped right back in after the legal issues were resolved. This was just a PR ploy. In the thick of the battle, Costco took out advertisements trying to lease restaurant pads on the property, even though it did not yet own the land, and even though Cottonwood was battling to hold on to its plans to build a church on the site. During my research for the *Orange County Register*, the private development consultant that finds sites for Costco throughout Southern California, Northwest Atlantic Partners, told me the company has to rely on redevelopment by cities to find sites because it is too hard and costly to otherwise find sufficiently large tracts of undeveloped land in the densely populated Los Angeles basin.[282] Clearly, then, Costco is pursuing a company policy that brings it the largest possible financial gain. If it cares about the costs it is imposing on forcibly removed property owners, it doesn't show it.

Costco was dealt a serious public-relations blow when the *Wall Street Journal*, the nation's highest circulation newspaper and one highly regarded in the financial community, printed a blistering editorial May 30, 2002, titled, "The First Church of Costco."[283]

"The Good Book instructs us to render unto Caesar what is his. But what do you do when Caesar casts his greedy eye on your local church—in order to replace it with a discount retailer?"

The editorial recounted the situation in Cypress, then made these observations: "[T]he whole point of property rights is that bureaucrats don't get to pick and choose who owns what. Ditto for businesses such as Costco, which should buy their land in the open market instead of relying on local governments to seize a juicy location at below-market prices.

"The powers of eminent domain are tricky enough when exercised for highways, schools or other public uses. But when invoked on behalf of a private business it represents the worst form of political collusion."

The editorial was right on point. Property rights are not a fiction. They don't exist only when government officials like the final outcome. They are there to allow individuals to pursue their own goals and desires, free from the demands of government officials. They are there to offer a level playing field. Costco shouldn't rely on government to pick and choose winners. The company should buy its land "in the open market." Unquestionably, as the *Journal* pointed out, the Cypress/Costco deal was an act of political collusion, a far cry from the use of eminent domain to build highways.

Apparently, the *Journal* editorial stung the Issaquah discount retailer. In a letter printed in the *Journal* on June 12, Costco CEO Sinegal fired back: "Had we been asked, we could have pointed out that we are not a party to any litigation, and do not have a contract to buy any land in Cypress, nor will we have until a judge or the parties themselves resolve their dispute. . . . We were wrongly painted in a negative light. I'm resisting the urge to fully defend our role in this—it might fill several pages detailing how you were misled and how Costco is being falsely portrayed as the villain in this dispute between the church and the city."[284]

Sinegal then blamed the church for buying the property, even though city officials had warned them against it—a fanciful explanation of what happened, but one that echoed the city's official line. It's an odd position given that the U.S. Supreme Court has upheld the right of property owners to do as they please with their property until the time it is taken by the government, as Gideon Kanner points out.[285] Here we had government officials and a corporate executive singing from the same hymnal in an unholy effort to deprive a church of its property. "The church went ahead and bought the land anyway, paying $14 million cash, in a highly speculative maneuver for any land developer, let alone a church," Sinegal continued. "Now, a key commercial corner sits vacant, frustrating the need of the city to increase its tax base to support schools and other services . . . " How public-spirited of Sinegal and Costco to be so concerned about the city of Cypress' tax base. This affirms one of my favorite maxims: The louder a person might bray about the public interest, the surer the public can be that private gain is behind the deal. "It is a general popular error to suppose the loudest complainers for the public to be the most anxious for its welfare," said Edmund Burke.[286] As explained in an earlier chapter, the church did nothing speculative. It bought property the old-fashioned, free-market way. It offered an acceptable price to four separate willing sellers. The land was zoned in such a way that a church was a specifically permitted use. The Costco retail plan, by contrast, was in violation of the land's zoning. The court eventually agreed with the church, and emphasized the obvious fact: A letter from a mid-level bureaucrat saying city officials might prefer another use for the property does not negate one's property rights, no matter how much Sinegal covets the land.

Most dubious, however, was Sinegal's solemn insistence that "we are not a party to any litigation, and do not have a contract to buy any land in Cypress, nor will we have until a judge or the parties themselves resolve their dispute." Well, technically, that is true.

Costco was not the legal party in the dispute. The official dispute was between the city and the church. But Costco was deep in the negotiations. Costco was trying to lease portions of the property to restaurants. The whole city retail center proposal was based, specifically, on the construction of a Costco. No one bothered hiding that fact. Fred Weinberg, a Las Vegas-based property consultant who advised Cottonwood, wrote in a June 12, 2002 letter to the *Journal*, "Costco, until June 10, had an exclusive right to negotiate for the property with the city." Furthermore, Weinberg wrote, "Costco tried to purchase the property directly from the church prior to any mention of eminent domain. Eminent domain came into the picture only when the church declined to sell the property."[287]

When a member of the public wrote to Costco to complain about its efforts to deprive Cottonwood of its property rights, Sinegal sent back a letter stating: "If we disappear from the picture, it will simply open the door for another retailer to take our place, but will not alter the city's position prohibiting the Christian Center to develop the Katella Avenue and Walker corner." He added: "Rest assured that we respect the good work that this Church does in the community, and would support their efforts to build a new facility in an appropriate location."[288] In Sinegal's view, "appropriate location" is not the location the church owns and has every right to develop, but one that Costco is not coveting.

If Costco is an innocent bystander, then why has it been involved in so many similar cases across the country? Costco has been involved in eminent domain cases in Lenexa, Kansas; Maplewood, Missouri; Port Chester, New York; East Harlem, New York; Kansas City, Missouri; and Lancaster, California. In Lenexa, a Costco attorney told the Planning Commission that the targeted neighborhood is "not much of a neighborhood anyway."[289] The *Kansas City Star* reported in June 2000 the following regarding a downtown Kansas City redevelopment project: "Costco, a membership-only wholesale store, nearly dropped out of the project. But city officials promised to hasten change by using condemnation powers if necessary to relocate a temporary-labor agency and a liquor store in the neighborhood."[290]

"Costco is the worst of any corporation out there in the case of eminent domain abuse," explains John Kramer, public-affairs director for the Institute for Justice.[291] "The first time they can say, 'oh well,'" explained IJ attorney Dana Berliner. "But by the time they get to No. 5 or No. 6, Costco can't claim ignorance any more."[292] "This is their MO," said Orange County Supervisor Chris Norby. "They expect this. This is a pattern."[293]

As an aside, the company expects subsidies also. In Orange County, California, alone, Costco has received more than $30 million in taxpayer subsidies, according to an August 12, 2002, *Orange County Register* report.[294] That's just one county. It's one thing when a company gains a competitive advantage through providing the best products at the best prices, quite another when it uses the government to extort property and money from private owners and taxpayers to pump up the bottom line. It might be legal, but this process is far from ethical. It's unfair forcing a small-business owner who must compete with Costco to also subsidize the discount retailer through his taxes, even worse when he has to move out of his store to make way for the company. Liberal critics of Costco often focus on the company's low prices that supposedly are unfair to small retailers and its non-union work force. In my book, that's no serious criticism. Free markets are dynamic. Creative destruction is part of the process. If a store cannot compete with a big discounter that has mastered the art of selling quality goods at low prices, tough. If an employee doesn't like his pay or benefits, he should work somewhere else. When the California Legislature tried to ban big-box stores as a sop to unions, I was outraged and editorialized against it.[295] Costco is in many ways a marvel. But it should not be allowed to subsidize its low prices on the backs of property owners and taxpayers.

The most damning account of Costco's eminent domain practices comes from a federal court, which in 2001 slammed an attempt by the city of Lancaster, California, to take a Costco competitor by eminent domain and hand the property to the company for $1. The case offers an insight into how Costco conducts business. Costco can say what it wants, but this published federal court ruling gives an insider view of how Costco operates. Serious critics of the company and of the eminent domain process in general would do well to carefully read the words of Judge Stephen V. Wilson.

The basics of the plan are simple. In 1983, the city of Lancaster— a desert community about sixty miles northeast of Los Angeles— created a redevelopment area based on a blight designation. As the court explained, the city claimed the land had insufficient public infrastructure, was prone to flooding and had faulty subdivision planning. That's safe to say, given that the land was vacant. It's the same old, same old: the city wanted to create a major shopping center to bring in property tax increment and sales tax, and went through the redevelopment process to accomplish this goal.[296]

In 1988, the city created a regional shopping center, the Power Center, and Costco became an anchor tenant. The shopping center was completed in 1991, and became home to Wal-Mart, Circuit City and other major stores. The city allowed its power of eminent domain to expire in 1995, but restored those powers in 1997, using the initial 1983 blight finding to justify its need for these powers. That in itself is an indictment of this redevelopment process. How could the Power Center—"the highest quality commercial retail property in Lancaster and one of the most prestigious shopping areas in the city," according to the court—realistically be called blight in 1997, based on blight findings in 1983 before anything was built there? Clearly, this is a legal fiction designed to give cities enormous powers.[297]

Here's where the situation gets juicy, and provides a revealing insight about Costco's *modus operandi*. In 1998, the 99 Cents Only

Store—a discounter that, to some degree, competes with Costco—moved into a vacant store next door to Costco in the Power Center. 99 Cents Only entered into a five-year lease with a fifteen-year option with the property owner, Burnham Pacific.

"Almost immediately after 99 Cents moved into the Power Center, Costco advised Burnham Pacific and Lancaster of its need to expand the size of its Lancaster operations," the judge explained. "Costco threatened to relocate in the city of Palmdale unless Lancaster provided Costco with additional space in the Power Center. Lancaster and Burnham Pacific began negotiating options by which Costco could expand its store and remain within the city of Lancaster. Significantly, Burnham Pacific advised Lancaster that 'the most efficient use of [Costco's] property would be an expansion to the south of their existing facility behind the 99 Cents Only Store.' Costco, however, demanded that it be allowed to expand into the space being occupied by 99 Cents."[298]

That point is significant: Costco was offered an alternative, by expanding south of the neighboring store, but refused. Costco was the party that insisted the city use eminent domain on its behalf. This is not mere speculation or the words of Costco's competitors or redevelopment critics. This is the official explanation offered in the federal ruling. Lancaster officials, fearing the loss of their anchor tenant to an adjacent community, agreed to use eminent domain to take the property, and then sell it to Costco for $1. That's right—one dollar. The city would pay Burnham Pacific $3.8 million in a "friendly" eminent domain proceeding—friendly, because the owner agreed to the deal. The use of government force allowed the owner to break its lease with 99 Cents Only Stores and gain certain federal tax advantages.

Unfortunately, from the city's standpoint, 99 Cents Only refused the buyout of its leasehold interest for $130,000. Dave Gold, the owner of Commerce, California-based 99 Cents Only Stores, was mad about the action on principle. He decided to fight back, using personal money rather than corporate money, arguing that a costly legal fight could hurt stockholders.[299] He wanted to do the right thing, regardless of the financial consequences, he said in an interview. The city hadn't expected a fight. It's speculation, but the city had to realize the difficult course it was pursuing if this matter ended up in court. The entire Power Center is part of a redevelopment area. The Costco store and the 99 Cents Only store were built by the same developer at the same time and are in the same condition. They are located next to each other, and city officials were on the record saying how much they liked 99 Cents Only. Even with lax standards for blight, it would be hard to make the case that the one building was so blighted that it ought to be given to the leaseholders of a nearly identical building next door.

So the city dropped its action two months before the case was scheduled for federal court. The city decided to give Costco a portion of a city park for its store instead of the 99 Cents Only property, and then argued to the court that its dispute with 99 Cents Only was moot.

But Gold insisted on having his day in court. The city, he said, refused to rule out eminent domain in the future, so unless he got a final court ruling, his business always would be at risk. The city's promises to leave him alone were not in writing. So how could the case be moot? The judge agreed that the mere suspension of the city's plan to use eminent domain did not make the case moot, and went on to issue a ruling that is one of the most significant federal rollbacks of eminent domain abuse nationwide in recent years.

Judge Wilson ruled, "In this case, the evidence is clear beyond dispute that Lancaster's condemnation efforts rest on nothing more than the desire to achieve the naked transfer of property from one private party to another. . . . In short, the very reason that Lancaster decided to condemn 99 Cents' leasehold interest was to appease Costco." In response to the ruling, Costco's chief legal officer, Joel

Benoliel, said that the company had no legal interest in the 99 Cents Only case, which sounds remarkably close to what Sinegal said with regard to Costco's role in the Cottonwood case.[300] Again, Costco wasn't a legal party to the case. Any idiot would understand that point. But it is clear from the court's ruling that the company was the driving force behind Lancaster's attempt to force 99 Cents Only out of its store and onto the street. The words "to appease Costco" were loud and clear. This eminent domain proceeding was not public in nature. It was for private gain, and Costco was the party insisting on the abuse of government police power.

Costco's attorneys weren't the only ones smarting from Judge Wilson's decision. Lancaster city attorney David McEwan told the *Wall Street Journal* in 2001: "The court has gone way beyond what the law permits. It's a troubling trend. I don't know where the courts are going with it. . . . 99 Cents produces less than $40,000 [a year] in sales taxes, and Costco was producing more than $400,000. You tell me which is more important."[301]

McEwan acts as if the Constitution grants one set of rights to property owners who pay large amounts of sales tax and another, lesser set of rights to those property owners who pay smaller amounts of taxes. The quotation shows how an attorney could be so immersed in redevelopment law that he forgets to read the simple words of the U.S. Constitution, upon which the nation's entire set of laws is supposed to be based. The main value in McEwan's words is his upfront admission that cities ought to be able to run roughshod over the property rights of anyone whose business pays a lower share of sales taxes. Which is more important? In the eyes of the justice system, neither one should be more important. Special favors and government power should not be used on behalf of one owner simply because a city bureaucrat likes how much tax that owner pays.

As Cottonwood's attorneys argued in their case against the city of Cypress, "If increasing government revenues were 'public use' enough to permit a taking under the fifth amendment, then the 'public use' requirement would be a dead letter, permitting the very uses it was designed to exclude. For then, any profit-making use—perhaps the most plainly 'private' imaginable use for taken property—would always satisfy the 'public use' requirement, simply because it could generate taxable profits."[302]

Costco Chairman Jeffrey Brotman told Forbes.com in a June 11, 2003, article: "We don't go to a city and say, 'We need this 15 acres, so why don't you condemn.' All the instances that we've been involved have all been urban renewal projects."[303] Unfortunately, the plain facts of the 99 Cents Only case make it clear Brotman is unaware of what his company's development practices are, or he is trying to deceive the public about them. Either way, Costco stockholders ought to be ashamed and ought to demand significant changes.

THE STADIUM RIP-OFF

The trend in these eminent domain cases is clear: Government officials use their power to benefit the nation's richest and most influential people at the expense of average folks. Costco's sales-tax bonanza trumps 99 Cents Only Stores' and Cottonwood's property rights. Atlantic City officials try to drive an elderly widow out of her house to benefit billionaire Donald Trump, the casino owner. General Motors uses its influence to destroy an entire neighborhood so that it can build a new assembly plant. But nothing epitomizes this "rob from the poor, give to the rich" strategy more than various cities' zeal to use eminent domain and public subsidies to enrich the elite club of owners of professional sports teams.

Team owners such as Alex Spanos of the San Diego Chargers, Al Davis of the Oakland Raiders, Jerry Jones of the Dallas Cowboys, Dan Snyder of the Washington Redskins and Peter Angelos of the Baltimore Orioles are not exactly poverty cases. These are the richest of the rich, yet ball club owners are notorious for threatening to leave cities that don't pay taxpayer-funded blackmail. The subsidies are bad enough, but eminent domain is an expected part of the process when new stadiums are being built to benefit wealthy magnates. Wealth is a great thing. I have nothing against billionaires or sports teams or entrepreneurship or enterprise. Those who berate the wealthy simply because they are wealthy are engaging in jealousy and greed themselves. But there is a great danger when wealthy business owners are able to leverage their wealth into political power that is wielded for personal gain. Building a retail empire is admirable, but properties should be purchased in the free market, with unwilling sellers left alone to pursue their own dreams. Likewise, stadiums to house sports enterprises are not public necessities. Sports teams are enjoyable pastimes, and although building a stadium might involve some adjoining public infrastructure (i.e., a road from the stadium to the freeway), these edifices should be financed and constructed solely by private investors. They should never be built on land taken by force.

Yet just as the term "public use" has been distorted to mean shopping centers and Costcos, so too has it come to mean privately owned sports stadiums. The most notorious case in which eminent domain is associated with a sports stadium is in Los Angeles, where city and federal officials cleared away a settled Mexican-American neighborhood just north of the city's downtown, known as Chavez Ravine. The area eventually was given to Walter O'Malley, owner of the Brooklyn Dodgers, who moved his franchise to Los Angeles and built Dodger Stadium on the property.[304]

The 170-acre area was an unusual rural-like enclave along the banks of the now-paved-over Los Angeles River, where immigrant families grew their own food and maintained modest but decent frame houses. Chavez Ravine is emblematic of redevelopment and eminent domain for a variety of reasons.

First, as foes of eminent domain abuse today point out, "blight" often is an interchangeable term for "African-American neighborhood" or "Mexican-American neighborhood." Often, especially in wealthier suburban communities, an older, predominantly minority neighborhood is assumed to be blighted, making it a target for redevelopment and eminent domain efforts. This is similar to what Jane Jacobs described in the North End of Boston, where a poorly planned but lively and safe ethnic neighborhood was the subject of much elite concern. So, this older Mexican-American community in Los Angeles was viewed as blight. It lacked sufficient infrastructure, city officials declared. The 1946 blight designation referred to "improper use of land, poor street patterns, a high proportion of substandard housing . . . ," according to a publication by the Center Theater Group of Los Angeles.[305] Of course, the city could have built new roads and sewers and electrical lines without bulldozing the entire neighborhood. It was hardly the fault of Chavez Ravine's residents that the city had neglected its responsibilities in that area. On several occasions, in fact, Chavez Ravine residents had met with city officials to lobby for improved public services. Note that the local residents bitterly opposed the redevelopment effort, even though they were given first dibs on brand-new apartments in the proposed Elysian Heights projects, which is a sign that conditions weren't nearly as bad as officials described them.

Second, Chavez Ravine was victimized by both forms of redevelopment discussed earlier in this book. There was the old federally funded urban-renewal side of the equation, in which officials cleared away old neighborhoods to put up ghastly high-rise housing projects. And then there is the new form of redevelopment, in which neighborhoods are cleared away in the name of tax generation, economic development and more innovative uses of the term "public use."

Chavez Ravine was first targeted for demolition by federal housing authorities who wanted to clear away the low-density, older homes and build a jam-packed neighborhood with 10,000 housing units, mainly in the form of thirteen-story housing projects, according to the Center Theater Group publication. The plan was approved in 1950, and would use $110 million in federal housing funds (about $1 billion in today's money). The plan to build East Coast-style federal housing projects in Los Angeles didn't sit well with city residents, and the battle over Chavez Ravine got caught up in debates about the Cold War and communist influence in general. Leaders of the city's housing authority were even called before the House Un-American Activities Committee, and some eventually lost their jobs for insisting on building socialist-style housing projects, the publication explained. Amid the controversy, opponents of the project pushed forward a referendum, and city residents overturned the public-housing plan. A new mayor, C. Norris Poulson, was opposed to the public-housing plan. The state Supreme Court insisted that the project move forward, whatever the outcome of the vote, and the city continued to clear residents out of their homes, with the last one removed forcibly by law enforcement officials in 1958.[306]

As the debate raged, the Dodgers' Walter O'Malley was playing Los Angeles off of Brooklyn to secure the best possible deal for his ball club. The city of Los Angeles, at the urging of its new mayor, put together a package of subsidies for the Dodgers, who eventually moved west. The team bought the old Chavez Ravine site and constructed Dodger Stadium. The original redevelopment plan required the property, cleared by eminent domain, to be used for public purposes. But part of the stadium plan included a forty-acre park, and supporters used that to justify the "public" purpose of transferring the land to a private team owner. Eventually, the Dodger deal went before city voters, who narrowly approved it. And the state Supreme Court upheld the use of the land for the stadium, explained *The Chavez Ravine Story*, by Carlos Saldana.[307] The rest, they say, is history, but

Chavez Ravine helped pave the way for the modern era, in which stadiums are generally viewed as public uses.

The story of Chavez Ravine remains a touchstone for the progressive movement, especially on the West Coast. Unfortunately, because progressives are not too fond of property rights, they draw the wrong lessons from the battle. Many accounts "blame" the McCarthy era for holding up the public-housing project on the site and for leading to the land's takeover by a wealthy baseball team owner. Yet, it's ridiculous to blame opponents of public housing for what took place. Given the nature of urban renewal, and the nightmares that high-rise housing projects became everywhere they were built, one could only say that opponents of the projects were right. Some progressives of the time supported bulldozing Chavez Ravine in the first place, in order to "improve" the lives of people who were perfectly content living where they were.

The problem was the ability of the government to level an entire neighborhood based on a blight finding. Once property rights were destroyed, and the residents were removed from their homes, the political situation changed, and public property became ripe for private profiteering. Had the founders' vision of property rights been upheld along the way, the neighborhood would still exist, although it no doubt would have improved dramatically over the years, just as the North End of Boston changed and improved mostly on its own.

Look behind many stadium deals and one will find that the land on which the new project was built was taken by eminent domain from other owners. Nicholas Kristof, writing an October 2002 column for the *New York Times*, discussed the Texas Rangers stadium deal that George W. Bush was involved in: "Local voters overwhelmingly approved the deal, so maybe we shouldn't get so exercised by star-struck local officials giving $200 million to rich baseball owners. But the most unseemly part of the deal was that Mr.

Bush and the Rangers' owners conspired with city officials to seize private property that would be handed over to the Bush group."[308]

"A copy of the secret agreement among Mr. Bush and the other Rangers owners shows that they intended to make money not just by running a baseball club but also by land speculation," wrote Kristof.

"For example, one owner found a nice chunk of land and sent a memo suggesting that it 'sounds like another condemnation candidate if you want to work the site into your master plan,' according to the court documents. Another of the owners' internal memos casts a proprietary gaze on a property and declares: 'We plan to condemn this land,' " Kristof added.

The *Boston Business Journal* in July 2000 included an interview with Herbert Gleason, who was hired that year by a neighborhood group that wanted information on eminent domain's use for a new Boston Red Sox stadium. Gleason had in the 1960s tried to expand eminent domain's use on behalf of a football stadium: "Gleason, now a lawyer with a private practice in Boston, helped draft legislation that would have allowed the Massachusetts Turnpike Authority to seize land for a 'public purpose'—namely, a privately owned football stadium." The legislation argued that eminent domain was valid because it would provide facilities for "groups dedicated to civic and social betterment."[309] The plan was struck down by the state's Supreme Judicial Court in 1969, but proponents of using eminent domain for private stadiums keep pushing forward, using the same arguments years later.

An organization called the League of Fans, a Ralph Nader-founded group opposed to public subsidies and eminent domain on behalf of NFL owners, offers on its Web site this description of the New York Jets stadium plan: "Local neighborhood groups say that it appears to be turning into a massive land grab to free the far West Side for developers and corporations to extend Manhattan's central business district into the Chelsea and Hell's Kitchen neighborhoods where taxpayer subsidies would be used, via eminent domain, to uproot and displace West Side neighborhood residents and local businesses."[310]

When a group of Los Angeles businessmen was negotiating in 2002 to bring a new NFL franchise to the city, one councilwoman argued that a plan to create a redevelopment area in South Los Angeles where a possible stadium would be located would not guarantee subsidies. "The only thing they could expect from the CRA [Community Redevelopment Agency] is help with eminent domain,"[311] she said, according to a 2002 Associated Press report. Apparently, we've reached the point where using eminent domain for stadiums is not even controversial.

Perhaps the most absurd use of eminent domain with regard to professional sports teams took place in Oakland, as the city attempted to use this police power to keep the Oakland Raiders from moving to Los Angeles. As Raymond Keating, chief economist for the Small Business Survival Committee in Washington, D.C., explained in a 1999 Cato Institute report: "The Raiders' move set faulty legal precedents for the future of sports leagues and team movements. First, and most obvious was the lower courts' outrageous acceptance of eminent domain in the case of sports teams. The state Supreme Court overturned the decision, however, with Chief Justice Rose Bird explaining:

"If a rock concert impresario, after some years of producing concerts in a municipal stadium, decides to move his productions to another city, may the city condemn his business, including his contracts with rock stars, in order to keep the concerts at the stadium? . . . May a city condemn any business and force it to stay at its original location? May a city condemn any business that decides to seek greener pastures elsewhere under the unlimited interpretation of eminent domain law that the majority appear to approve?' "[312]

It's a bizarre take on property rights when owners of sports stadiums implore cities to take property that gets in the way of their new stadium plans, and when cities use eminent domain to keep the teams from moving elsewhere. Perhaps a stricter following of the U.S. Constitution would spare so many people the anguish of such foolish abuses. Although the focus of this book is eminent domain, the abuse of taxpayer subsidies by stadium owners is significant also. Generally, if something is a public enough use to qualify for subsidies, it is public enough to allow government agencies to use eminent domain on its behalf. The subsidy story reinforces the subject of this chapter: the degree to which private corporations will lobby government for special privileges. I'll always defend businesses when they use lobbyists and attorneys to fight against excessive regulations and taxation. These are necessary defensive actions in a world in which special-interest groups always lobby for higher benefits paid for by higher taxes imposed on the other guy. What I object to here is the use of the political process to divert direct subsidies toward private enterprises.

Sports team owners developed their teams without significant public involvement in the first half of the century, wrote Doug Bandow, a senior fellow at the Cato Institute, in an October 2003 article in the *Washington Post*. "Yet the willingness of political elites to sacrifice taxpayers on the omnipresent sports altar spans the country. Oregon faces a serious budget crisis, but that didn't stop the Legislature from recently approving $150 million for a new baseball stadium in a bid to win the Expos for Portland. In Oakland, Al Davis, the irrepressible owner of the Raiders football team, won a $34.2 million verdict against the city stadium for failing, he argued, to deliver on its promise of sold-out games. In San Diego, meanwhile negotiations continue between the city and the Chargers, who want a new stadium—eight years after the city renovated the old one."[313]

Bandow points to $20 billion worth of subsidies to sports teams nationwide since mid-century.

Since when is a stadium a public use? It is, indeed, a public venue, in that members of the public can attend high-priced sporting events at such stadiums or arenas. But we're not talking a freeway or water-treatment facility or a school. We're talking about a private venture, albeit a big and complicated one well liked by many people in any given metropolitan area. The Web site of supporters of the San Diego Chargers stadium proposal champions the idea that stadiums are public uses because they bring in so much local revenue. This is similar to what advocates of redevelopment say when they are justifying the use of eminent domain on behalf of a shopping center or downtown-revitalization project.

But tax revenue does not make a public use. "If property ownership is to remain what our forefathers intended it to be, if it is to remain a part of the liberty we cherish, the economic by-products of a private capitalist's ability to develop land cannot justify a surrender of ownership to eminent domain,"[314] explained one Illinois appeals court justice in dissenting in an appeals court case involving a taking for economic-development purposes.

Supporters of stadium subsidies are as inventive as supporters of redevelopment projects who twist the language to their ends. Various case studies and economic analyses show that stadium projects mainly spread money around a region. People spend a few hundred dollars at a football game, but that money generally would have been spent on other entertainment in the region. The stadium might shift money from the suburbs to downtown, but that hardly justifies a public commitment to build such a facility. Stadiums sit empty much of the year.

Writes Bandow: "Public finance experts Roger Noll of Stanford and Andrew Zimbalist of Smith College found in a recent study that 'no recent facility appears to have earned anything approaching a reasonable return on investment and no recent facility has been self-financing in terms of its impact on net tax revenues.' . . . Economists Robert Baade of Lake Forest College and Allen Sanderson of the University of Chicago have looked at ten metropolitan areas that brought in sports teams, and found no net employment increase, as spending was simply realigned."[315]

Ironically, the pro-subsidy, pro-Chargers Web site, www.ftballiance.org, offers all the evidence opponents need to oppose these colossal wastes of taxpayer dollars. Under the heading, "Economic Impact of the Loss of an NFL Team," the site features this impact: "Many other cities did not want to spend tax dollars to keep teams in their cities and ended up spending hundreds of millions of dollars to try to win new teams." Here is another option: Governments don't spend any money now to save the team, and don't spend any money in the future to lure a new one. Then everyone wins, except of course for the team owners who are so eager to tap into public funds. The Web site includes facts on stadium financing in other cities, ranging from 100 percent public contributions in Oakland, St. Louis and Atlanta, to "only" 17 percent in New England, 27 percent in Washington and 23 percent in North Carolina.[316]

Property-rights scholar Richard A. Epstein argues that the same Fifth Amendment standards that apply to takings ought to apply to "givings" as well. Writing about a 2002 plan by Chicago Mayor Richard Daley to use $632 million in public funds to renovate the private Soldier Field stadium used by the Chicago Bears, Epstein argues in a May 5, 2002, *Chicago Tribune* article: "Public assets, such as prime lakefront real estate, should not be given away for a song to private interests, any more than corporate assets should be transferred to the firm's president at bargain rates." He refers to an Illinois Supreme Court decision restricting eminent domain for private uses, and wonders: "The Illinois Supreme Court should be aware of the same facile justifications for givings as well as takings.

In both settings, the legislature creates a fatal mismatch between the individuals whom it benefits and burdens with its actions."[317] The law, after all, prevents gifts of public funds, which makes it more amazing that such "givings" take place so often.

When it comes to stadiums, cities and states are rarely reluctant to take property from private owners. Buried in a news story about a January 2004 plan by Anoka County, Minnesota, officials to create a redevelopment plan for a new Minnesota Vikings stadium, along with hundreds of acres of other entertainment and office uses, is this statement: "The county proposal provides a menu of funding options. . . . These include bonding, a countywide sales tax, a stadium district with sales, lodging, food and beverage taxes on businesses within the development, while creation of a tax-increment financing district is also an option for the city of Blaine. . . .

"Over and above that, the proposal calls for the city of Blaine to exercise its eminent domain powers, if necessary, to assemble the land for the project," reports the *Anoka County Union* on January 15, 2004.[318]

The same arm-twisting goes on everywhere. In 2001, a Massachusetts state judge rebuked the city of Springfield for its efforts to condemn property and subsidize a minor-league baseball team: "From the evidence, particularly through the mayor's testimony and the documentary exhibits, it appears the disappointment over the city's inability to attract a minor league affiliated baseball franchise set into motion a series of events and decisions on the part of certain officials, organizations, and individuals to bring some type of professional baseball team to Springfield through whatever means possible. Baseball became the all-consuming goal and the propriety of public funding to obtain that goal became, at best, secondary."[319]

Whenever government becomes consumed with a project, whether it is luring a baseball stadium, a discount retailer or an auto mall, the property rights of individuals always get sacrificed.

Unfortunately, too many judges allow this alliance to continue between government officials who have eminent domain and taxing powers and private profiteers who promise cities the moon, the sun and the stars if only the officials use those powers on their behalf.

THE REDEVELOPMENT INDUSTRY

The ultimate beneficiaries of eminent domain may be wealthy business owners, but the process of blighting and taking property and floating public debt to pay for new developments on the property is profitable to another class of people: the consultants, attorneys, bond brokers, appraisers and housing organizations that are built around the redevelopment process.

There is significant money in representing cities and advancing eminent domain plans. Prestigious law firms and consulting groups even conduct costly seminars teaching new people how to blight properties on behalf of local governments. Sometimes, these blighting techniques can get quite creative. Certain developers also specialize in exploiting the lucrative financial incentives created by redevelopment law.

California's law requires that 20 percent of the tax increment in any given redevelopment area be used for "affordable housing." That means government-subsidized housing projects. Many of the cities that use redevelopment for tax and retail purposes don't want to build housing projects for poor people in their affluent communities, so they, essentially, squander the money on loft projects for college students. In one case, the wealthy golf-course community of Indian Wells gave its affordable-housing credits to the poor neighboring city of Coachella.[320]

In Chapter 2, I wrote about the non-profit housing organization that lobbied in favor of the project to bulldoze a neighborhood and turn it into a theme park. To Jamboree Housing, it was far better to eliminate real affordable, market housing so that tax increment would be created and diverted to its company, to build subsidized affordable housing. This gives you an idea of the type of counterintuitive thinking that goes on in the redevelopment industry.

So much government money is available from condemning properties, floating bonds and building new developments that the process attracts a particularly unprincipled group of players. Some attorneys hired by cities think nothing about employing hardball corporate legal tactics against small-business owners and homeowners without the resources to fight back.

"So many people benefit from the deal, that making the deal happen is the main concern of everyone involved," explains California attorney Eric Norby. "If nothing happens, no one gets paid."[321]

The consultants who look for "blight" in a community have every incentive to find it. The brokers who secure public debt to pay for the projects have every reason to make the projects sound as financially feasible as possible. The lawyers know that cities want to take properties and pay as little for them as possible, so like Cypress, California's attorney, Bill Wynder, they advance the most aggressive legal theories possible. This should be expected, of course, but it's a key point to remember when trying to figure out a way to change the system. Powerful interest groups such as the League of Cities have a vested interest in the status quo. Organizations such as the California Redevelopment Association are well-funded to oppose serious reform.

According to the California controller's report, $3.3 billion was spent by the state's redevelopment agencies in fiscal year 1997–98, according to *Redevelopment: The Unknown Government.* "Over a quarter of that money pays for the interest on debt. That's $871 million into the pockets of bondholders, at the expense of California taxpayers. This is a powerful motive for bond lawyers and brokerage houses to keep pushing redevelopment schemes and lobbying against needed reform," according to the book.[322]

When eminent domain and redevelopment are being sold to the community, the redevelopment industry typically talks about blight removal and the need to rebuild crumbling inner cities. But when one reads their own publications, one sees how realistic these planners and consultants are about the process. The American Planning Association includes a description of redevelopment that's almost identical to the description offered by redevelopment's critics in its September 2002 Policy Guide:

"Redevelopment is now seen by local agencies as almost exclusively a tool for economic development rather than a tool for physical redevelopment. This has affected almost everything about how it functions, from where it is located in the city government, to how eminent domain is used, to how we define blight, to how it is perceived by stakeholders, to the type of property which is condemned."[323] The APA, like other defenders of redevelopment and eminent domain, is concerned by recent court rulings and public backlash against the process. There is too much at stake not to fight back, and it will be interesting to see the novel theories that the redevelopment industry will promote to allow it to continue along its merry old way.

SAME OLD 'LEGAL PLUNDER'

The redevelopment system reminds many observers of musty old political and economic philosophies that have long been debunked. One such philosophy was popular in Europe in the mid-nineteenth century and was even favored by the Whig party in the United States around the same time. It was called mercantilism, and is best known for its theory of imports and exports. Mercantilists believed a country would grow richer by increasing exports and decreasing imports. But the system was defined by a powerful central state that worked in concert with established, private interests.

The free-market economist Murray Rothbard called it "a system of statism which employed economic fallacy to build up a structure of imperial state power, as well as special subsidy and monopolistic privilege to individuals or groups favored by the state."[324] That's the key: The government was in the game of picking economic winners and losers. The "public good" was always the justification, but private gain was the name of the game. Author Edgar Lee Masters referred to the system as one that "doles favors to the strong in order to win and to keep their adherence to the government."[325]

This close partnership between government and private corporations was a main feature of fascist ideology. As Professor Thomas DiLorenzo, of Loyola College in Baltimore, explains in a June 1994 article in the *Freeman*, most people naturally associate fascism with the racist totalitarian systems of Nazi Germany and Mussolini's Italy. "But there was also an economic-policy component of fascism, known in Europe during the 1920s and '30s as 'corporatism,' that was an essential ingredient of economic totalitarianism as practiced by Mussolini and Hitler."[326]

Under this philosophy, a small elite of business and government leaders would create a unified economic policy, as opposed to the "disorderly" forms of business developments that took place in market economies. "The whole idea . . . is to make citizens subservient to the state and to place power over resource allocation in the hands of a small elite," wrote DiLorenzo.

Compare that idea to the founders' original intent. Here's DiLorenzo again: "The U.S. Constitution was written by individuals who believed in the classical liberal philosophy of individual rights and sought to protect those rights from governmental encroachment. But since the fascist/collectivist philosophy has been so influential, policy reforms over the past half century have all but abolished many of these rights by simply ignoring many of the provisions in the Constitution that were designed to protect them."

Of course, we could simply describe abusive government policies in the way that French economist Frederic Bastiat described them in his classic 1850 book, *The Law.* He called laws that rob from Peter and pay Paul "legal plunder." And he argued that plunder, or theft, was far worse when it took place under the protection of the law than outside of it. "It is impossible to introduce into society a greater change and a greater evil than this: the conversion of the law into an instrument of plunder," Bastiat wrote.[327]

"No society can exist unless the laws are respected to a certain degree. The safest way to make laws respected is to make them respectable. . . . There is in all of us a strong disposition to believe that anything lawful is also legitimate. This belief is so widespread that many persons have erroneously held that many things are 'just' because law makes them so,"[328] Bastiat wrote.

That's certainly reminiscent of the redevelopment process, which is routinely defended as something perfectly legal. Unfortunately, as Bastiat understood, "Sometimes the law defends plunder and participates in it. Thus the beneficiaries are spared the shame, danger and scruple which their acts would otherwise involve. Sometimes the law places the whole apparatus of judges, police, prisons, and gendarmes at the service of the plunderers, and treats the victim—when he defends himself—as a criminal."[329]

Perhaps the most compelling statement on the dangers of businesses participating in legal plunder comes from Professor Tibor Machan of Chapman University, writing in the *Laissez Faire Electronic Times*: "The moral of the story is that while the free market is just and usually fair, many in business do not, by any stretch of the imagination, give it their support, quite the contrary. In the end, though, they will regret this because as politicians and bureaucrats can conspire against small business with big ones, so they can undo the big guys as well, should that suit their fancy."[330]

Even Costco ought to take heed of those words.

9. THE MEDIA FINALLY WAKE UP

Instead of considering the editor of a newspaper, as an abstraction, with no motive in view but that of maintaining principles and disseminating facts, it is necessary to remember that he is a man, with all the interests and passions of one who has chosen this means to advance his fortunes, and of course, with all the accompanying temptations to abuse his opportunities, and this too, usually, with the additional drawback of being a partisan in politics, religion, or literature.

— James Fenimore Cooper[331]

Journalists tell themselves and the public that they are the watchdogs of American liberties, exposing greed, corruption and abuse. That's sometimes true, but in reality journalists have their own biases and outlooks, and the story of eminent domain abuse had rarely been told until the last few years because of such biases. Recently, thanks to the increasing outrageousness of many eminent domain actions and the efforts of some lawyers and activist groups, media coverage has improved. The problem had gotten so bad that the media has had to take some notice.

"The media has either not given attention to the matter or has been outright hostile," argues attorney Gideon Kanner. In his representations of property owners in court, he often must also battle journalists who are so biased in favor of government actions on behalf of the environment that they distort the news and attack property owners.[332] Kanner cites the controversy over the federal government's efforts to buy Pacific Lumber Company's 7,500-acre Headwaters Forest, comprising old-growth redwoods in Northern California. "No rational person can honestly dispute that, on principle, government acquisition and preservation of irreplaceable natural resources is a good thing," Kanner wrote, in a September

2000 *Environmental Law Reporter* article.[333] But the environmentalists involved in the matter "vociferously asserted that the land's owner had no right to log it, and that the government should gain control and eventually ownership of Headwaters without paying for it. Amazingly, this unblushingly voiced demand that the government ignore the Fifth Amendment—and the Eighth Commandment, if you are of a religious bent—far from being treated as the outlandish attack on constitutional rights that it was, enjoyed support from the mainstream press that encouraged such government conduct and evidently emboldened it to give it a try."

As Kanner explained in his *ELR* article, the *Wall Street Journal* tried to depict the property owner as the one trying to blackmail—the *Journal* called it "greenmail"—the federal government into paying for the property, even though the federal judge compared the government's tactics to those of Cosa Nostra. The company's new chief executive, Charles Hurwitz, was portrayed as a greedy corporate raider who was trying to rape the environment and shake down the U.S. government. Kanner cites many examples, including the *Journal* depiction of the battle this way: "Hurwitz wants the U.S. government to pay him hundreds of millions of dollars for 4,500 acres of the ancient redwoods, in a remote California grove known as the Headwaters Forest." No mention of property rights, of course. *Newsweek* depicted the company's CEO as a man who "began attacking the company's birthright: thousands of acres of so-called old-growth redwoods." *Rolling Stone* looked at it this way: "It's a story about Michael Milken, junk bonds, Ivan Boesky, Drexel Burnham Lambert, enormous conglomerates—and between 10,000 and 12,000 acres of virgin redwoods."[334]

That's typical of the media's bias, especially when the story is framed as a conflict between the environment and a corporate profit seeker. But whatever the truth about Hurwitz's corporate activities, the case at hand was about guaranteeing just compensation for property taken by the government. The media was squarely on the side of the government. "The press took it as axiomatic that it was evil and indeed somehow illegal for PALCO to use its own land for its historical use of timber harvesting . . . There was simply no respectable legal basis for asserting that this government land acquisition should not have been accompanied by payment of just compensation," Kanner added. Instead of acting like the public watchdog, he wrote, the media acted like the environmentalists' lapdog.[335]

Yet the media is incapable of seeing its bias in such matters. As ABC's John Stossel said during a January 2004 California speech, talking to the media about bias is like talking to a fish about water: "Water. What water?"[336] Of course, there are other reasons the media have traditionally not given property owners a fair shake.

Bernard Goldberg, the CBS News veteran reporter who broke ranks with his colleagues by exposing media bias in a *Wall Street Journal* article and subsequently in the books, *Bias* and *Arrogance*, blames the lack of good coverage on redevelopment and other topics on the merging of entertainment with news. "Once upon a time, the networks did serious documentaries. . . . They realized these things don't sell. They still do one-hour shows called *48 Hours, 20/20, Primetime* and *Dateline*. But they do what they have to do to get ratings. They used to do documentaries on Social Security . . . Now the worst thing I've seen on TV was Diane Sawyer's interview with Britney Spears. Nothing rivals that. . . . I'm not against interviewing celebrities, just celebrities who have nothing to say,"[337] he said in an interview.

Until the recent *60 Minutes* episode mentioned earlier, property rights and eminent domain just couldn't rival Britney Spears. In the newspaper industry, a similar dynamic is at work. An increasing amount of news coverage is devoted to entertainment. Another major focus among the major dailies is "community journalism." The idea doesn't sound bad: getting more deeply entrenched in the community, listening to different voices and creating more of a grass-roots-style journalism. This is what the focus groups and media consultants tell the editors to do. By and large, newspapers—except for the elite newspapers—have followed such advice. The result is dismal. Instead of doing hard news, newspapers are focused on community festivals, stories that pander to ethnic groups, feel-good stories about neighborhood groups and charities, and lots of big pictures. It's the *USA Today*-ization of the newspaper business.

For all the focus on the community, reporters routinely miss the big community stories that involve property rights and eminent domain, except perhaps for the occasional short "he-said, she-said" news story about a redevelopment project. More often than not, however, the matter has been ignored by all media outlets—TV, newspaper, radio.

There's not one dynamic going on in the media, of course. There are thousands of newspapers, television stations, magazines and radio programs. There's little doubt, at this point, however, that a liberal bias permeates the media. As Goldberg explains, the bias isn't a simple Republican-Democrat matter, in which the national news media slant stories to benefit one party over another. It's a matter of overall outlook, of how journalists perceive the world. If a reporter, say, believes that government is a force for good in the world, then he is more likely to cover a proposed new government program in a way that's different from someone who views government in the way that America's founding fathers viewed it. Reporters are professional enough to include quotations from people on both sides of any given issue, but the way they frame the story often is driven by the way they see the world. That's why the predominance of liberal reporters, no matter how fair or professional they try to be, leads to slanted news coverage.

The biggest bias in the media comes in the form of story selection. Let's take an example related to the topic of this book. A mayor proposes a plan to redevelop a city's downtown. There are a variety of legitimate news stories that could be sparked by such a proposal. But typically, newspapers and local TV stations will examine the new jobs that will be created, and won't look at, say, the amount of debt that will be accrued, or the impact of using eminent domain to clear away existing businesses. Some of this has to do with laziness or a lack of sophistication on the part of reporters and editors. After all, it's easier to take the city's press releases, interview city officials and business leaders, and craft a story about the promises of the new project than it is to figure out all the financial and legal details surrounding it. That's especially true in small media markets. But much of the coverage is driven by the tendency of liberal reporters to believe in the goodness of government officials and the rightness of government actions.

In some ways, one might think that media that tend toward the left would be sympathetic to the plight of small business and homeowners tormented by eminent domain, especially because so many times those targeted by cities are ethnic minorities or elderly people. Goldberg said one of the recurrent themes from his years in the national TV news business is the desire by reporters to identify and side with the "underdog." "Generally speaking, if the media is not rooting for the small guy, I'm shocked," he said, in response to my question about the lack of media interest in eminent domain.[338]

Here's where another dynamic kicks in. Goldberg said that if the reporters aren't too sophisticated and the right people at city hall take them aside and tell them that the eminent domain victims are against progress, and the plan will improve the city for everybody, they are likely to go with a story that emphasizes that approach.

This reality touches on the nature of coverage of eminent domain: It is almost always local. A neighborhood in Garden Grove, California, is under siege, or a church in Cypress, California, or a neighborhood in Ohio or Minnesota, or a handful of small businesses in a town in Alabama. It's usually left to the local newspapers to discuss what is going on. Often, only the community weeklies, rather than the big metropolitan daily, get in on the action. And in small cities, newspapers often serve more as civic boosters than watchdogs. They are among the Leaders Of Our Town, or LOOT.

MEDIA BOOSTERS

In my past experience at a small Midwestern newspaper—an experience typical at small newspapers—reporters covering the city beat were typically strong supporters of the city administration. The local TV station was, likewise, part of the boosterism. When plans emerged to redevelop an old industrial site, the news reports featured artists' renderings of the project across the front page, and the TV station interviewed Chamber of Commerce types boasting about the expected new revenue and urban revival. Rarely was a critic even found—outside of the editorial page. The mayor's administration referred to opponents of his projects as people who were "negative," and who were too selfish to want what's best for the whole community. It was hard for opponents of eminent domain and redevelopment to get their voices heard.

Some recent court decisions have started to affect news coverage, said the Institute for Justice's Scott Bullock. But until recently, "most editorial pages do civic boosterism, saying 'This will be wonderful and is needed for the community. Yes, there are problems with eminent domain, but let's hope the parties work it out.' They display no cynicism. They never look back at previous disasters.' "[339] The best examples he could think of were the *Baltimore Sun,* which lobbied heavily for expanded eminent domain powers in Baltimore, and the *Pittsburgh Post-Gazette*, the major Pittsburgh daily, which was a cheerleader for Mayor Tom Murphy's plans to use eminent domain to remove businesses in the Fifth and Forbes area of downtown and replace them with a subsidized development. Both newspapers have a decidedly liberal philosophy on the editorial pages, but it's the sort of liberalism that stands up for big government and "the community" rather than the sort that stands up for the little guy.

The *Post-Gazette's* editorials are astonishing. On June 24, 1999, when downtown redevelopment plans were just beginning, the editorial page opined:

"It will take courage, coherent planning and foresight on the part of elected leaders and urban planners if Downtown is to become a dynamic urban core.

"A vital Downtown will take courage to create because, as competition intensifies for scarce parcels of land, somebody will have to say 'no' to projects that offend the overall vision—and stick to that 'no.'

"Without coherent planning, Downtown will become a mishmash of disparate elements. Some projects will conflict with or duplicate existing uses."[340]

That's almost something one would expect out of Pravda before the fall of communism. We mustn't have disparate elements—as in different buildings owned and planned by individuals rather than by the central government—and someone—i.e., government officials—has to have the courage to say no. The *Post-Gazette* never mentions whether private property-rights have any bearing on this process at all.

On November 3, 1999, the *Post-Gazette* weighed in with an editorial titled "Blight flight: Eminent domain has served Pittsburgh well.":

"Blight is in the eye of the beholder. Is a tawdry street with a triple-X movie house, where shady characters gather and drug deals go down, an example of blight? Is a downtown retail corridor, which has lost stores, customers and vitality, a blighted area?

"Is a warehouse district full of old, dingy buildings blighted enough to be replaced by a riverfront park and signature fountain that draw more than a million people a year?

"The answers are yes, if you believe in a city's need to reinvent itself.

"State Rep. William Robinson wants to curb the power to do that by cutting the use of eminent domain. But his is a solution for a problem that doesn't exist."[341]

What world is the *Post-Gazette* editorial writer living in? Would the newspaper gladly give up its office building should a mayor want to reinvent its location? And what is a city's right to reinvent itself? I recall references to property rights in the Constitution, but never to a government having a right, let alone a right that comes at the expense of individual property owners. The newspaper doesn't even admit that eminent domain could be a problem to its victims. Nope, it's a problem that doesn't exist. It gets even wilder. Here's the newspaper's explanation of the process of taking property from one private owner and giving it to another from another *Post-Gazette* editorial: "Eminent domain, the legal process that balances private rights and the public interest, begins with a declaration of 'blight.' It continues through a series of steps in which government can obtain on behalf of its citizens privately held land in exchange for just compensation to the owner."

The language is Orwellian. Eminent domain is the process of taking property from private owners and giving it to the government or to other private owners. It is not the process that "balances private rights and the public interest." What kind of balance is it when the government gets to take whatever it wants and give it to whomever it wants? That's not balance, but raw power. Is the government really obtaining property on "behalf of its citizens" or on behalf of private interests favored by government officials and newspaper executives? The editorial never even questions whether just compensation is truly paid.

The *Post-Gazette* continued with its frequent editorials on behalf of the project, at one point lambasting the pro-eminent domain mayor for not being more aggressive with his redevelopment efforts. When private-property owners delayed redevelopment, the newspaper called on the owners to "cut a deal and exit now."[342] It lambasted property owners for holding up progress. Regarding another redevelopment project that allowed eminent domain, *Post-Gazette* columnist Brian O'Neill on January 16, 2002, pooh-poohed concerns about eminent domain and explained that the city only seeks "flexibility to offer tax breaks, and it's hardly the only municipality making flights to 'blight' to do so."[343]

This type of editorializing is common. So is news coverage that arrives at similar conclusions. A *Philadelphia Inquirer* news story from December 19, 2003, titled, "Redevelopment plan a boon for Clementon,"[344] doesn't mention eminent domain, but does matter-of-factly talk about subsidies. The whole article promotes the project as a positive development, and doesn't bother quoting anyone who disagrees with the deal.

An article in the March 28, 2003, *Arizona Republic* is titled: "Redevelopment is key to future."[345] Here's a sampling of it: "Scottsdale is down to just 4,000 acres of vacant land outside of its vast desert and mountain preserves. The limited room for growth is forcing the city to think inward and redevelop older parts of the community.

"'Scottsdale needs to find a relationship with redevelopment that doesn't feel so dirty,' said Rick Kidder, public policy director for the Scottsdale Area Chamber of Commerce." The entire piece is a promotion for new redevelopment efforts. The article notes, "Scottsdale leaders admit they've struggled with redevelopment, but that Arizona lacks the tools many other states have to lure inner-city developers."[346]

These are typical examples, and they are from major metropolitan dailies, not little local newspapers that lack sophistication. The locals are even worse, and one can find story after story, editorial after editorial, that put the most simplistic, pro-development spin on every redevelopment project, whether or not it includes the power of eminent domain. When the city of Cypress, California, was planning to use eminent domain to acquire the Cottonwood Christian Center property and transfer it to Costco, the local Cypress newspaper, the *News Enterprise*, served as a virtual mouthpiece for the city government, even taking on the *Orange County Register* editorial page, which—atypical for major newspaper editorial pages—defended the property and religious rights of the Cottonwood church.

A couple of samples are as entertaining as they are illustrative of the knee-jerk "defend the city government" attitudes typical in many newspapers: "War has been officially declared. The *Orange County Register*, whose philosophy is just to the right of John Birch, through its senior editorial writer, Steven 'Lap Dog' Greenhut, an obviously frustrated true eastern liberal, in an editorial piece done last Sunday said that the government and the people of Cypress were not better than a communist block nation," the newspaper opined in April 2002.

"The paper in short has called for a Holy Jihad in defense of a poor multi-million dollar business called Cottonwood Christian Center against the government and the good people of Cypress,"[347] it added.

Never mind how one could be to the right of John Birch and a true eastern liberal at the same time. This is a window into what local citizens have to go through when their rights are imperiled. Instead of having their causes championed by the local media, they often are attacked and humiliated by that media. Often, it's because the local editors and reporters are part of the "in crowd." In small communities, reporters and city officials often travel in the same crowd, have drinks together and are friends with one another after hours. It can be exhilarating to be a player and not just an observer, but it's hard for reporters to step back and suddenly relate to the victims of city actions and not just the officials themselves.

In small communities, especially, the city manager and mayor and redevelopment director are among the elite. They are smart and well-dressed, articulate and comfortable talking to reporters. The small-property owners often are angry (it's not hard to understand why), inarticulate and from a different social class than the city officials. The reporters naturally feel akin to their friends in city hall, often disdaining the local complainers and writing them off as gadflies. As a newspaper writer, I often have to work hard to understand what a poor, unsophisticated, uneducated caller is complaining about. It's hard work distinguishing the guy with a real beef from a lunatic. Reporters have this problem, too, and they often take the easy route of listening to those who speak most clearly, and those often are the official government voices.

Generally, the media have shown a lack of interest in the problem. Notice how aggressive newspapers and TV stations can be when it comes to unearthing stories of supposed discrimination. There isn't an ethnic disparity anywhere (i.e., Latinos underrepresented as neurosurgeons) that hasn't been the focus of a two-part series. But reporters aren't exactly turning over the rocks looking for property-rights abuses. It's hard enough getting them to notice when people are calling up the newspaper and demanding coverage. The *Orange County Register* editorial page is libertarian, and has an abiding interest in property rights, so we naturally look for these types of stories, but others aren't looking. The *Post-Gazette* is a more typical example, although the suburban-based *Pittsburgh Tribune-Review*, which has a conservative editorial page, wrote some scathing anti-eminent domain editorials, according to the Institute for Justice. Sometimes it only takes one media voice to help organize opposition to eminent domain and redevelopment abuses, but that voice too often is lacking. Not until the grass roots gets a political campaign going to stop a plan, or organizes hundreds of people to show up to a council meeting, does a reporter typically wake up. It's a combination of liberal bias, dependence upon official sources, laziness, and a lack of understanding of the subject. And, for as eager as newspaper reporters are to "afflict the comfortable," they rarely want to afflict the city managers and mayors whom they depend upon for information.

When problems start, and the natives get restless, reporters serve up those boring "he-said, she-said" articles. "Officials say that the redevelopment plans will bring jobs and a broader tax base, but local critics contend that the project should be built without subsidies and without taking people's private property by eminent domain . . . " That's about as good as readers will typically get. My favorite article of this sort comes, once again, from the *Pittsburgh Post-Gazette*. Titled "Redevelopment official admits eminent domain is unpopular," the article from September 2003, includes this incisive observation: "Anytime there's the potential for property to be acquired through eminent domain, obviously there are going to be people who are not excited about the idea. . . . In this case, it's Marcella Calverny, the property owner."[348]

That's pretty obvious.

LOCATION, LOCATION

Using eminent domain to redevelop downtown Pittsburgh, right in the newspaper's front yard, certainly made the story one that could not easily be ignored. Even though the *Post-Gazette* was an enthusiastic backer of the plan, property owners at least received some attention. And other media sources were less supportive of the plan. But sometimes a redevelopment project, even one that includes an egregious abuse of property rights, falls through the cracks because it is occurring off the beaten media track.

Lake Elsinore, California, is an older city of about 30,000 on the eastern fringes of the greater Los Angeles area. It is semi-rural, separated from the sprawling Riverside County suburbs by about ten miles in each direction and nestled in a valley of dry, desert-like hills.

Even though it sits on a lake, Lake Elsinore is not a wealthy or picturesque town. It is mostly blue-collar and has its share of older bungalows and trailers, a vestige of the days when this was a booming resort community for Angelenos. The city has a sad and sordid past, but when the lake dried up—it is full again—the resort dried up with it. Although a few new developments ring the city, it is hard on its heels, and city officials always are looking for new ways to redevelop the area. As Southern California communities become increasingly hostile to new growth, Lake Elsinore remains a pro-growth hotbed.

The city's downtown-redevelopment project mostly succeeded in knocking down many historic buildings and leaving parking lots in their place. A new tax-built ballpark, home to the AAA Lake Elsinore Storm, is attractive, but has been a financial disaster for the city. Developers on occasion get an idea to restore the area, given the lake location. But the ideas usually flop, given that the city is too far to Los Angeles County for commuters, and hemmed in by the Santa Ana Mountains, making the trip to Orange County work destinations long and hazardous.

As mentioned previously, in 1999, the county of Riverside decided to quietly promote a plan to redevelop a large area of unincorporated land near the city. The county had no developer lined up, but it was clearly setting the stage to strip away hundreds of modest but mostly well-kept homes on nearly 3,000 acres. Officials said they were just going to use tax-increment financing to help fund infrastructure in the area. But the neighborhoods were close to the lake and close to a planned commercial zone by the freeway, which made the proposal suspicious. It was pretty hard to see how tax increment—the increase in the property taxes from the day the redevelopment area is designated—would lead to all the promises the county was making. The increase, officials said, would be used for new roads, sewers and sidewalks. But older homes, many of them trailers and doublewides, wouldn't increase in value anywhere near the amount needed to finance the plans, without some new developer coming in with a big project.

The redevelopment report from 1999 was even more Orwellian than most of these reports tend to be. For instance, the plan explained that "[e]ven though the Sub-Area is blighted, the existing owners of property and businesses continue to have equity that can be tapped to revitalize areas." That raised the specter of the county using code enforcement to force local residents to fix up their properties to the standards established by the government. Then there was this kicker: "In the event a participant fails or refuses to rehabilitate or develop his/her real property pursuant to this Plan and/or the participation agreement as an alternate thereto, the real property, or any interest therein, may be acquired by the Agency subject to the limitations set forth in this Plan, and sold or leased for rehabilitation or development in accordance with this Plan."[349] In other words, if you refuse to fix things up, the property will be confiscated.

After a controversy ensued, the county vowed to restrict the use of eminent domain. But the fine print told a different story: The use would only be restricted in predominantly owner-occupied areas, but since the area was, according to the agency but not the local residents, 85 percent rental properties, eminent domain could be used.

As you can see, there are any number of enterprising stories that could be done by a reporter with the slightest inquisitive spirit. Even if one doesn't care about property rights in concept, one could get exercised about the idea of kicking hundreds of elderly people out of their homes. Or about the deceptive way the county was pushing forward the plan. Or about the eerie, totalitarian language in the redevelopment report. And then there was a great underdog story. The man who organized his neighbors, Les Poppa, financed his campaign out of his meager life savings.[350]

But no one was interested. The Riverside *Press-Enterprise*, the major daily newspaper in the area, wrote a couple of news stories on the controversy, but that was about it. The *Los Angeles Times* ignored the issue. Lake Elsinore is out of the coverage area of the *San Diego Union-Tribune*, the *San Bernardino Sun* and the *Orange County Register*. TV crews weren't about to tackle this one. The Riverside County Board of Supervisors was bolstered in its arrogance, I believe, because of the lack of oversight of what it was doing. When Poppa and a group of residents drove to Riverside to appear before the board, they were granted a total of three minutes to make their case. Fortunately, attorney Bob Ferguson of Claremont took the case and eventually beat back the redevelopment area. But the fight was long, costly and done mostly without news coverage.

I made the trip to Lake Elsinore, explaining to my editor that the story was relevant in Orange County because redevelopment is a statewide issue. County and city redevelopment agencies may operate locally, but they are officially state agencies, and redevelopment abuse in any community was justification for redevelopment reform in Sacramento. My article was criticized by the Riverside County board, but it bolstered local activists and helped them get legal help and financial support. But it was only one column printed in a newspaper that doesn't circulate in the affected communities. Imagine what could have happened had the local newspapers decided to do their job and serve as watchdogs.

Cottonwood Christian Center attorney Andrew Guilford, of Sheppard Mullin Richter and Hampton in Costa Mesa, California, said the *Register's* coverage and my columns kept the heat on city officials during the process in the city of Cypress.[351] It helped frame the debate as one about property rights and not just tax revenue. It helped bring crowds out to the council meetings, and inflicted a cost on council members who insisted on supporting the eminent domain plan. I'm not suggesting the columns were the decisive factor in the resolution of the matter. The judge and the attorneys who argued the case before him had far more to do with the final conclusion. In Garden Grove, the publicity, not just from the *Register* but from the *OC Weekly* (Orange County, California) and to a lesser extent the *Los Angeles Times*, exacted a price from the officials who were pursuing the plan and probably had more to do with the favorable outcome. It's hard to measure such things. But without an active media covering, investigating and criticizing (in columns, letters to the editor and editorials) the eminent domain plan, the property owners are at a greater disadvantage.

There were times during the above-mentioned debates that I sensed a change in opinions and attitudes. Early in the process, Garden Grove and Lake Elsinore homeowners were despondent, believing there was nothing they could do to even get their voices heard, let alone stop the bulldozers. The full resources of the city and county were allied against the property owners. They weren't getting notices they should have been getting. When they did hear from the government, it was hard to understand what was going to happen to their property. Nothing beats a good lawyer, of course. But nothing beats proper media attention for building a confident and aggressive defense against these abuses, and for keeping property owners energized during the long legal battle.

I'm left wondering how many property owners have suffered alone because reporters and editors have been too lazy or biased to engage in these debates. It helps when there is a second major newspaper in an area, especially if that newspaper has a more conservative editorial-page approach. Sometimes the alternative weeklies are helpful. Big newspapers such as the *Post-Gazette* epitomize the establishment-left type of journalism, where the government is seen almost always as a force for good and progress. That makes it hard for reporters and editorial writers to identify with the little guy. But the alternative weeklies generally tilt further to the left, and often are outraged by the cozy relationships between corporations and redevelopment officials. The *OC Weekly* didn't pay attention to Cottonwood, probably because it didn't want to defend the property rights of a conservative Christian congregation. But the newspaper did an admirable job covering the Garden Grove situation, as well as other eminent domain and redevelopment situations.

The *Pittsburgh City Paper* gave a more jaundiced look at the mayor's downtown-redevelopment plan, bemoaning the predominance of national chain stores and the destruction of historic buildings.[352] Smaller communities, of course, rarely have any diversity of media opinion.

In 2001, I appeared on a panel of editorial writers at a Society of Professional Journalists convention in Anaheim. In my discussions, I criticized the state's redevelopment law, and one would have thought that I had said something totally out of bounds.

The other editorial writers from mid-size and large California newspapers were in general agreement that redevelopment, and eminent domain, were good for the state. I didn't hear much support from journalists attending the session. Only one unlikely source—a college journalism professor in the audience—expressed any support for my criticisms of redevelopment. Is it any surprise that these editorial writers, who decide what they are going to cover and how they are going to cover it, rarely delve into the problems associated with redevelopment and eminent domain?

That doesn't mean nothing critical is ever said about redevelopment. The *Los Angeles Times* generally stayed on the sidelines during the Cottonwood debate. But the newspaper's Orange County edition did support Judge Carter's decision slapping the hands of city of Cypress officials. "A no-nonsense legal opinion issued last week delivers a strong but necessary message to bargain-hunting retailers and cash-strapped cities intent on using eminent domain to clear land for tax-generating storefronts," the newspaper wrote on August 11,

2002.[353] It wasn't too harsh on the city, however: "But it isn't fair to cast Cypress City Council members as uncaring bigots. The city has gone as far as tabulating the number of churches per capita to show that residents needn't travel far to find a place to worship. It's clear that the eminent domain action was driven by economics. Simply, put, big retail stores generate sales tax revenue and places of worship generally don't."

My sense at the time was, gee, thanks for weighing in—*after* the judge ruled and after all the heavy lifting was done. But at least the *Times* figured out that the church had a good point. Better late than never, but if the congregants of Cottonwood had been depending on the *Times'* defense of their rights to help save their church, they would have been disappointed. The *Times* lauded the city for tabulating the number of churches per capita, as if it's up to city officials to decide when there are enough churches in their city. Apparently, to the city and the *Times,* one church is as good as another. The evangelical Protestants who attend Cottonwood shouldn't worry about the loss of their property rights when there's a Catholic church or Presbyterian one across town. At least the editorial recognized that sales taxes were guiding development decisions.

By contrast, we at the *Orange County Register* hammered city officials during the height of the debate. We featured a column, with a photograph of the site, on the cover of the Commentary section long before anyone else was talking about the matter. We helped set the tone of the debate, pushing property rights and redevelopment abuse to the top of the agenda. We didn't pull punches. After the city invoked eminent domain against the church property, I wrote in a June 2, 2002 column:

"The city's ad hominem attacks on the church, its grandiose legal justifications, officials' unsavory self-congratulation and the 'mind-numbing bureaucratic banality,' as one Cottonwood attorney described it, cannot divert attention from the obvious fact: City officials are perpetrating an egregious act.

"The contrast between the city's bureaucratic banality and Cottonwood's presentation was stunning. The church made a simple case. As Pastor Bayless Conley explained, the church owns the land. Had the city wanted it, it could have gone through the trouble of assembling the parcels and buying it in the many years it sat vacant. The church does good work saving souls, providing social services, meeting community needs. Its value cannot be measured in terms of sales-tax dollars.

"Besides, the land has been vacant so long, it's absurd to argue that the city of Cypress' economic future and the services it provides are dependent on building a Costco rather than a church."[354]

This isn't meant to pat myself on the back or laud my own employer. I merely want to point out the importance of the media in treating these takings with the seriousness they deserve. Giving voice to victims of eminent domain has an impact on the debate and the process, even if most of these matters eventually are settled in court. Politicians do sometimes change their mind based on media pressure. Clearly, Garden Grove officials reacted to that pressure when they backed down from their plan. Bruce Broadwater, in the midst of an election for higher office, actually was the third vote in favor of a January 2004 measure to limit eminent domain in the city. His council colleague, Mark Leyes, the author of the amendment, was sure that Broadwater was reacting to media portrayals of him as "the Bulldozer."[355]

IT'S NOT ALL BAD

The media story isn't entirely bad. Some reporters have pursued serious stories about redevelopment and eminent domain abuse, even when a brouhaha over a particular taking isn't brewing.

I first learned about redevelopment in September 1998, about a month after I moved from Ohio to California. I learned about it by reading a feature article in the *Orange County Register*, written by Tiffany Horan. The subject, appropriately enough, was Garden Grove. There was no big eminent domain dispute at the time. The story, " 'Renaissance' built on Garden Grove subsidies," was a piece that investigated the finances behind redevelopment, looking at financial trouble the city had gotten itself into because of multimillion-dollar payments to hotels and developers: "While many agree that the city is looking much nicer, big subsidies used to lure development have led to a redevelopment agency budget crunch: The agency predicts a $2.2 million deficit in 2000.

"About $3.4 million of agency-owned land must still be sold to balance this year's budget.

"The agency is using $4.5 million in city money (which is separate from redevelopment money) for expenditures this year."[356]

The redevelopment project promised hotel-room rates of $189 a night, but they were instead around $85, according to the article. The redevelopment agency loaned one developer $480,000, "with no set terms for repayment." Then the agency pledged another $275,000 to the developer for maintenance and other expenses. The simple reporting of the financial arrangements, sans editorializing, was striking: "In 1984, the redevelopment agency obtained $8.6 million in tax-exempt financing on behalf of the Westar Associates . . . The agency also bought the parking lot for $900,000, leasing it back to Weststar for $1 a year. In 1995, the agency sold the lot back to Westar for $62,500."

And the eminent domain issue was referred to as well: "While some of the properties due to be torn down for Riverwalk [a then-proposed tourist development] are ragged, the center—home to Rite-Aid, Max Foods, Burger King and El Pollo Loco—is described as an 'attractive, contemporary community shopping center' by the consultants who prepared the Riverwalk Environmental Impact Report."[357]

The article was balanced, extensively quoting city officials explaining why the property sell-offs and deficits are justified. But it was hard to finish that story without at least recognizing that there's more to these development projects than ribbon cuttings and new tax revenue. It was an example of what reporters should do—delve into the details of these complex, taxpayer-funded deals. Eminent domain almost always is part of them, but the property-rights abuses always start with complex subsidized financial relationships between governments and developers offering promises.

On January 30, 2002, the *Los Angeles Times* published an in-depth look at redevelopment and its failure in North Hollywood. The story also focused on the financial aspects of redevelopment, rather than on property takings. But this is essential: Properties are blighted and transferred to developers based on economic rationales and development promises. Uncover the truth about redevelopment—that it is all about private enrichment, and it rarely redevelops the area as promised—and the pressure for eminent domain will subside.

The story, "Heady Plans, Hard Reality,"[358] came to this conclusion:

"Two decades and $117 million in public money later, efforts by the city of Los Angeles to rescue suburban North Hollywood from creeping blight have largely struck out, a *Times* computer analysis has found.

"North Hollywood had seemed a promising candidate in 1979 for one of the city's most ambitious redevelopment projects ever . . . But the meager results logged so far in North Hollywood offer a cautionary tale to hundreds of other California communities that are investing more than $1.5 billion annually in hopes of reviving fading areas.

"The number of vacant and deteriorating homes—a key indicator of blight—has doubled in the twenty years that the city's Community Redevelopment Agency has been on the job in North Hollywood. Only a fraction of the new homes and businesses the

CRA pledged to build have been erected, and plywood boards still protect shut-down storefronts.

"Of perhaps greater significance, North Hollywood's recovery has lagged behind other depressed areas in Los Angeles that improved without any money from the city's CRA, according to the *Times* analysis of census, property and employment data."[359]

Those are some shocking conclusions. The area is worse off than it was before the redevelopment started. Areas that did not use government redevelopment have done better than this area that has relied most heavily on it. Foes of redevelopment and eminent domain abuse wouldn't be surprised. I've interviewed enough home and business owners in redevelopment areas to know the dynamic. Once an area is termed blighted and placed in a redevelopment area, everything stops. Property owners stop investing in their properties. Everyone waits for the government to spearhead the project. And the developers involved in the deal often take the taxpayers to the cleaners. Yet to see it on the front page of a major newspaper was shocking, especially given the ramifications of the story on the many other cities undertaking projects similar to the one in North Hollywood.

As good as these articles are, they are too rare. For every article on the real results of redevelopment, there are scores about the wonderful new project that's coming to our city.

TRUTH GETS OUT

After the *Wall Street Journal* began writing about the problem in the late 1990s, the truth started to get out. It's hard for anyone to ignore the *Wall Street Journal*. The groundbreaking story, which some credit for shifting coverage of the eminent domain situation nationwide, came on the front page of the *Journal* in 1998: "Take and Give: Condemnation Is Used To Hand One Business Property of Another—Tactic by Local Governments Seeking Jobs and Taxes Is Protested as Unfair—BMW Yes, Mitsubishi No."[360]

I excuse the endlessly long headline on the fact that in 1998, the story about eminent domain abuse had rarely if ever been told. The piece was direct and shocking:

"When a developer decided to bring Home Depot and Costco stores to New York's East Harlem, the state of New York had a simple message for William Minnich and his cabinetmaking business: Get out. . . .

"Local and state governments are now using their awesome powers of condemnation, or eminent domain, in a kind of corporate triage: grabbing property from one private business to give to another. A device used for centuries to smooth the way for public works such as roads, and later to ease urban blight, has become a marketing tool for governments seeking to lure bigger business. Cities now undertake about eighty business projects a year involving condemnations, twice as many as a decade ago. . . . "

In March 2001, *Reader's Digest* featured an article, "Kiss Your House Good-Bye."[361] It brought the issue to a wide audience. In August 2003, *Reader's Digest* featured another piece called "Home Wreckers: Greedy developers can seize your property and do it legally."[362] The influence of that original *Journal* story could still be felt [Note: the family name is "Minnich"; the business name is "Minic."]:

"William Minnich's father founded his furniture making business, Minic Custom Woodwork, in 1927. For nearly a quarter-century, the company operated out of a building he owned on 117th Street in New York City. Until 1998, Minnich imagined the family business would remain there indefinitely." But then he read in the *New York Times* about a redevelopment project in his Harlem neighborhood that would feature a Home Depot and other shopping—and it meant the seizure of his company's land.

The left-leaning *Village Voice*[363] ran an article describing the efforts to redevelop the Minnich property, focusing on the lack of due process afforded owners whose property is being taken. It quoted

Bill Minnich: "This is our last-ditch attempt. You get your three minutes at the hearing and that's it. For the little guy, while they're stealing his property, he doesn't even know he's out of the game."

From about 2000 to the present, the number of stories on the matter has increased exponentially. A simple Web search will yield hundreds of recent stories on the matter. Most of them are surprisingly sympathetic toward the victimized property owner, refreshingly harsh toward the developers and government officials. Many of them are fairly balanced, of course, but a balanced portrayal of this issue still leaves readers outraged. Who are you going to sympathize with most: a developer saying he wants some land to bring in more tax revenue for the city, or an elderly widow fighting to save a family homestead filled with a lifetime's worth of memories?

A sea change in news coverage was occurring. A long feature in the September 14, 2003 *Detroit News*[364] found that Michigan was fourth in the nation in its use of government condemnations for the benefit of private owners. Maryland was No. 1 with 1,237, California No. 2 with 858, Ohio No. 3 with 421, Michigan No. 4 with 311, Kansas No. 5 with 162, and Detroit was the most condemnation-happy city in the nation. As the article explained, "Michigan became even more assertive about eminent domain after the state Legislature passed a law in 2002 that strengthened local governments' hand in areas designated as 'blighted.' "

On July 11, 2003, Forbes.com included a short business article called, "Domain Abuse." It spotlighted several companies that have been notorious beneficiaries of the process. Increasingly, national columnists are noticing the abuse of eminent domain. Columnist Doug Bandow explains in a 2002 syndicated column:

"In Madison, Illinois, the Gateway International Raceway wanted [to expand its] parking lot. So it hired a quasi-government agency to seize the land. In an important victory for property owners everywhere, the Illinois Supreme Court has said no. Four years ago, the

Raceway decided that it needed more parking. So it went to the Southwestern Illinois Development Agency (SWIDA) which, in the name of 'development,' proposed taking the property of the next-door metal recycling facility. The U.S. Constitution requires that any taking be for a 'public use,' but here government sought to grab land at the behest of a private party. So SWIDA claimed the property seizure would ease traffic congestion, which was in the public interest.

"By that standard, there is little that doesn't count. Taking my neighbor's land so I could build a bigger house would ease traffic congestion."[365]

Perhaps the biggest news story for opponents of eminent domain abuse came in September 2003 when *60 Minutes* featured its piece on Lakewood, Ohio, Mesa, Arizona, and New York City. First, Mike Wallace interviewed Jim and Joanne Saleet of Lakewood, among the heroes I discussed in Chapter 1. "The city of Lakewood is trying to use eminent domain to force the Saleets out to make way for more expensive condominiums. But the Saleets are telling the town, 'Hell no! They won't go.' "[366]

"The bottom line is this is morally wrong," Jim Saleet told the news program. "We talked about this when we were dating. I used to point to the houses and say, 'Joanne, one of these days we're going to have one of these houses.' And I meant it. And I worked hard."

As *60 Minutes* explained, the city set a standard for blight that was broad enough to enable it to clear out a lovely neighborhood in order to bring in new development with a better tax base. So any house that didn't have three bedrooms, two baths, a two-car attached garage and central air conditioning was blight. That encompassed 90 percent of the city's homes, including the mayor's. These are historic neighborhoods. Two-car attached garages were not built in the early part of the century. Few homes near Lake Erie have central air conditioning, given the cool summer temperatures. The best part of the special was when Wallace interviewed Lakewood Mayor Madeleine Cain, who admitted that the blight designation is a "statutory" term that has nothing to do with actual blight. She admitted that her house would be blighted also.

Here's a key portion of the show's transcript, as provided in the Institute for Justice's December 2003, *Liberty & Law* newsletter:

"Wallace: My understanding is that using the criteria that are in place, more than 90 percent of the houses in Lakewood could be deemed blighted, including the houses of the mayor and of every one of the City Council members. True? Do you have two bathrooms?

"Mayor Cain: No

"Wallace: Blight. Two-car garage?

"Mayor Cain: No.

"Wallace: Blight. Is the garage attached?

"Mayor Cain: No.

"Wallace: Blight. And your lot size; is it under 5,000 square feet?

"Mayor Cain: Oh, well under."

The news program then featured Randy Bailey, whose brake shop was being taken in Mesa, Arizona, because the city wanted to relocate a hardware store to Bailey's prime location. It interviewed Ken Lenhart, owner of Ace Hardware. "Lenhart wants a much bigger store. He could have negotiated with Bailey, but instead, he convinced the city of Mesa to buy Bailey's land through eminent domain and then sell it to him," according to a *60 Minutes* news report about the show.

Then *60 Minutes* zeroed in on New York City:

"And this isn't happening just in small towns. In New York City, just a few blocks from Times Square, New York state has forced a man to sell a corner that his family owned for more than 100 years. And what's going up instead? A courthouse? A school? Nope. The new headquarters of the *New York Times*.

"The world's most prestigious newspaper wants to build a new home on that block, but Stratford Wallace and the block's other property owners didn't want to sell. Wallace told *60 Minutes* that the newspaper never tried to negotiate with him. Instead, the *Times* teamed up with a major real estate developer, and together they convinced New York state to use eminent domain to force Wallace out. How? By declaring the block blighted."[367]

It was devastating. Even Bernard Goldberg, the onetime CBS newsman and critic of the networks' political bias, said he sent an email to one CBS official praising the show.[368] It wasn't slanted, he said, but gave both sides the chance to make their cases. One side's case was so poor—the side of those who would use eminent domain for private gain—that he naturally sided with the victims of the process. He thought it was a fabulous piece.

A COMMON LINK

There's a link between these compelling stories, from *60 Minutes* and the *Detroit News* and Doug Bandow and the *Village Voice* and *Reader's Digest* and, literally, hundreds of other sources. In every one, the Washington, D.C.-based Institute for Justice is mentioned as a source. Indeed, the Institute, a small group of libertarian attorneys and activists, has managed to put the issue on the map through a concerted nationwide media strategy.

John Kramer, the Institute's director of communications, agrees that newspapers traditionally have taken a civic-booster approach to redevelopment and have treated eminent domain victims as obstacles to progress.[369] He notes that newspapers have financial self-interest when new business comes to town. "A lot of editorial pages come around when they see it positioned as David v. Goliath." Kramer and attorneys Dana Berliner and Scott Bullock have gone to editorial boards and explained that all other rights hinge on property rights. There are no sudden conversions, of course, but Kramer has seen a willingness by newspapers to more fully consider the impact of eminent domain on individual lives. He has seen editorial writers conclude that if other people's property rights aren't safe then their own property rights aren't safe.

The *Day*, the daily newspaper in New London, Connecticut, he said, was the biggest booster of a redevelopment project that would have taken property even though city officials didn't know yet what they intended to do with it. "After a couple of editorial board meetings, they took a harder look at the issue," he said in an interview. Typically, the Institute is providing a side of the story that editorial boards and reporters aren't used to hearing. "The only people they are used to hearing from are not the homeowners, but the sophisticated developers. We go in and level the playing field." Kramer is confident that when both sides are heard, even journalists will side with the abused property owners. Developers love to keep the discussions of eminent domain muted, he said, but the Institute is able to push this issue onto the media radar screens.

Even with the *Pittsburgh Post-Gazette*, Kramer said the Institute had some success. The paper continued to shill for the redevelopment project, but after meeting with the editorial board the newspaper opened up the op-ed page to columns by the Institute and homeowners disagreeing with the plan. The Institute makes a point of putting its clients front and center, in order to put a sympathetic face out there with the discussions of this legal concept. Kramer said the clients personalize the message, humanize the issue and dramatize the outrage behind the taking of property from one owner to give to another.

The proof is in the newspapers and on the TV shows. This story has been covered like never before, and almost always, the recent news stories have at least allowed the victims to speak. That's a far cry from the days when journalists ignored the issue, or listened only to the civic boosters. Most important, perhaps, is the extensive research the Institute has provided that offers not only a national perspective, but local examples of the problem. Berliner's book, *Public Power, Private Gain* is an easy-to-read compilation of eminent domain abuses in virtually every state.[370] All a reporter needs to do is look up the section on his state to find compelling and well-researched examples.

60 Minutes was a harder nut to crack. Kramer pitched the idea to a Washington-based CBS correspondent more than three years ago, he said. But the correspondent said there wasn't anything she could do until Berliner's book was out. She wanted to be sure it was a big enough problem. After the book came out, Kramer took it to the correspondent, but she no longer was interested. He talked to six different *60 Minutes* correspondents and producers, but no luck. He finally decided he needed to talk to the big guy, Producer Don Hewitt. But no one gets to talk to Hewitt. At least that's what everyone told him. Kramer, however, had Hewitt's number, and put together a quick and focused pitch, summoning up all his nerve.

"He seemed incredulous," Kramer said.[371] "He said, 'I can't believe this is happening in America. Send me more information.'" Kramer said he followed up, and a week later *60 Minutes* officials came to Washington and met with Institute attorneys. The Institute for Justice outlined the facts, and had citations for everything. Kramer made suggestions about the most compelling stories, and, ultimately, producer Bob Anderson and correspondent Mike Wallace put together the segment described above. "They are master storytellers," Kramer noted. Indeed, the news show has probably done more than all the previous publicity of every sort combined to explain eminent domain to the general public.

"The change has been drastic," Kramer said. "When we started this in the mid-1990s, with the Vera Coking case [Donald Trump's attempt to take her Atlantic City, N.J., property for his casino parking lot], we were pushing the story out to the media. We had to explain eminent domain. Reporters said, 'Oh, it's only used for roads.' Now we get as many calls coming in as going out. . . . Just getting the information out is important. Developers want to keep it low-key. It's strictly a backroom thing for them. That makes them profitable, but it doesn't make them right." Supporters of eminent domain, he notes, rely on imprecise language to make their case. Public use really is a public benefit, which really ends up meaning private gain. They use complex language—redevelopment, blight determinations, economic imbalances—to obfuscate the issue and keep the public in the dark or utterly confused. But his side relies on precise, simple words, Kramer explains. Public is public. Eminent domain is a form of theft. What's going on is a threat to individual rights and liberties.

Fortunately, that simple language is increasingly getting out, over the Orwellian phrases and cant that the *Pittsburgh Post-Gazette* and others have specialized in. Thanks to the Institute for Justice, some writers and many diligent attorneys, the story of eminent domain abuse at last is getting told.

10. FIGHTING BACK AND WINNING

We make war that we may live in peace.

— Aristotle[372]

Property owners have scored some significant victories against the special interests and government officials who seek to abuse eminent domain on behalf of their pet projects. The victories always are hard-fought. When a neighborhood or a business is targeted for redevelopment, this much is certain: You're not going to save your property, or secure a fair-market price for it, unless you fight back.

What do you do when the unthinkable happens and your lovely home overlooking a park or your successful print shop is deemed "blighted" and slated for removal?

The natural first response is despair. As Steven Strooh of Des Moines Blue Print explained in Chapter 3, the principals in his company felt a cloud of doom hovering over their dreams and aspirations. The Saleets, who battled the city of Lakewood, Ohio, said they felt their idyllic life slipping away. They were hanging on by their fingertips.

But don't let the despair last long. The key to success is not to feel overwhelmed by the powerful forces allied against you. Property owners must get organized quickly. Typically, city officials hide their plans as long as legally possible to blunt opposition to them. They like to unveil the redevelopment project and get the bulldozers out within months, rather than fight in court for years.

In this chapter, we'll look at the four main approaches that have yielded some success. The first is community organizing. It's the old, "united we stand, divided we fall" axiom. The second is adopting a legal strategy. There is nothing frivolous about hiring an attorney to protect your constitutional rights. Some attorneys will offer pro bono or discounted help to property owners; others will work on a contingency basis for those seeking a higher amount of compensation for the property. That means that even lower-income property owners can gain access to the legal system. The third approach is political. Organized homeowners can put redevelopment to a referendum, as the homeowners in Lakewood did, or they can storm city council meetings, as homeowners in Garden Grove, California, and Crystal Heights, Minnesota, did. Don't downplay the impact it can have on council members if hundreds of angry people show up at public meetings to voice their displeasure. Other property owners have organized to defeat pro-eminent domain candidates at the polls. This isn't always feasible, and it's hard to defeat a well-entrenched incumbent. But political activism is worth a try. The fourth necessary approach revolves around the media. Savvy opponents of eminent domain tell their story to anyone who will listen. They approach newspaper and television reporters, they start Web sites and email lists, they blanket the neighborhood with brochures and flyers, they get on talk-radio shows. As I described in Chapter 9, despite certain media biases, media coverage of the issue is becoming more sympathetic to property owners in eminent domain cases. In Lakewood, a *Cleveland Plain Dealer* article led eventually to a *60 Minutes* piece, and the rest is history. But even in communities that can't gain regional or national media coverage, publicity is essential.

Here's a look at some of the success property owners have had in fighting back against eminent domain abuse.

LEGAL EAGLES

Property-rights activists and redevelopment officials rarely are in agreement on anything, except for this one point: The courts have started, however slowly, to slap down cities or other condemning agencies that go "too far."

The Institute for Justice says that property owners win 40 percent of their cases these days, which is a far cry from the times when they rarely won at all. About twenty redevelopment projects have been defeated nationwide in recent years and several laws have passed state legislatures that are making it harder to use eminent domain for private use.[373]

Specifically, the courts are putting stricter limits on the definition of "public use," and are occasionally overturning eminent domain uses that are clearly for private benefit. They sometimes are looking askance at government's clever redefinition of "public use," as the Constitution describes it, to "public benefit." This isn't happening all the time, as the Kansas Supreme Court's decision with regard to the Target distribution center makes clear, but it is happening enough to get the notice of property owners and government agencies.

Practically speaking, the increase in legal action and political victories is inflicting a cost on local agencies. Sure, those agencies often move forward despite the publicity and costs. They are spending taxpayer dollars, after all, rather than their own money. The Cypress City Council, for instance, was un-swayed by mounting bad publicity and lengthy legal action. It didn't soften its stance until it was rebuked in no uncertain terms by the court. Even then, the city attorney wanted to appeal the decision. But other cities no doubt saw what Cypress went through. Other officials realized there would be a cost for pursuing high-profile eminent domain actions. That's especially true now that the media have put at least some spotlight on the process.

Although the ruling by the federal court in the Cypress case was to grant a preliminary injunction, it was a published federal court decision. That cannot be ignored. Just like RLUIPA (Religious Land Use and Institutionalized Persons Act) cannot be ignored. City officials get worried whenever a church mentions that federal statute, given the amount of success religious groups have had with it in the courts.

It's unclear, however, whether the tide is turning, and a more constitutional understanding of property rights is emerging, or whether the abuses have gotten so blatant and numerous that property owners were bound to have some success at stopping them. "What might be happening," says Notre Dame Law Professor Nicole Garnett, quoted in a Reason online article in February 2003, "is we are cycling back into the 'too much' use of eminent domain. Now that economic development incentives are everywhere, cities and states are using eminent domain as another incentive. We are seeing an uptick in takings challenges because we are seeing more eminent domain cases, and we are seeing more cases reining in abuses."[374]

Skeptics also note that some of the court victories are procedural more than philosophical, and that many of the victories have come at such a high price to property owners that cities and other government agencies remain as brazen as ever. The legal situation Gideon Kanner described remains in effect: Courts still view condemnees as enemies of the nation, as greedy people unwilling to give in for "the good of the public." That hasn't changed. Their ability to receive just compensation, Kanner says, is just as bleak now as it always has been. Individuals will almost always get higher payouts if they go to court than if they refuse to fight, but there are still large expenses they must pay, and the courts and especially the legislatures have yet to address that issue.

"People who receive grossly inadequate offers are more likely to go to court and to win," Kanner said.[375] His point: The worse the offer, the more likely a victim of eminent domain will fight in court, and the more cases we will see of courts granting better compensation. That's not a sign of progress, per se, but of an increased brazenness of officials in trying to buy properties as inexpensively as possible. Increasingly, we are seeing condemning agencies offer zero for businesses or amounts below what the owners paid for their properties. When business owners receive such low offers they have no choice but to fight in court, and often enough they win. But Kanner, who edits the journal *Just Compensation*, argues that there are many small cases that owners are unwilling to fight in court. Many people believe they cannot fight city hall, so they don't bother.

Nevertheless, property owners have more and more legal precedents to depend upon as they battle to save their properties.

Illinois Stops 'One Stop Shopping'

In 1987, the Illinois Legislature passed the Southwest Illinois Development Authority Act, designed to promote economic development in two economically depressed counties outside St. Louis. This glorified redevelopment agency had the expressed purpose of using public funds to encourage new private businesses, in the service of creating jobs and a broader tax base. The agency could issue bonds and use eminent domain to foster these goals. But the Southwest Illinois Development Authority (SWIDA) was not any old redevelopment agency. To make eminent domain proceedings easier, the agency used what is known as the "quick take" process for fostering economic development. It was simple one-stop shopping. "All applicants had to do was fill out a form, pay a fee, add a commission to SWIDA based on the value of the property, and voila, the redevelopment agenda would condemn someone else's land and hand it over," explains the Buckeye Institute's Sam Staley, in a February 2003 Reason online article.[376] "Of course, it wasn't quite that simple—the St. Clair County board had to approve the transfer—but the message was clear: 'If you need land, we'll get it for you.' "

In 1996, SWIDA had issued $21.5 million in revenue bonds to fund the Gateway International Motorsports Corp.'s racetrack. The company had taken a small, local racetrack and turned it into a 50,000-seat facility and wanted to expand the track to lure Winston Cup NASCAR events,[377] according to a Georgetown University presentation by attorney Timothy S. Hollister. As it expanded its seating areas, it needed more parking. Gateway had lost a lease to some of the land it used for parking, so it looked next door to a 148.5-acre site owned by National City Environmental, an environmentally sound auto-metal shredding and landfill operation.

This was empty land that was the key to NCE's future. When its landfill filled up, it planned to expand onto that site. Gateway officials approached the company about buying the site, but NCE officials weren't interested in selling it. So Gateway filled out a quick-take application form. Its rationale was that the land would increase the value of the racetrack, and that constituted "economic development." The company paid an application fee, agreed to pay SWIDA an acquisition fee of between 6 percent and 10 percent of the price paid for the property, and to pay for all costs associated with the taking, the court explained. The St. Clair County board approved the application, explaining that Gateway's success "would enhance the public health, safety, morals, happiness and general welfare of the citizens of southwestern Illinois by increasing the tax base in the area and generating additional tax revenues."[378] Well, it would increase everyone's happiness perhaps, except for the owners of the NCR facility and their eighty to 100 employees.

That was early February. By the end of March, SWIDA filed a complaint against NCE to condemn the property. NCE argued that the taking was unconstitutional because it was for an obviously private use, according to the court. The circuit court ruled in SWIDA's favor, agreeing that the parking facility addressed serious public-safety issues because racetrack patrons would no longer need to walk across a highway from the parking area to the track. SWIDA was created for economic-development purposes, and Gateway filled out the application packet based on economic-development rationales. But when it came time to go to court, suddenly, the property was also being taken based on a pressing public-safety issue. Public safety, economic development, whatever. Government agencies seeking to take property by force, and the private companies seeking to benefit from the government's police powers, will use any argument a court might accept.

But as the Illinois high court noted: "Ron Wolter, president and general manager of Gateway International Raceway, testified that by turning the 148.5 acres owned by NCR into parking for the racetrack, Gateway would grow and profits would increase. Wolter acknowledged that Gateway had discussed developing a parking garage facility to meet its needs but that it would be much less expensive to have SWIDA take the property in question from NCE and give it to Gateway for ground parking."[379]

In other words, the power of the state was being used to wrest property from an unwilling seller simply so another private business could build a parking facility in the most cost-effective way. Apparently, using such reasoning, any one of us should be allowed to take our neighbor's property if it's more cost effective to build a family-room addition that way.

An appeals court overturned the trial court decision. The appeals court saw no genuine public benefit, but only an attempt to bolster private, corporate profits. In a concurring opinion, one justice argued: "If a government agency can decide property ownership solely upon its view of who would put that property to more productive or attractive use, the inalienable right to own and enjoy property to the exclusion of others will pass to a privileged few who constitute society's elite. The rich may not inherit the earth, but they most assuredly will inherit the means to acquire any part of it they desire."[380]

That's exactly right. In 2001, however, the Illinois Supreme Court, by a 4–3 vote, overturned that appeals court ruling, arguing that condemnation was appropriate as long as it was "rationally related to economic development."[381] But the court granted NCE a rehearing, and in April 2002 reversed its own decision. Four years later, NCE prevailed in court.

The Southwest Illinois Development Authority contends that the safety and economic development benefits of its new parking lot are a public purpose, and that "any distinction between the terms 'public purpose' and 'public use' has long since evaporated and that the proper test is simply to ask whether a 'public purpose' is served by the taking," the Illinois Supreme Court explained. But the court disagreed that the difference between the two terms is semantic. The court acknowledged that a blurring of the terms has taken place—as does anyone, supporter or foe of eminent domain, who has watched the process since the 1950s. Nevertheless, the court ruled that, unlike the taking of slum properties allowed in the *Berman* decision, the taking of vacant land to give to a racetrack owner results "not in a public use, but in private profits." Although acknowledging that economic development is an important public purpose, the court argued that such "goals must not be allowed to overshadow the constitutional principles that lie at the heart of the power with which SWIDA and similar entities have been entrusted. . . . While the activities here were undertaken in the guise of carrying out its legislated mission, SWIDA's true intentions were not clothed in an independent, legitimate governmental decision to further a planned public use. SWIDA did not conduct or commission a thorough study of the parking situation at Gateway. Nor did it formulate any economic plan requiring additional parking at the racetrack. SWIDA advertised that, for a fee, it would condemn land at the request of 'private developers' for the 'private use' of developers. In addition, SWIDA entered into a contract with Gateway to condemn whatever land 'may be desired by Gateway.' "[382]

The Illinois Supreme Court also argued that although the Legislature gave SWIDA its power, and the court wouldn't question the Legislature's authority in granting eminent domain powers, "the government does not have unlimited power to redefine property rights. . . . The power of eminent domain is to be exercised with restraint, not abandon."[383] Finally, a court that is willing to put a check on unconstitutional legislative actions.

California Dreaming

In California, in three separate cases, the courts challenged the government's expansive definition of blight. The cases showed that there is, at some point, a limit to what can be called blight. The cases involved redevelopment plans in the California cities of Diamond Bar, Murrieta and Mammoth Lakes.

I referred to the Diamond Bar decision in Chapter 2, in which the court struck down a blight finding based on peeling paint and other modest problems. The court actually held the city to normal blight standards—as opposed to the expansive descriptions of blight typically used by cities. The city's official publications bragged that the city was affluent and free from blight, so the court wasn't about to let city officials have it both ways.

In Mammoth Lakes, the court struck down a blight finding that referred to this rural mountain community as blighted because of excessive urbanization. The town was trying to find an excuse to blight its entire downtown and replace it with a tourist-oriented downtown. Likewise, in Murrieta, the city's attempt to call blighted thousands of acres of mostly rural land near the intersection of two freeways was rebuked by the trial court and the appeals court. As the Los Angeles *Daily Journal* explained in 1999, the city wanted to gain control of a prime area that was starting to be developed. In fact, that's often what redevelopment and eminent domain are all about—cities trying to gain revenue and control over areas that are starting to boom economically. They talk about blight, as did Murrieta, but really all they want is to benefit from economic growth that already is taking place on its own. Like Mammoth Lake officials, Murrieta officials were stuck arguing that an essentially rural and unblighted area was urban and blighted, because California's

Community Redevelopment Law demands that both factors exist before granting vast redevelopment powers. In this case, the city was opposed by the county of Riverside, which feared losing revenue from the area. The courts agreed with the county, ruling that the city relied on "jargon" to justify its redevelopment area and provided no proof of "true blight,"[384] according to the *Daily Journal*.

"The uniform message from the courts in all of the cases was that redevelopment—the power to acquire land, repackage it for development and incorporate various forms of subsidy—is meant to be used on truly blighted land, not merely on any property that city officials want to designate," wrote columnist Dan Walters,[385] in a March 29, 2001, column.

In the Lake Elsinore case discussed in Chapters 1 and 9, the trial court allowed the redevelopment area, but the appeals court ruled in favor of the residents, questioning how an area comprising so much vacant land could conceivably be called urbanized,[386] according to Berliner's book, *Public Power, Private Gain*.

The Constitution State Rediscovers the Constitution

The Connecticut Supreme Court found a city's blight finding to be so weak that it took the unusual—and laudable—step of requiring the city to return the property it seized to the original owner. The case, *Pequonnock Yacht Club, Inc. v. Bridgeport*, "involved two acres in Bridgeport that the plaintiff owned and operated as a private yacht club and marina for nearly ninety-five years," according to John J. Louiszos and Patricia M. Gaug, writing in the November 2002 *Connecticut Lawyer*.[387] As the authors explain, the property owners sought to be included in the redevelopment plan and were willing to work with the developer to fix up the property and to be made part of a fifty-acre development known as Steel Point. But the city refused, insisting that the two-acre site be condemned and transferred to the project's developer. The site was not even an integral part of the city's redevelopment, but appears to have been added as an afterthought.

The court agreed that it was unreasonable to insist on the taking of a non-blighted property and to have failed to work with the owner to integrate the property into the redevelopment plan. The court, according to the *Connecticut Lawyer* article, held "that the requirement that the taking of property that is not itself in a sub-standard, blighted condition be essential, requires the redevelopment agency to consider integration of the property into the plan without a taking, because the taking will only be essential if the agency finds that the property cannot be successfully integrated into the overall plan in a manner that allows the plan to achieve its objectives. . . . The decision also appears to place the burden of estab-lishing that the taking is essential on the redevelopment agency."[388]

On the same day—October 25, 2001—the Connecticut Supreme Court issued another groundbreaking decision reining in the power of eminent domain in the *Aposporos v. Urban Redevelopment Commission of Stamford* case. In that case, the court argued that blight designations have a time limit. The owners of Curley's Diner in downtown Stamford argued that the city could not use a 1963 blight finding to incorporate their property into a redevelopment area in the mid-1980s, wrote Louiszos and Gaug.[389] It's an important deci-sion because governments will routinely rely on old blight rulings to condemn properties, even if the area has changed dramatically over the years. The ruling also spotlights the degree to which these rede-velopment plans can drag on, leaving property owners in a state of limbo, depriving them of the fair use of their property for decades.

The city created its downtown redevelopment plan in 1963, but did very little about redeveloping the area. In the 1980s, officials became concerned about competition to the shopping district from a new mall elsewhere in the city, according to the *Connecticut Lawyer* article, and commissioned a study which recommended the acquisition of four new properties, including the diner. The city tried to find developers to acquire the properties in 1988, "but a downturn in the real estate market led to the unavailability of financing, and thus the project fell through. Almost a decade later, the project was reborn with a new private developer and, in November 1999, the defendants began the process of acquiring the plaintiffs' property."[390] The owners were denied an injunction at the trial court, which saw nothing wrong with the way the city acted. But eventually the state Supreme Court overturned the decision, arguing that an "amendment to a redevelopment plan approved decades after the original plan was adopted that addresses conditions and seeks to achieve objectives that were not contemplated in that plan . . . effectively constitutes, and should be subject to, the same procedural requirements as, a new redevelopment plan." The state Supreme Court had not reviewed a redevelopment taking for nearly three decades.[391] That says volumes in and of itself. That the court, in unanimous decisions, upheld the rights of property owners was a sign of real progress, even if the cases were based largely on the procedural matters of blight findings.

Colorado Supremes Slap Down Wal-Mart

The Colorado Supreme Court on March 1, 2004, dealt a blow to Wal-Mart's plans to build a store on property seized from private owners. The court "ruled that the Arvada Urban Renewal Authority could not use eminent domain to take Columbine Lake from its owners, reversing an earlier ruling by Jefferson County," reported the *Sentinel and Transcript Newspapers* on March 6, 2004.[392] "According to an application filed with the city of Arvada, 20 percent of the lake would have been filled in to accommodate a Wal-Mart Supercenter in the Arvada Marketplace shopping center . . . . "

The court's ruling was significant, even if it wasn't a tour de force of constitutional reasoning. Essentially, the court reasoned that the city could not rely on an old blight finding to condemn a private property. If the redevelopment area cured the blight condition, then a new blight finding would be needed to take any property within the redevelopment area. The court explained as follows in March 2004:

"[W]e hold that AURA [Arvada Urban Renewal Authority] no longer has any statutory authority to condemn the quarry lake parcel. . . . [N]either the lake parcel nor the Arvada Marketplace parcel is subject to the City of Arvada's 1981 blight finding. Thus, the statutory basis for AURA's authority to condemn the lake parcel—the elimination of blight—is no longer present. Without a statutorily recognized public purpose, AURA is powerless to exercise its condemnation power over the quarry lake parcel unless the City of Arvada makes a new determination that the area AURA seeks to condemn, in its current condition, is blighted."[393]

The Federal Courts Weigh In

Two federal decisions, referred to previously in this book, have an even greater impact across the United States. The most significant is the *99 Cents Only Stores* case against the city of Lancaster, California. In Chapters 7 and 8, I referred to language in the case describing Costco's predatory behavior. The judge's words stood in stark contrast to the claims of the company, which denied involvement in pushing cities to take property for its own private benefit. The city of Lancaster was condemning the neighboring property occupied by 99 Cents Only Stores in order to give it to Costco for $1. Costco had threatened to move to another city if it wasn't granted that specific property for its planned expansion. Here's the key part of the ruling that cities across the country are going to have to keep in mind:

"In this case, the evidence is clear beyond dispute that Lancaster's condemnation efforts rest on nothing more than the desire to achieve the naked transfer of property from one private party to another. Indeed, Lancaster itself admits that the only reason it enacted the Resolutions of Necessity was to satisfy the private expansion demands of Costco."[394] The court found such a taking to violate the public-use clause of the Fifth Amendment.

In the Cottonwood case, the federal judge granted the preliminary injunction stopping the city of Cypress, California, from taking the church property and giving it to Costco, based in part on the 99 Cents Only case reasoning, and also on the probability that the federal RLUIPA statute would apply in this case. Even though California law places blight findings beyond review, the judge pointed to the *99 Cents Only* decision, which finds that "such findings are relevant under federal law only insofar as they bear upon the court's public use analysis under the Fifth Amendment."[395] The court is insisting that the use of eminent domain be subjected to the Constitution, and not merely to the court's legalistic definitions of blight. The new use must be public, regardless of past blight findings.

"The framers of the Constitution . . . might be surprised to learn that the power of eminent domain was being used to turn the property over to a private discount retail corporation," wrote Judge Carter in granting the Cottonwood injunction.[396]

ALL POLITICS IS VOCAL

While you wage a legal fight, don't slow down your political activism. Had the Garden Grove, California, homeowners in Chapter 2 kept quiet and accepted their fate, they would now be living in a redevelopment area, awaiting the eventual taking of their properties to make way for a theme park—or whatever final plan would be accepted by the city's bureaucrats. They organized, and even though they had little money, they were able to bring about 800 opponents of the plan to the City Council meeting. The anger and activism convinced all five council members to keep their neighborhood out of the redevelopment area. Since that time, debates on the Garden Grove City Council have more frequently revolved around how far to go to restrict eminent domain in the city, rather than how far to go to expand it. This is a significant improvement.

In Pittsburgh, after the targeted downtown business owners gained the help of the Institute for Justice, and a year-long controversy ensued, Nordstrom, a movie theater owner and the key developer pulled out of the redevelopment deal. This caused the mayor to declare his support for a new project that would proceed without the use of eminent domain. That decision was the result of political organizing, threatened lawsuits and pressure applied to the stores and developers that were poised to build on confiscated land.

In Cypress, California, city officials were belligerent, and Costco was unmoved by complaints by church members whose property would be taken to make way for a new discount store. But a judge's ruling chastening the city and the retailer convinced officials to go back to the drawing board and come up with a compromise that allowed the construction of the church and the store on nearby sites. Without eminent domain, more compromises like that would take place. There would be true win-win situations, but with the power of eminent domain available, city officials and greedy developers are apt to look toward that power first, and leave compromises for the later stages.

The Lakewood, Ohio, property owners scored an amazing victory: They stopped the specific developer's plan, removed from office the mayor who was advocating the plan and removed the blight designation from their neighborhood.

Bob Smith, the Libertarian Party of Minnesota official who helped Crystal Heights residents save their homes, said his organization is working to build support for property rights on one city council after another. That's a great approach: Develop allies before any redevelopment plan is proposed.

Politics, Publicity and the Courts

Often, legal actions, publicity campaigns, community organizing and political activism work together. As mentioned earlier, the city of Mesa, Arizona, tried to force Randy Bailey to vacate his brake-repair shop so that Ken Lenhart, owner of an Ace Hardware Store, could buy the prime corner property at about 50 percent of market rates. "Lenhart wants a much bigger store," according to *60 Minutes.* "He could have negotiated with Bailey, but instead, he convinced the city of Mesa to try to buy Bailey's land through eminent domain and then sell it to him." Bailey lost the case in Superior Court, but on October 1, 2003, the state Court of Appeals ruled that the eminent domain action was against the Arizona Constitution's clear prohibitions on taking private property for private use. This constitutional protection is perhaps the strongest in the nation.

The Arizona Constitution states the matter in elegant simplicity: "Private property shall not be taken for private use, except for private ways of necessity, and for drains, flumes, or ditches, on or across the lands of others for mining, agricultural, domestic or sanitary purposes. No private property shall be taken or damaged for public or private use without just compensation having first been made . . . which compensation shall be ascertained by a jury, unless a jury be waived . . . Whenever an attempt is made to take private property for a use alleged to be public, the question whether the contemplated use be really public shall be a judicial question, and determined as such without regard to any legislative assertion that the use is public."[397]

It's a far cry from federal court decisions that say that if a legislature determines an action to be a public use, then the courts have little reason to object. The court of appeals in the Bailey case explained the facts at hand simply: "The city is attempting to exercise its power of eminent domain to take the Bailey property and package it with adjacent parcels of land for sale to private developers who intend to build retail, office and restaurant facilities." Given those facts and the clear words of the Constitution, the court made these findings:

"The framers of our Constitution understood that one of the basic responsibilities of government is to protect private property interests. The Constitution contains no language suggesting that protection of such interests from an improper exercise of eminent domain is any less important, or less fundamental, than the other rights protected in the Constitution." The court referred to the limitations of private takings in Article 2, Section 17, then concluded: "Taking one person's property for another person's private use is plainly prohibited, with a few specific exceptions not applicable here." Then the court referenced the line stating that the judiciary has the right to make the determination of whether a taking is for public or private uses. "The intended use of the property is fundamentally for private development. The developers and other private parties would be the primary beneficiaries rather than the public. The anticipated benefits to the public do not outweigh the private nature of the intended use."[398]

That ruling, combined with bad publicity from *60 Minutes* and other media, no doubt contributed to the City Council's 7–0 vote in January 2004 against appealing the decision to the state Supreme Court. This was the best of all worlds: a principled court and active opposition convinced sensible council members to forget about their eminent domain plans.

The Way From San Jose

In San Jose, California, a preliminary ruling against the city, combined with active resistance by targeted business owners, convinced the redevelopment agency to drop its plans to condemn an ethnic-oriented shopping center in the eastern part of the city and hand it to a developer to build a new shopping hub. In San Jose, owners of the family-type businesses in the Tropicana center were going to be forced out of business to make way for a new fancier shopping center. Middle-class business owners were being forced to give up their businesses to benefit a wealthy developer. Here's how the San Jose Coalition for Redevelopment Reform explains the situation:

"During the year, the City Council, acting as the RDA [redevelopment] agency, issued Exclusive Negotiating Agreements and then Developer Disposition Agreements (DDA—Done Deal Already) to Blake Hunt Developers of Walnut Creek to take over the Tropicana Shopping Center from its owners who had spent more than $9 million of their own money to renovate the Center, and voted to spend hundreds of thousands of dollars on relocation and appraisal consultants to treat the property as if the agency already owned it and to give the chosen developers a subsidy of $50 million for this property and one across the street."[399]

Following a two-and-a-half-year fight, the city finally withdrew its condemnation action in October against the business owners after "a six-page tentative decision issued . . . by Judge Gregory H. Ward," reported the *Silicon Valley/San Jose Business Journal* on October 21, 2003.[400] "In that decision, the judge ruled that the city had failed to fully meet its burden of proof for exercising its right of eminent domain. In particular, the judge said that the administrative record of the city's actions in the case did not show that the redevelopment agency and its board had properly balanced the joint goals of minimal private injury and the common good."

Atlantic City Officials Gambled and Lost

Perhaps the first case that started the counter-revolution took place in Atlantic City, New Jersey. Donald Trump asked the city redevelopment agency to take Vera Coking's house so he could use it as a limousine parking lot for one of his casinos. To Trump, Coking was in the way of progress. So were Banin Gold Shop and Sabatini's Italian restaurant. Notice, however, how it's always the beneficiaries of the eminent domain plans and subsidies who describe the actions as "progress." These business and homeowners didn't think the plan was progress, so they fought the 1994 condemnation action, arguing that the use was private, not public, according to the book, *Public Power, Private Gain*.[401] This was the first Institute for Justice case that got national attention. It was an ideal case to show the public what eminent domain abuse was all about: Trump vs. an elderly widow. The court said the parking lot could be a public use, according to the Institute for Justice book, but said that once the lot was transferred Trump could do whatever he wanted with it, including expand his casino. The court eventually rejected the taking, and the owners are still there.

Organizing ABCs

Keep these points in mind as you organize your neighbors:

A. Build Broad Coalitions.

One of the beauties of this debate is that it unites people of various political backgrounds. It's important to build coalitions. The politicians on city councils always have political perspectives, so it's wise to build a campaign that unites right and left, one that promotes the ideas of property rights and human rights, to draw as much support as possible. A great example of that involves the new fight to overturn the old *Poletown* decision. Attorneys from the conservative Pacific Legal Foundation in Sacramento, California, have joined with attorneys from the liberal American Civil Liberties Union Fund of Michigan to file a friend of the court brief in a Michigan Supreme Court case known as *Wayne County v. Hathcock*.[402] Wayne County, home to the city of Detroit, is trying to condemn 1,300 acres of land around the Detroit airport to build a business park. The county has based its arguments on the *Poletown* decision, which allowed Detroit to bulldoze an entire thriving neighborhood to make way for a new Cadillac plant. The case has been the law of the land in Michigan, allowing scores of government agencies to justify virtually any taking in the name of economic development in the past two decades.

"*Poletown* was hastily written and has led to oppressive and unfair results," argues the PLF and ACLU brief. "*Poletown* created an inequitable policy of corporate welfare, allowing wealthy and powerful interests to take other people's land for their own profit—usually at the expense of the poor and underrepresented. *Poletown* is inconsistent with the history and meaning of the Public Use Clause, which formerly limited eminent domain to cases involving use by the public."[403] The brief documents the many Michigan cases that have followed the *Poletown* precedent. Even when courts were sharply critical of *Poletown* and of modern efforts to redistribute land to private parties in the name of economic development, they were forced to follow the state Supreme Court precedent. And *Poletown*, of course, has given inspiration—if that's what one might call it—to courts in other states justifying similar abuses of property rights.

The key problem with *Poletown* is that, as the brief explains, it nullifies the Constitution's public-use clause. "The argument for permitting private takings is that by improving economic conditions generally, the public is benefited in a general way. But if any general benefit to the public can satisfy the public use limitation—even when such benefits are incidental to a private company's profit and success—then that limitation would be nullified, because every successful business provides some sort of benefit to the public."[404]

This joint Pacific Legal Foundation/American Civil Liberties Union effort advances the core arguments of conservatives and liberals, and yet is not contradictory to either side's values. The case for property rights is stated soundly and clearly: "America's founders believed government existed to preserve the lives, property and welfare of the people, not to redistribute assets to accomplish the government's purposes."[405] So is the case for protecting the weak and the poor from the powerful and the rich: "In the absence of a realistic check on private redistributions through eminent domain, developers have become a new kind of robber baron, confident that they may take property whenever doing so serves their practically un-reviewable reading of public interests." That's the beauty of property rights: They protect poor and rich alike. They are the foundation of all other rights. So the fight against eminent domain can be fought vigorously from both sides against the middle. This effort in particular offers a blueprint for others who want to wage similar fights in other places.

B. Go On the Offensive

Most efforts to battle eminent domain abuse have, understandably, centered on the court system. When a person is facing the loss of his property, he knows that only the courts can stop it, or at least guarantee a higher amount of compensation. But, ultimately, more battles are going to have to be fought in state legislatures, in Congress and through the initiative process if Americans are going to stop these abuses before they happen. It's far better to strip government officials of their ability to use eminent domain for private uses then it is to fight a rear-guard action after a taking has occurred.

Unfortunately, even in cities where eminent domain abuses are rampant, it's hard to gain a political majority to make meaningful change. In Garden Grove, California, after the fiasco over the theme park, Councilman Mark Leyes has been trying to get his fellow council members to approve an initiative that bans the use of eminent domain for single-family properties. It was modeled on this language from a statute in the Los Angeles County city of Lawndale: "The redevelopment agency shall not use its power of eminent domain to acquire property which is zoned for residential purposes and/or developed with residential structures with four units or less, except that the agency may use its eminent domain powers to acquire property with the consent of all owners of the property."[406]

The simple, direct approach seems effective. Any number of initiatives or legislative proposals could be advanced to trim back the abuse of eminent domain. Specific bans on eminent domain for certain types of properties, or requirements that all redevelopment debt or eminent domain proposals go before voters, are other suggestions. A federal constitutional amendment forbidding the transfer of private property to other private owners would be wonderful, but the constitutional amendment process would take years, and there probably wouldn't be enough pro-property-rights legislators to allow this to happen. Every state has embraced "economic development" and is eagerly trying to win businesses from other states. Political powers would be aghast at the thought of eliminating what they describe as one "tool" in their economic-development and tax-generating arsenal.

In most Western states, especially California, the initiative process is the main way that any substantive change gets accomplished. Oregon had a successful property-rights initiative, called Measure 7, pass in November 2000. It didn't deal with eminent domain, per se, but it is easy to envision a similar measure that would deal with the subject of this book. Measure 7 stated that "If the state, a political subdivision of the state, or a local government passes or enforces a regulation that restricts the use of private real property, and the restriction has the effect of reducing the value of a property upon which the restriction is imposed; the property owner shall be paid just compensation equal to the reduction in the fair market value of the property."[407]

This passed in one of the nation's most liberal states, a state whose largest city has drawn a "green line" around its metropolitan boundaries, restricting growth and property rights by government edict. If an initiative this defiantly in favor of property rights can pass in Oregon, it ought to be able to pass anywhere. Unfortunately, the Oregon Supreme Court overturned the vote of the people, arguing that it made two non-related changes to the Constitution, and a proper initiative must restrict itself to one change. Furthermore, because the measure exempted porn-shop owners from the compensation, the court ruled that the measure restricted free speech. As supporters of Measure 7 explain, the porn exemption was included after a similar measure was defeated in Washington state after opponents argued that the law would invalidate restrictions on porn shops. In both states, the porn issue is a red herring. Simply put, environmentalists used that issue to undermine these proposals, because environmentalists thrive on the state's ability to restrict private-property use in order to promote growth controls and other environmental policies.

In various state legislatures, some simple changes to the law have been proposed. As mentioned earlier, New York Gov. George Pataki rejected a bipartisan bill that would have simply required proper public notice before an eminent domain action proceeded against a property owner. In Nevada, a bill was moving forward that would have forced the government to pay for a property owner's legal fees if the owner fought an eminent domain proceeding. In Colorado, bills were moving forward in the 2004 legislative session that would deal with the problem in the most obvious way: allowing eminent domain only for traditionally public uses. As bill sponsor Rep. Shawn Mitchell, R-Broomfield, told the *Denver Post* on January 4, 2004: "If the city or the state comes to take my land, it darn well better be for the city and state's public use—a courthouse, a road, a school—not just because they'd rather see someone doing something else on my land."[408] The Municipal League instantly vowed its opposition to the plan, but the *Post* reports that the plan was gaining interest from the governor and widespread support. Most of the support was coming from Republicans, but a strong contingent of Democrats was expected to support some version of the bill.

The Mitchell bill would outlaw the transfer of property to private owners. An alternative measure, introduced by Rep. Lois Tochtrop, D-Westminster, Colo., would tighten the definition of "blight," so that it could not be used for vacant or agricultural land,[409] according to a January 12, 2004, article in the *Denver Post*. That's not nearly as firm a restriction as the Mitchell plan, but at least the debate in Colorado is centering on the right things, on the need to rein in government power rather than expand it. At least the state could set a precedent followed throughout the country.

The Institute for Justice's Berliner points to six states that have passed legislative restrictions on the use of eminent domain. This is progress, however tentative and slow.

The U.S. Congress has been a dead zone when it comes to needed eminent domain reform. A Republican-sponsored energy bill would allow the Federal Energy Regulatory Commission to condemn private property to build new transmission lines.[410] Western governors feared that new federal eminent domain powers would bulldoze state efforts to protect private property. In this case, the Republicans backed the bill, and the Democrats were mostly opposed. But Democratic opposition wasn't driven by any great love of property rights, but out of opposition to Republican energy-development policies.

C. Be Positive, Not Just Reactive

The California Legislature has been approaching the solution from an interesting but promising direction. Although an outright restriction on eminent domain abuses would be the best place to start, the Legislature is trying instead to address the fundamental reason for eminent domain abuse. The catchwords in California are "the fiscalization of land use." Members of both major parties agree that the state's limitation on property taxes, and follow-up legislation that gave big cities preferential treatment in the disbursement of tax revenue, has made smaller cities and suburban areas dependent on sales tax to fund their government services. As a result, cities subsidize big-box stores, such as Wal-Mart and Costco, and are driven to abuse eminent domain to clear sites for these sales tax-generating behemoths. California politicians, including Gov. Arnold Schwarzenegger, have debated a plan that rearranges the way cities receive funds from Sacramento. Various proposals have been floating around, and each has a slightly different take on the problem. But each essentially does the same thing: takes away or reduces the sales tax cities receive and sends the money to the state government. In exchange, the state government would send cities a roughly equivalent amount of property taxes. This way, the argument goes, cities would no longer have the incentive to condemn massive amounts of private property. They would get more revenue from allowing houses to be built than from subsidizing Costco. The details need to be worked out, but the concept is sound. It wouldn't ban cities from abusing eminent domain, but it would take the air out of redevelopment agencies and create fewer reasons for eminent domain abuses to take place.

"Today, local governments hold on to only a tiny fraction of the property taxes collected within their boundaries—often keeping only 15 percent—but collect a full 1 cent of the sales tax collected on each $1 of taxable sales generated there," California Assemblyman John Campbell, a Republican, former Assemblyman Bob Hertzberg, a Democrat, and Anaheim Mayor Curt Pringle, a Republican, wrote in a February 1, 2004, *Orange County Register* column. "As a result, city and county officials have been increasingly motivated to promote developments that generate sales-tax dollars. These skewed incentives that lead officials to focus on their bottom line rather than the needs of their communities have contributed to California's dire housing shortage, long commutes, and the rapid spread of 'big box' stores and megalithic shopping centers across the state."[411]

They've also contributed to the abuse of eminent domain to make way for those big-box stores and shopping centers.

Mayor Pringle, however, isn't waiting for a change in the sales-tax/property tax system before changing his city's approach to redevelopment and eminent domain. In a model that could be followed around the country, this conservative Republican has built a coalition with two other council members—Richard Chavez, a liberal Democrat, and Tom Tait, a libertarian-oriented Republican. Together, the three of them have rejected the use of eminent domain and taxpayer subsidies for economic development purposes. They have charted a course that puts property rights and individual freedom ahead of the city's narrow fiscal concerns.[412]

For instance, in a large area of commercial and vacant land around Angels Stadium and the Arrowhead Pond of Anaheim, home to the Anaheim Angels baseball team and Mighty Ducks hockey franchise, respectively, the council members envision the emergence of a regional downtown. That's typical of what other city officials do—envisioning development plans for underused areas. But here's what's different. Instead of using redevelopment to subsidize plans envisioned by the city, Anaheim is encouraging private developers to come to it with their own plans. Anaheim wants the market to drive the process, not government planners, and it will not use eminent domain to take property from unwilling sellers for non-public uses, period. Mayor Pringle related in an interview a story about a meeting with developers, in which the developers said something to this effect: "Sometimes it's hard to acquire properties." The mayor's response: "You better figure out how to do it on your own."[413] If more cities took this bold approach, perhaps developers would be more creative and more respectful of other people's property.[414]

D. *Know What You Want To Do*

The Pioneer Institute, a Boston-based free-market institute, offers some concrete ideas for fixing eminent domain abuses, in a research paper on the topic:[415]

- Require the condemning agency to undertake a rigorous cost-benefit analysis before using eminent domain.
- Require all notices and explanatory materials to be provided in plain English (and other languages, as necessary) to eminent domain victims.
- Provide pre-taking appraisals to property owners.
- All "orders of taking" should include the name of condemnees, so that victims get proper notice.
- Open public records on these takings for forty years to assure accountability.
- Ensure judicial review of whether the taking is for a "public use."
- Make jury trials available in all cases that are contested.
- Award good will to businesses.
- Remove caps on relocation payments.
- Require full compensation for legal fees.
- Provide fair-market interest payments to condemnees who must wait a long time to receive their compensation.

This seems like a good template for legislative changes that activists can push for in their own states.

E. *Don't Lose Sight of Principles*

The key to winning these battles is to always remind people of the basic principles of the American experiment. As scholar Richard A. Epstein explains in a *Chapman Law Review* article in April 2003, "Once a court believes in the basic proposition that the purpose of government is to protect ordered liberty in all aspects of life, then there is only one way in which it can undertake constitutional interpretations. It must first begin with a broad presumption in favor of the protection of liberty and property, and then require the state to show some strong justification as to why the liberty ought to be limited or abridged."[416] Creating additional profits for Costco or Donald Trump or a billionaire sports-team owner clearly does not meet that standard.

F. Keep It Simple

Such concepts can sound complex. But one needn't be a constitutional scholar to understand them. The 1942 children's book, *The Little House*, tells a simple story: "Once upon a time there was a Little House way out in the country. She was a pretty Little House and she was strong and well built. The man who built her so well said, 'This Little House shall never be sold for gold or silver and she will live to see our great-great-grandchildren's great-great-grandchildren living in her."[417]

But the world changed, and the Little House in the country has watched the surveyors, who built roads for horseless carriages, come. Then the Little House watched the farm fields get paved to make way for houses and stores. Then the Little House watched high rises go up around her, and then highways and trains and skyscrapers, until the Little House was nothing but a shabby little place in the midst of a big city. Finally, along came the great-great-granddaughter of the man who built the Little House. She bought the place and moved it back out to the country where they all could be happy.

Today, the Little House would have been taken by force and bulldozed well before the area became a city. Today, the men and women who make such decisions don't believe that property is special, at least not other people's property. They don't believe that a person has the right to build a house with the intent that it will be lived in and cared for by that person's great-great-granddaughter. They believe that the Little House, or the Little Business or the Little Church, is worth nothing more than the cost of the bricks and mortar. They believe that people's dreams should be bulldozed any time a wealthier person, backed by the plans of government officials, has a better idea.

Even a child can understand that this is wrong. And even a city official might understand that abusing eminent domain is not worth the trouble, if more people fight back, if more legislators support reforms and if more courts rule in the property owner's favor.

RESOURCES

The following organizations offer information in the area of eminent domain abuse, redevelopment, free markets and property rights:

Acton Institute
161 Ottawa NW
Grand Rapids, MI 49503
www.acton.org

Allegheny Institute
305 Mt. Lebanon Blvd., Suite 208
Pittsburgh, PA 15234
www.alleghenyinstitute.org

American Land Rights Association
30218 NE 82nd Ave.
P.O. Box 400
Battle Ground, WA 98604
www.landrights.org

Becket Fund for Religious Liberty
1350 Connecticut Ave. NW, Suite 605
Washington, DC 20036
www.becketfund.org

Buckeye Institute
88 E. Broad St., Suite 1120
Columbus, OH 43215-3506
www.buckeyeinstitute.org

Cato Institute
1000 Massachusetts Ave. NW
Washington, DC 20001-5403
www.cato.org

Coalition for Redevelopment Reform
P.O. Box 446
San Jose, CA 95103
www.coalitionforredevelopmentreform.org

· Defenders of Property Rights
1350 Connecticut Ave. NW, Suite 410
Washington, DC 20035
www.defendersproprights.org

Evergreen Freedom Foundation
P.O. Box 552
Olympia, WA 98507
www.effwa.org

Foundation for Economic Education
30 S. Broadway
Irvington-on-Hudson, NY 10533
www.fee.org

Goldwater Institute
500 E. Coronado Rd.
Phoenix, AZ 85004
www.goldwaterinstitute.org

Grassroot Institute of Hawaii
1413 South King St., Suite 1163
Honolulu, HI 96814
www.grassrootinstitute.org
www.hawaiireporter.com

Heritage Foundation
214 Massachusetts Ave. NE
Washington, DC 20002-4999
www.heritage.org

Hoover Institution
Stanford University
Stanford, CA 94305-6010
www-hoover.stanford.edu

The Independent Institute
100 Swan Way
Oakland, CA 94621-1428
www.independent.org

Institute for Justice
1717 Pennsylvania Ave. NW, Suite 200
Washington, DC 20006
www.ij.org
www.castlecoalition.org

John Locke Foundation
200 W. Morgan St.
Raleigh, NC 27601
www.johnlocke.org

Ludwig von Mises Institute
518 W. Magnolia Ave.
Auburn, AL 36832-4528
www.mises.org
www.lewrockwell.com

Municipal Officials for Redevelopment Reform
Citizens United for Redevelopment Education
www.redevelopment.com

Pacific Legal Foundation
10360 Old Placerville Rd., Suite 100
Sacramento, CA 95827
www.pacificlegal.org

Pacific Research Institute
755 Sansome St.
San Francisco, CA 94111
www.pacificresearch.org

Pioneer Institute
85 Devonshire St.
Boston, MA 02109
www.pioneerinstitute.org

Property Rights Foundation of America
P.O. Box 75
Stony Creek, NY 12878
www.prfamerica.org

Public Policy Institute of California
500 Washington St., Suite 800
San Francisco, CA 94111
www.ppic.org

Reason Public Policy Institute
3415 S. Sepulveda Blvd., Suite 400
Los Angeles, CA 90034
www.rppi.org

State Policy Network (directory of think tanks)
P.O. Box 5208
Richmond, CA 94805-5208
www.spn.org

Sutherland Institute
150 E. Social Hall Ave., Suite 650
Salt Lake City, UT 84111
www.sutherlandinstitute.org

NOTES

Introduction 1: Eminent Domain Is Theft By Another Name

1. George Bernard Shaw, quoted by The Independent Institute, www.onpower. org/quotes/s.html (accessed March 9, 2004).
2. *United States v. General Motors*, 323 U.S. 373, 379 (1945).
3. Dana Berliner, *Public Power, Private Gain*, (Washington, D.C.: Institute for Justice, 2003), 2.
4. Eric Carpenter, "Double Jeopardy," *Orange County Register*, October 2, 2002.
5. Gideon Kanner, "Making Just Compensation Just," quoted by Virginia Property Rights Coalition, www.vapropertyrights.org/justcompgideonkan-ner.html (accessed March 14, 2004).
6. Attributed to John Fund by Scott Bullock of the Institute for Justice, interview by author, telephone, January 2004.
7. *99 Cents Only Stores v. Lancaster Redevelopment Agency*, CV 00-07572 SVW (June 25, 2001).
8. Jane Jacobs, quoted in Project for Public Spaces biography, Quotables, http://pps.org/info/placemakingtools/placemakers/jjacobs#quotable (accessed March 14, 2004).
9. *Random House College Dictionary, Revised Edition* (New York: Random House, 1975), 433.
10. "Eminent Domain," *60 Minutes*, September 26, 2003.
11. Ayn Rand, *Capitalism: The Unknown Ideal* (New York: New American Library, 1966), as quoted by Ayn Rand Institute, www.aynrand.org/objectivism/ rent_control.html (accessed March 14, 2004).
12. *Declaration of Independence*: "We hold these truths to be self-evident, that all men are created equal, that they are endowed by their Creator with certain unalienable Rights, that among these are Life, Liberty and the pursuit of Happiness. That to secure these rights, Governments are instituted among Men, deriving their just powers from the consent of the governed . . . "
13. JoAnne Saleet, interview by author, telephone, March 6, 2004.
14. Ibid.
15. Erick Trickey, "How the West End Was Won," *Cleveland* magazine, January 2004.
16. Ibid.

17. JoAnne Saleet, interview by author, telephone, March 6, 2004.

18. Ibid.

19. Ibid.

20. V. David Sartin, "West End developer cancels offer to buy land," *Cleveland Plain Dealer*, January 12, 2004.

21. JoAnne Saleet, interview by author, telephone, March 6, 2004.

22. Erick Trickey, "How the West End Was Won," *Cleveland* magazine, January 2004.

23. Manny Ballestero, interview by author, telephone, March 7, 2004.

24. Ibid.

25. Bob Smith, interview by author, telephone, March 6, 2004.

26. Bob Smith, quoted in www.noforce.org (accessed March 14, 2004).

27. Justin Piehowski, "EDA throws out Crystal Heights plans," *Crystal Sun Post*, January 22, 2004.

28. Les Poppa, interview by author, telephone, March 11, 2004.

29. Ibid.

30. Author first heard this comparison used by attorney Chris Sutton of Pasadena in the late 1990s.

31. Gideon Kanner, comments to author, February 2004.

Chapter 2: We're From the Government and We're Here for Your Home

32. Llewellyn Rockwell Jr., "Wall Street Socialism," WorldNet Daily, December 2, 1998.

33. Steven Greenhut, "Neighborhood Watch," *Orange County Register*, June 16, 2002.

34. Katherine Nguyen, "Theme park raises concern," *Orange County Register*, June 7, 2002.

35. Ibid.

36. Ibid.

37. Nick Schou, "The Ride of Their Lives," *OC Weekly*, June 14–20, 2002.

38. City of Garden Grove, Calif., "Opportunity to serve on and second election of the project area committee for the proposed amendment to the redevelopment plan for the Garden Grove Community Development Project," letter to residents, January 28, 2002.

39. Steven Greenhut, "Neighborhood Watch," *Orange County Register*, June 16, 2002 (reprinted in its entirety with permission from *Orange County Register*).

40. Jim Tortolano, "The Boom of World War II and Modern-Day Garden Grove," *Garden Grove Journal*, November 30, 2003.

41. Manny Ballestero and neighbors, interview by author, in person, June 2002.
42. *Beach-Courchesense v. City of Diamond Bar* (2000) 80 Cal.App.4th 388, 95 Cal.Rptr.2d 265.
43. *Redevelopment: The Unknown Government*, (Fullerton, Calif.: Municipal Officials for Redevelopment Reform, April 2004), www.redevelopment.com, 4.
44. Ibid., 4.
45. Manny Ballestero, interview by author, in person, spring 2002.
46. City of Garden Grove, "Finding the Right Balance," video, June 2002. Not only did they use city funds, but officials also had police officers distribute the video door to door.
47. Nick Schou, "The Ride of Their Lives," *OC Weekly*, June 14–20, 2002.
48. Vik Jolly, "A Riverwalk of sorts feasible, experts say," *Orange County Register*, January 6, 2000.
49. Tiffany Horan, "'Renaissance' built on Garden Grove subsidies," *Orange County Register*, September 3, 1998.
50. Bruce Broadwater, "Milt Krieger Believes The Best Way To Solve Problems in Garden Grove Is To Spend More Taxpayer Money. And His Handling of the Alicante Hotel Boondoggle Proves it," campaign mailer, date unknown.
51. Author's observations, Garden Grove City Council meeting, June 25, 2002.
52. Ibid.
53. Ibid.
54. Garden Grove Firefighters Local 2005, letter distributed outside council meeting, no date on letter.
55. Steven Greenhut, "Garden Grove Neighbors Triumph," *Orange County Register*, June 30, 2002.
56. Frederic Bastiat, What *is Seen and What is Not Seen* (July 1850), quoted by the Foundation for Economic Education, The Library of Economics and Liberty, www.econlib.org (accessed March 14, 2004).
57. John Adams, quoted by www.marksquotes.com.

Chapter 3: Unjust Compensation

58. Gideon Kanner, comments to author, February 2004.
59. Steven Strooh, interviews by author, telephone, January 2004.
60. Ibid.
61. Ibid. Also, Gideon Kanner, comments to the author, February 2004; he explained: "The U.S. Supreme Court and lower federal courts hold that it is legal for federal agents to come onto private property, seize it, and tell its owner 'sue me.' Also, Congress can simply pass a bill declaring that particular land (described in the bill) is now federal property, and its owners have

six years to sue for compensation in the U.S. Court of Federal Claims in Washington." In California, Kanner adds, the government can take possession of property on three days notice if it claims to have an urgent need for the property.

62. California law, quoted from Oliver Vose Sandifer Murphy & Lee of Los Angeles, article on just compensation, www.eminentdomainlaw.net (accessed March 14, 2004).

63. Yae Hong, interview by author, telephone, September 2001.

64. Steven Greenhut, "Garden Grove's empire-building," *Orange County Register*, September. 30, 2001.

65. Ibid.

66. Ibid.

67. Oliver Vose Sandifer Murphy and Lee Web site, www.eminent domainlaw.net (accessed March 14, 2004).

68. Gideon Kanner, "Making Just Compensation Just," quoted by Virginia Property Rights Coalition Web site, www.vapropertyrights.org/just-compgideonkanner.html (accessed March 14, 2004).

69. Gideon Kanner, "Ethics? We Don't Have To Show You Any Stinkin' Ethics. This is Eminent Domain" (unpublished article provided to author, February 2004).

70. John C. Murphy, interview by author, telephone, January 2004.

71. Ibid.

72. Sean O'Connor, "Getting a Fair Shake," Sheppard Mullin Richter & Hampton Web site, Nov. 11, 1999, http: //www.smrh.com/publications/pubview.cfm? pubID=109 (accessed April 25, 2004).

73. Sean O'Connor, interview with author, in person, January 2004.

74. Editorial, "Mississippi Churning," *Wall Street Journal*, January 4, 2002.

75. Based on the author's reporting on topic involving the city of Anaheim's initial plan to acquire older apartment buildings known as the Jeffrey-Lynne complex. Because Anaheim Council Members Lucille Kring and Tom Tait refused to vote for eminent domain on principle, the project had to proceed without its use, June 1999.

76. John C. Murphy, interview by author, telephone, February 2004.

77. Ibid.

78. Ibid.

79. Gideon Kanner, "Making Just Compensation Just."

80. Ibid.

81. *United States v. 320 Acres of Land, More or Less, Etc.*, 605 F.2d 762 (5th Cir. 1979)

82. Gideon Kanner, "Ethics? We Don't Have To Show You Any Stinkin' Ethics. This is Eminent Domain."

83. Sean O'Connor, interview by author, in person, January 2004.

84. Manny Ballestero, interview by author, telephone, January 2004.

85. Ibid.

86. Alan Lutz, interview by author, in person, January 2004.

87. Gary Mulligan, interview by author, in person, January 2004.

88. Zaheera Wahid and John McDonald, "No longer city's 'hostage,' bar can improve building," *Orange County Register*, January 8, 2004.

89. Gary Mulligan, interview by author, in person, January 2004.

90. Carrie Coolidge, "Sell Cheap or Die," *Forbes*, December 22, 2003.

91. Dana Berliner, interview by author, telephone, December 2003.

Chapter 4: Property Rights Are Human Rights

92. William Pitt, as quoted by Martin Anderson, *The Federal Bulldozer: A Critical Analysis of Urban Renewal, 1949–1962* (Cambridge, Mass.: The MIT Press, 1964), 184.

93. Gideon Kanner, comments to author, February 2004. Kanner added that "Grotius was disputed by the German, Puffendorf, who argued that the correct term should be 'imperium,' not 'dominium.' The British use the term 'compulsory purchase,' and everyone except us says 'expropriation,' except for Australians, who say 'resumption' because under their law, land was granted by the king on condition that royal title may be resumed on payment of compensation."

94. Terry L. Anderson and Laura E. Huggins, *Property Rights: A Practical Guide to Freedom and Prosperity* (Stanford, Calif.: The Hoover Institution Press, 2003), 7–8.

95. John Locke, *The Second Treatise of Civil Government* (1690), www.constitution.org/jl/2ndtreat.htm, Chapter 5, Section 26.

96. Gideon Kanner, comments to author, February 2004.

97. Marco Bassani, "The Real Jefferson," www.Mises.org, May 27, 2002.

98. Tibor Machan, interview by author, telephone, February 2004.

99. Dana Berliner, *Public Power, Private Gain*, 135.

100. Alice Beasley, "When Government Takes Private Property: Public Uses and Private Benefits," *Western City*, May 2003, www.westerncity.com/May03 LegalNotes.htm (accessed March 14, 2004).

101. Chris Sutton, interview by author, telephone, December 2003.

102. Ibid.

103. Ibid.

104. Steven Hill, "Bill of Rights Protects Property, Not People," *Seattle Post-Intelligencer*, date unknown, www.giantleap.org/envision/bill.htm (accessed, December 7, 2003).

105. Chris Sutton, comments to the author, February 2004.

106. Bernard Siegan, *Property and Freedom*, (New Brunswick, N.J.: Transaction Publishers, 1997), 14.

107. Ibid., 14

108. Tibor Machan, interview by author, telephone, February 2004.

109. Ibid.

110. Chris Sutton, interview by author, telephone, November 2003.

111. Gideon Kanner, interview by author, telephone, January 2004.

112. Sarah H. Gordon, *Passage to Union: How the Railroads Transformed American Life, 1829–1929*, (Chicago: Ivan R. Dee, 1996), 59.

113. *Missouri Pacific Railway Co. v. State of Nebraska*, 164 U.S. 403 (1896).

114. Ibid.

115. Martin Anderson, *The Federal Bulldozer*, 185.

116. Ibid, 185–186.

117. Dana Berliner, *Public Power, Private Gain*, 2.

118. Karen Samples, "Fights brew over use of eminent domain," *Cincinnati Enquirer*, January 10, 2002.

119. Eric Felten, "Kiss Your House Good-bye," *Reader's Digest*, March 2001.

120. Patrick Poole, "Sell your land or we'll take it," WorldNetDaily, June 24, 2000.

121. Brad Cooper, "Critics: Public power used for private gain," *Wichita Eagle*, April, 29, 2003.

122. Patrick Poole, WorldNetDaily, June 24, 2002.

123. David Greenberg, "David Greenberg on rights and freedom," CIVNET (Center for Civic Education), March–April 1999.

124. The Associated Press, December 23, 2003: "Millions of Chinese who have plunged into capitalism by starting businesses and investing in stocks will be guaranteed their right to property for the first time since the 1949 revolution under a constitutional amendment proposed by China's communist leaders."

125. Ayn Rand, *The Pull Peddlers*, quoted by Larry Salzman, http://criterion.uchicago.edu/issues/iv2/salzman.html (accessed March 14, 2004).

126. *Rindge Co. et al. v. Los Angeles County, 262 U.S. 700 (1923)*. Thanks to Chris Sutton for explaining the significance of this case to author.

127. Ibid.

128. Ibid.

129. Ibid.

130. Chris Sutton, interview by author, telephone, November 2004.

131. Aesop, *The Wolf and the Lamb*, (The Harvard Classics), www.bartleby.com /17/1/2.html (accessed March 14, 2004).

132. *Berman v. Parker*, 348 U.S. 26 (1954).

133. Ibid.

134. Ibid.

135. Ibid.

136. Ibid.

137. Ibid.

138. *Hawaii Housing Authority v. Midkiff*, 467 U.S. 229 (1984).

139. Ibid.

140. Ibid.

141. Gideon Kanner, comments to author, February 2004.

142. *Hawaii Housing Authority v, Midkiff*, 467 U.S. 229 (1984).

143. Ibid.

144. Ibid.

145. Gideon Kanner, comments to author, February 2004.

Chapter 5: The New Urban Renewal: As Bad As the Old Urban Renewal

146. Jane Jacobs, *The Death and Life of Great American Cities* (New York: Vintage Books, 1961), 17.

147. Jon C. Teaford, "Urban Renewal and Its Aftermath" (Housing Policy Debate, Fannie Mae Foundation 2000), 449.

148. Ibid. A widely used term. For an early reference to it and an excellent look at urban renewal at the time it was occurring: Arthur R. Simon, "New Yorkers Without a Voice: A Tragedy of Urban Renewal," *Atlantic Monthly*, April 1966, www.theatlantic.com/issues/97jan/urban/simon.htm (accessed March 14, 2004).

149. Jon C. Teaford, "Urban Renewal and Its Aftermath," 443.

150. Ibid., 445.

151. Martin Anderson, *The Federal Bulldozer: A Critical Analysis of Urban Renewal, 1949–1962*, (Cambridge, Mass.: The MIT Press, 1964), 5.

152. Ibid., 218.

153. Jon C. Teaford, "Urban Renewal and Its Aftermath," 458.

154. Alexander von Hoffman, "Why They Built Pruitt-Igoe," (the Joint Center for Housing Studies at Harvard University, policy paper, 2000), http://www.soc.iastate.edu/sapp/PruittIgoe.html (accessed March 14, 2004). Hoffman writes: "St. Louis's Pruitt-Igoe housing project is arguably the most infamous public-housing project ever built in the United States. A product of the postwar federal public-housing program, this mammoth high-rise development was completed in 1956. . . .

"Only a few years later, disrepair, vandalism, and crime plagued Pruitt-Igoe. The project's recreational galleries and skip-stop elevators, once heralded as architectural innovations, had become nuisances and danger zones. Large numbers of vacancies indicated that even poor people preferred to live anywhere but Pruitt-Igoe. In 1972, after spending more than $5 million in vain to cure the problems at Pruitt-Igoe, the St. Louis Housing Authority, in a highly publicized event, demolished three of the high-rise buildings. A year later, in concert with the U.S. Department of Housing and Urban Development, it declared Pruitt-Igoe unsalvageable and razed the remaining buildings."

155. For a description of this planning ideology by supporters, see the Congress for the New Urbanism, www.cnu.org.

156. Dana Berliner, interview with author, telephone, December 2003.

157. Ibid.

158. Dana Berliner, *Public Power, Private Gain*, 166.

159. Bob Ferguson, interview with author, telephone, March 12, 2004.

160. Author lives several miles from the downtown and gets to observe it closely.

161. Jenny Nolan, "Auto plant vs. neighborhood: The Poletown battle," *Detroit News*, archives, no date, www.detnews.com/history/poletown/poletown.htm (accessed March 14, 2004).

162. Ibid.

163. *Poletown Neighborhood Council v. City of Detroit*, 304 N.W. 2d 455, 410 Mich. 616 (1981).

164. Ibid.

165. Ibid.

166. Jeanie Wylie, *Poletown: A Community Destroyed*, (Urbana, Ill.: University of Illinois Press, 1990).

167. Daniel Patrick Moynihan argued that as the public began to increasingly tolerate deviant behavior, such behavior became normal, and that began a slide downward. With property rights, it's not hard to see a parallel, as Americans increasingly tolerate more government intrusions and think of them as normal.

168. *Redevelopment: The Unknown Government*, 6.

169. Tiffany Horan, "Garden Grove schools won't let agency off hook," *Orange County Register*, September 16, 1998.

170. Steve Westly, *State of California Community Redevelopment Agencies Annual Report* (fiscal year 2001–02), 487.

171. For information about Prop. 13 visit the Web site for the Howard Jarvis Taxpayers Association, named after the man who led the Prop. 13 battle, www.hjta.org.

172. Gideon Kanner, comments to author, February 2004.

173. Chris Potter, "If Looks Could Kill," *Pittsburgh City Paper*, 2000.

174. Dana Berliner, *Public Power, Private Gain*, 176–177.

175. Eric Montarti, interview by author, telephone, November 2003.

176. Eric Montarti, "Tax Increment Foolishness" (The Allegheny Institute for Public Policy), June 10, 2002.

177. Eric Montarti, "A Brief Lesson in Tax Increment Financing," *Point of View*, September/October 1999.

178. City of Rapid City, S.D., "Tax Increment Financing Committee," www.rcgov.com/planning/committeeminutes /tif/tifcover.htm (accessed December 15, 2003).

179. Eric Montarti, interview with author, November 2003.

180. State of Nebraska Department of Economic Development, "Tax Increment Financing," http://crd.neded.org/pubs/tif.html (accessed December 15, 2003).

181. State of South Carolina, "Code of Laws: Title 31 – Housing and Redevelopment," www.scstatehouse.net/code/t31c007.htm (accessed May 22, 2004).

182. Spokane, Wash., Area Economic Development Council, "Tax Increment Finance Summary," www.spokaneedc.org/incentives/tif.php (accessed December 15, 2003).

183. State of Arkansas, "Tax Increment Financing," www.1-800-arkansas.com/incentives/tax_increment.htm (accessed December 15, 2003).

184. Yvette Shields, "Chicago Thinks Outside the TIF to Develop Its 'Golf Course,'" *Bond Buyer*, October 2, 2002.

185. C. Vernon Gray, *Tax Increment Financing: An Alternative Economic Development Financing Technique*, (Issue brief: Presidential Initiative Task Force on Economic Development, National Association of Counties, January 2000), 6.

186. Jane Jacobs, *The Death and Life Of Great American Cities*, (New York: Vintage Books, 1961). Perhaps the best book ever written for those interested in urban planning and freedom.

187. Ibid., 15–16

188. Ibid., 15.
189. Ibid., 15.
190. Ibid., 11.
191. Misc. authors, "Downtown Anaheim gets a boost," *Orange County Register*, January 26, 2004.
192. Chris Norby, interview with author, in person, December 2003.
193. Ibid.
194. Ibid.
195. Frank Hotchkiss, interview with author, in person, January 2004.

Chapter 6: The Eminent Domain Mentality

196. C.S. Lewis, *The Screwtape Letters*, preface, quoted by Steven Greenhut, "Cypress' white-collar crime," *Orange County Register*, June 2, 2002.
197. Guy B. Adams and Danny L. Balfour, *Unmasking Administrative Evil*, (Thousand Oaks, Calif.: Sage Publications, 1998).
198. Institute for Justice, "Saving the Skin of Property Owners In Connecticut: New London Residents Fight Eminent Domain Abuse," Litigation Backgrounder, no date, 4.
199. Ibid., 4.
200. Connie Cass, "Cities seize private land for development," *Portsmouth Herald*, May 9, 2003.
201. Ibid.
202. Lucette Lagnado, "Pfizer's Vision for a Research-Center Area Remains Far From Realized in Bitter Town," *Wall Street Journal*, September 10, 2002.
203. Institute for Justice, "Connecticut Supreme Court Permits Eminent Domain Abuse; A Majority Rules Against Homeowners in New London," news release, March 3, 2004.
204. City of Garden Grove, Calif., "What are the Community-wide benefits of Redevelopment?", www.ci.garden-grove.ca.us/ departments/comm_development/redevben_html (accessed November 25, 2003).
205. American Planning Association, *Policy Guide on Takings* (adopted by the APA Board of Directors, April 11, 1995), 3.
206. Sam Staley, "Wrecking Property Rights," Reason Online, February 2003.
207. Vera Vogelsang-Coombs, "LTI Speaker Links Ethics to Credibility of Local Officials," National League of Cities, August 20, 2001, http://www.nlc.org/nlc_org/site/newsroom/nations_cities_weekly/display.cfm?id=FF04C91C-D233-4405-AF4A976C0834DCD5 (accessed May 9, 2004).
208. Ibid.

209. California Redevelopment Association, www.ca-redevelopment.org (accessed March 14, 2004).

210. Dean Starkman, "Take and Give," *Wall Street Journal*, December 2, 1998.

211. Douglas Kendall and Timothy Dowling, letter to the editor, "The Need for Eminent Domain," *Wall Street Journal*, December 22, 1998.

212. Gideon Kanner, letter to the editor, "Eminent Domain, or Just Greed?" *Wall Street Journal*, January 11, 1999.

213. *General Building Contractors L.L.C. and Robert D. Tolbert v. Board of Shawnee County Commissioners of Shawnee County, Kansas*, The Supreme Court of Kansas No. 89, 02.

214. Ibid. Gideon Kanner said, in comments to the author, February 2004, that this decision is legally wrong: "The power of eminent domain is an inherent power of the state that lies dormant in the law delegating that power to cities, counties and other entities. So if the power has not been delegated to an entity subordinate to the state, that entity may not exercise it."

215. Dana Berliner, *Public Power, Private Gain*, 175–176.

216. Editorial, "Coatesville's bad idea," *Philadelphia Inquirer*, May 22, 2002.

217. Pateen Corcoran, "Coatesville ordinance debated," *West Chester (Pa.) Daily Local News*, June 26, 2002.

218. Bajeerah Lowe, "Judge upholds Saha petitions," *West Chester (Pa.) Daily Local News*, August 27, 2003.

219. Bajeerah Lowe, "Pa. court rejects Saha suit," *West Chester (Pa.) Daily Local News*, December 14, 2003.

220. Ibid.

221. Dick Saha, interview with author, telephone, March 9, 2004.

222. Gina Zotti, "Sahas' remark upsets group," *West Chester (Pa.) Daily Local News*, March 12, 2004.

223. Malia Zimmerman, "The Demise of an Entrepreneurial Dream," *Hawaii Reporter*, September 6, 2002.

224. Ibid.

225. Ibid.

226. The Associated Press, August 22, 2003.

227. Fred Guarino, "Eminent Domain Settlement Reached – Eight of 10 Landowners Agree to Sell," *Shelby County (Ala.) Reporter*, www.shelbycountyreporter.com/articles/2004/01/08/news/news04.txt (accessed Jan. 8, 2004).

228. David Olson, "Koreans condemn inn's forced sale," *Herald (Wash.)*, January 16, 2004.

229. 1 Kings 21: 1–23 (Revised Standard Version, as quoted in www.bible.com). Author learned of this passage from Gideon Kanner.

Chapter 7: God Doesn't Pay Taxes

230. Steven Greenhut, "Cypress continues its unholy war," *Orange County Register*, April 14, 2002.
231. Ibid.
232. City of Cypress, "New Economic Era Begins for Community," www.ci.cypress.ca.us/community_develpmnt/redevelopment/city_view_1 003.htm (accessed December 23, 2003).
233. Ibid.
234. Reporting by the author for the *Orange County Register.*
235. Ibid.
236. Jim Hinch, "Values versus value," *Orange County Register*, September 1, 2002.
237. City of Cypress, letter.
238. Roger Faubel, interview by author, telephone, February 2004.
239. Author attended meeting.
240. Jim Hinch, "Fight with city inspired church," *Orange County Register*, February 21, 2003.
241. Steven Greenhut, "Cypress' white-collar crime," *Orange County Register*, June 2, 2002.
242. City of Cypress, "City of Cypress Outlines Detailed Defense in Court Papers," news release, July 22, 2002.
243. *Cottonwood Christian Center v. Cypress Redevelopment Agency; City of Cypress; Does 1-10*, Case No. SA CV 02-60 DOC (ANx), August 6, 2002, www.cottonwood.org (accessed March 14, 2004).
244. Ibid., 8.
245. Ibid., 17.
246. Ibid., 24.
247. Ibid., 24.
248. Ibid., 25.
249. Ibid., 25.
250. Ibid., 30.
251. Ibid., 30.
252. Ibid., 32.
253. City of Cypress, "Federal Court Issues Preliminary Injunction to Preserve the 'Status Quo' Between Cypress and Cottonwood," news release produced by The Terpin Group, Los Angeles, August 6, 2002.

254. Paige Austin, "Resolution in Cottonwood church case," *Orange County Register*, September 19, 2002.

255. Bayless Conley and Mike Wilson, interview by author, in person, January 2004.

256. Booker T. Washington, *Up From Slavery: An Autobiography* (1901), www.bartleby.com, Chapter 5, Section 8.

257. Andrew Guilford and Sean O'Connor, interview by author, in person, January 2004.

258. Juliet V. Casey, "Church's zoning victory turns sour," *Las Vegas Review-Journal*, July 18, 2002.

259. Martin Lasden, "Holy Zoning," *California Lawyer*, July 2002.

260. H.R. 4084, introduced in the U.S. House of Representatives, March 23, 2000.

261. Lewis Carroll, *Alice's Adventures in Wonderland*, (Millennium Fulcrum Edition 3.0), http://www-2.cs.cmu.edu/People/rgs/alice-table.html (accessed May 9, 2004), Chapter 3.

262. Jessica DeStefano, "CDA Seeks to Acquire Church," *Westbury (N.Y.) Times*, January 14, 2000.

263. Dana Berliner, *Public Power, Private Gain*, 151.

264. Jessica DeStefano, *Westbury Times*, January 14, 2000.

265. Ibid. Also, Julie Foster, "Testing the Faith, WorldNetDaily, 2000.

266. Jim Lesczynski, "Meet The New Power Brokers," The Empire Page, 2002.

267. Jacob Sullum, "One man's blight," Creator's Syndicate, October 10, 2000, www.Townhall.com/columnists/jacobsullum/printjs20001010.shtml (accessed March 14, 2004).

268. Property Rights Foundation of America, www.prfamerica.org.

269. Phil Reisman. "Pataki ignores chance to improve eminent domain law," *The Journal News (N.Y.)*, October 5, 2003.

270. *City of Los Angeles v. Spencer Chadwick*, No. B054922, Court of Appeal, Second District, Division 1, December 12, 1991. Thanks to Chris Sutton for providing a copy of this decision, which was not published by the state Supreme Court.

271. Ibid., 285 Cal. Rprtr. 192 (Cal. App. 2 Dist. 1991).

272. Ibid., 285 Cal. Rprtr. 191: "The Supreme Court ordered that the opinion be not officially published."

273. Scott P. Richert, "A Nightmare on Elm Street," *Chronicles*, October 2003, www.chroniclesmagazine.org.

Chapter 8: Corporate Welfare Queens

274. H.L. Mencken, *Prejudices, Fourth Series* (1924), quoted in Libertyhaven.com.

275. Scott Bullock, interview with author, telephone, January 2004.

276. Ibid.

277. Eric Norby, interview with author, telephone, January 2004.

278. Ira Carnahan, "Domain Abuse," Forbes.com, June 11, 2003.

279. Dennis Foley and Courtney Perkes, "Santa Ana, county collide over dealership expansion," *Orange County Register*, January 16, 2004.

280. Eminent Domain, *60 Minutes*, September 28, 2003.

281. Fred Weinberg, letter to the editor, "Story Behind Costco, A City and a Church," *Wall Street Journal*, June 27, 2002.

282. Steven Greenhut, "Costco's big-box political clout," *Orange County Register*, June 23, 2002.

283. Editorial, "The First Church of Costco," *Wall Street Journal*, May 30, 2002.

284. Jim Sinegal, letter to the editor, "Costco Isn't the Villain In Church/City Dispute," *Wall Street Journal*, June 12, 2002.

285. Gideon Kanner, comments to author, February 2004.

286. Edmund Burke, quoted in http://www.conservativeforum.org/authquot.asp?ID=254 (accessed March 14, 2004).

287. Fred Weinberg, letter to the editor, *Wall Street Journal*, June 27, 2002.

288. Copy of letter forwarded to author by recipient, no date.

289. Mike Hendricks, "Costco plan could carry steep price," *Kansas City Star*, February 14, 2001.

290. *Kansas City Star*, June 2000.

291. John Kramer, interview by author, telephone, February 2004.

292. Steven Greenhut, "Costco's big-box political clout," *Orange County Register*, June 30, 2002.

293. Ibid.

294. Martin Wisckol, "Cities offer deals in bulk," *Orange County Register*, August 12, 2002.

295. Editorial, "Over-legislating," *Orange County Register*, Sept. 12, 1999.

296. *99 Cents Only Stores v. Lancaster Redevelopment Agency*, CV 00-07572 SVW (AJWx), June 25, 2001.

297. Ibid.

298. Ibid.

299. Dave Gold, interview by author, telephone, 2001.

300. Dean Starkman, "Cities Often Misapply Eminent-Domain Rule," *Wall Street Journal*, July 31, 2001.

301. Ibid.

302. Cottonwood legal brief, Sheppard Mullin Richter & Hampton LLP, Costa Mesa, Calif., June 23, 2002.

303. Ira Carnahan, Forbes.com, June 11, 2003.

304. Various news accounts, including brochure and time line from the Center Theater Group, www.centertheatergroup.com; and Carlos Saldana, *The Chavez Ravine Story*, 1992-2003, www.toonist.com/burrito/cine.html (accessed March 14, 2004).

305. Ibid.

306. Ibid.

307. Ibid.

308. Nicholas Kristof, *New York Times*, October 2002, quoted in Wampum, www.wampum.blogspot.com, September 16, 2003.

309. Author unknown, "Eminent domain for Sox? That's Gleason's territory," *Boston Business Journal*, week of July 17, 2000.

310. League of Fans, "Summary of Current National Football League Stadium Deals," September 9, 2003.

311. No byline, "Financial feasibility," *Sports Illustrated* online edition, May 15, 2002.

312. Raymond J. Keating, "Sports Pork: The Costly Relationship Between Major League Sports and Government," (Cato Institute Policy Analysis), April 5, 1999, www.cato.org/pubs/pas/pa339.pdf (accessed March 14, 2004).

313. Doug Bandow, "Surprise! Stadiums Don't Pay, After All," *Washington Post*, www.cato.org, October 19, 2003.

314. *Southwestern Illinois Development Authority v. National City Environmental, LLC*, Docket N. 87809-Agenda 16, opinion filed April 4, 2002.

315. Doug Bandow, "Surprise!", October 19, 2003.

316. The Fans, Taxpayers and Business Alliance, "New Stadiums In Other Cities," www.ftballiance.org (accessed March 14, 2004).

317. Richard A. Epstein, "Not too late to stop Soldier Field giveaway," *Chicago Tribune*, May 5, 2002.

318. Peter Bodley, "Anoka County officials hand deliver county's comprehensive Vikings stadium plan," *Anoka County Union*, January 2004.

319. Justice Constance Sweeney, quoted in "The Power To Take: A Primer on Eminent Domain" (The Pioneer Institute for Public Policy Research, 2001 Policy Dialogue, No. 42, Boston), 5.

320. Eric Norby, interview by author, telephone, February 2004.

321. Ibid.

322. *Redevelopment: The Unknown Government*, 20.

323. The American Planning Association, *September 2002 Policy Guide.*

324. Thomas J. DiLorenzo, "Mercantilism," The Ludwig von Mises Institute, www.mises.org/fullarticle.asp?record=152&month=5 (accessed Jan. 2, 2004).

325. Ibid.

326. Thomas J. DiLorenzo, "Economic Fascism," *Freeman*, June 1994.

327. Frederic Bastiat, *The Law* (1850), http://www.lexrex.com/ informed/otherdocuments/thelaw/main.htm (accessed Jan. 3, 2004), Section 9, "The Results of Legal Plunder."

328. Ibid., Section 9, "The Results of Legal Plunder."

329. Ibid., Section 18, "The Law Defends Plunder."

330. Tibor Machan, "Big Business Isn't Always Capitalist," *The Laissez Faire Electronic Times*, April 29, 2002.

Chapter 9: The Media Finally Wake Up

331. James Fenimore Cooper, *The American Democrat*, (New York: A. Knopf, 1931), 163.

332. Gideon Kanner, interview by author, telephone, January 2004.

333. Gideon Kanner, "Redwoods, Junk Bonds, and Tools of Cosa Nostra: A Visit to the Dark Side of the Headwaters Controversy," *Environmental Law Reporter*, September 2000.

334. Ibid.

335. Ibid.

336. John Stossel, speaking to the Orange County Forum, January 2004.

337. Bernard Goldberg, interview by author at Tait and Associates in Santa Ana, Calif., January 2004.

338. Ibid.

339. Scott Bullock, interview by author, telephone, December 2003.

340. Editorial, "Saying no: Public officials need to stand fast for Downtown," *Pittsburgh Post-Gazette*, June 24, 1999.

341. Editorial, "Blight flight: Eminent domain has served Pittsburgh well," *Pittsburgh Post-Gazette*, November 3, 1999.

342. Editorial, "Garden view/The theater owner should cut a deal and exit now," *Pittsburgh Post-Gazette*, April 23, 2002.

343. Brian O'Neill, "A blight idea for rejuvenating the East End," *Pittsburgh Post-Gazette*, January 16, 2002.

344. Edward Colimore, "Redevelopment plan a boon for Clementon," *Philadelphia Inquirer*, December 19, 2003.

345. Kristen Go, "Redevelopment is key to future," *Arizona Republic*, March 28, 2003.

346. Ibid.

347. Editorial, "Supporting Cypress," *News Enterprise*, April 2002. The newspaper also featured an editorial cartoon of this writer as a dog being led on a leash by the church pastor. A June 26, 2002, editorial hurls the worst possible insult, perhaps: "Greenhut is an easterner . . . in fact a real live Yankee."

348. Lynda Guydon Taylor, "Redevelopment official admits eminent domain is unpopular," *Pittsburgh Post-Gazette*, September 14, 2003.

349. Riverside County, "Report to the Board of Supervisors for Redevelopment Project Area No. 1-1986, Amendment No. 1, Lakeland Village/Wildomar Sub-Area, June 22, 1999" (Prepared by GRC Redevelopment Consultants Inc., Diamond Bar, Calif.), 148, 14.1.

350. Steven Greenhut, "Storm over Elsinore," *Orange County Register*, January 23, 2000.

351. Andrew Guilford, interview with author, in person, January 2004.

352. Chris Potter, "Big Mac Attack," *Pittsburgh City Paper*, 2001.

353. Editorial, Orange County Perspective, "The Real Issue is Revenue," *Los Angeles Times*, August 11, 2002.

354. Steven Greenhut, "Cypress' white-collar crime," *Orange County Register*, June 2, 2002.

355. Mark Leyes, interview by the author, telephone, January 2004.

356. Tiffany Horan, "Renaissance" article, *Orange County Register*, September 3, 1998.

357. Ibid.

358. Times staff writers, researched by T. Christian Miller and Patrick McGreevy, "Heady Plans, Hard Reality; $117-million redevelopment effort left North Hollywood no better after 20 years than some similar areas that got no such aid, data show. Officials defend agency," *Los Angeles Times*, January 30, 2000, A1.

359. Ibid.

360. Dean Starkman, "Take and Give," *Wall Street Journal*, December 2, 1998.

361. Eric Felten, "Kiss Your House Good-Bye," *Reader's Digest*, March 2001.

362. Tucker Carlson, "Home Wreckers," *Reader's Digest*, August 2003.

363. J.A. Lobbia, "Property Rights and Wrongs," *Village Voice*, December 20–26, 1999.

364. Dale Buss, "Metro Detroit businesses fight government property grabs," *Detroit News*, September 14, 2003.

365. Doug Bandow column, April 17, 2002.

366. *60 Minutes* report about the program, from its Web site, www.cbsnews.com.

367. Ibid. *60 Minutes* online description of the program, not the transcript of it.

368. Bernard Goldberg, interview by author, January 2004.

369. John Kramer, interview by author, telephone, February 2004.

370. Dana Berliner, *Public Power, Private Gain*.

371. John Kramer, interview by author, February 2004.

Chapter 10: Fighting Back and Winning

372. *The Columbia World of Quotations* (1996), quoted by www.Bartleby.com.

373. Jacob Sullum, "Exposing eminent domain abuses," Creator's Syndicate, April 25, 2003.

374. Sam Staley, "Wrecking Property Rights," Reason online, February 2003.

375. Gideon Kanner, interview by author, telephone, February 2004.

376. Sam Staley, "Wrecking Property Rights," Reason online, February 2003.

377. Timothy S. Hollister, Shipman & Goodwin LLP, Hartford, Conn., "Satisfying The 'Public Use' Requirement of Eminent Domain" (Georgetown University Law Center Continuing Legal Education/Environmental Law & Policy Institute program, Litigating Regulatory Takings Claims, Berkeley, Calif., October 10-11, 2002).

378. *Southwestern Illinois Development Authority v. National City Environmental*, Docket No. 87809-Agenda 16, opinion filed April 4, 2002.

379. Ibid.

380. *SWIDA* case, as quoted by Timothy Hollister and Amy Souchens, "Eminent Domain and Condemnation: How Far is Too Far" (International Municipal Lawyers Association presentation), 11.

381. *SWIDA* case, as quoted by Timothy Hollister, "Satisfying the Public Use Requirement."

382. *Southwestern Illinois Development Authority v. National City Environmental*, Docket No. 87809-Agenda 16, opinion filed April 4, 2002.

383. *Loretto v. Teleprompter Manhattan CATV Corp.*, 458 U.S. 419, 439, 73 L. Ed. 2d 868, 885, 102 S. Ct. 3164, 3178 (1982).

384. Kenneth R. Styles, "Blight Lite: Overview of redevelopment in California and discussion of whether a city can establish a redevelopment," *Daily Journal*, 1999, www.msandr.com (accessed January 24, 2004).

385. Dan Walters, "Opportunists Gut Spirit of Redevelopment," *Sacramento Bee*, March 29, 2001.

386. Dana Berliner, *Public Power, Private Gain*, 23.

387. John J. Louiszos and Patricia M. Gaug, "From the Diner to the Yacht Club: Connecticut Redevelopment Law after Aposporos and Pequonnock Yacht Club," *Connecticut Lawyer*, November 2002, 22.

388. Ibid., 22.

389. Ibid., 20.

390. Ibid., 20.

391. Ibid., 22.

392. Jeff Francis, "Court rules against Wal-Mart," *Sentinel and Transcript Newspapers*, www.Jeffconews.com; March 6, 2004.

393. *The Colorado Supreme Court, Arvada Urban Renewal Authority v. Columbine Professional Plaza Association, Inc.*, March 1, 2004.

394. *99 Cents Only Stores v. Lancaster Redevelopment Agency, CV 00-07572 SVW (AJWx)*, June 25, 2001.

395. Ibid.

396. Ibid.

397. Article 2, Section 17.

398. *Randall E. Bailey and Melissa M. Bailey v. The Honorable Robert D. Myers, Judge of the Superior Court of the State of Arizona, in and for the County of Maricopa*, 1 CA-SA 02-0108, filed Oct. 1, 2002, Cause No. CV 2001-090422.

399. Coalition for Redevelopment Reform, www.coalitionforredevelopmentreform.org (accessed January 21, 2004).

400. Ibid.

401. Dana Berliner, *Public Power, Private Gain*, 135. See also Dana Berliner, *Government Theft: The Top 10 Abuses of Eminent Domain, 1998-2002* (Washington, D.C.: Institute for Justice).

402. *County of Wayne v. Edward Hathcock*, Supreme Court Nos. 124070-124078.

403. Pacific Legal Foundation and ACLU Fund of Michigan, Brief Amicus Curiae in Support of Defendants-Appellants in *County of Wayne v. Edward Hathcock*, et al., January 12, 2004, www.pacificlegal.org (accessed January 12, 2004), 1.

404. Ibid., 3.

405. Ibid., 5.

406. Language based on a city ordinance in Lawndale, Calif.

407. Measure 7, Oregonians In Action, www.oia.org (accessed January 30, 2004).

408. Adam Schrager, "Eminent domain is target of bill," *Denver Post*, January 4, 2004.

409. Alicia Caldwell, "State eminent-domain curbs on table," *Denver Post*, January 12, 2004.

410. Tom Morton, "Eminent domain a high wire in energy bill," *Casper Star Tribune*, November 4, 2003.

411. John Campbell, Bob Hertzberg and Curt Pringle, "Time to fix state tax system," *Orange County Register*, Feb. 1, 2004.

412. Steven Greenhut, "Anaheim's new deal," *Orange County Register*, July 27, 2003.

413. Curt Pringle, interview by author, February 27, 2004.

414. Editorial, "A welcome push for freedom in Anaheim," *Orange County Register*, January 27, 2004.

415. Michael Malamut, "The Power to Take: The Use of Eminent Domain in Massachusetts" (White Paper, The Pioneer Institute for Public Policy Research), www.pioneerinstitute.org/research/whitepapers/wp15cover. cfm (accessed January 7, 2004). The bullet points are based closely on the language used in the paper.

416. Richard A. Epstein, "The Necessary History of Property and Liberty," *Chapman Law Review*, April 2003.

417. Lee Burton, *The Little House*, (Boston: Houghton Mifflin Company, 1942), 1.

INDEX

Adams, John, 51

Ainsworth, Leonard, 53, 54, 55

Allegheny Institute for Public Policy, 94, 125

American Civil Liberties Union, 266, 267

American Planning Association (APA), 143–44, 215

Anaheim, California, 133–34

Anderson, Bob, 246

Anderson, Martin, 90, 110–11

Anoka County, Minnesota, 212

Anoka County Union, 212

Aposporos v. Urban Redevelopment Commission of Stamford, 258

appraisers, 70, 71, 72, 77

Arizona Constitution, 13, 263, 264

Arizona Republic, 226

Arizona State Court of Appeals, 263

Arkansas, and Tax Increment Financing, 127–28

Arvada, Colorado, case, 259–60

Arvada Urban Renewal Authority (AURA), 259, 260

Atlantic City, New Jersey, case, 84, 265–66

Baade, Robert, 211

Bailey, Randy, 243, 263

Ballestero, Manny, 19–20, 22, 31, 36, 40, 74–75

Baltimore Sun, 223

Bandow, Doug, 209, 210–11, 241–42, 244

Bassani, Marco, 82–83

Bastiat, Frederic, 49, 217

Beach-Courchesne v. City of Diamond Bar, 39

Beasley, Alice, 84

Becket Fund, 170

Belmer, David, 165, 169

Berliner, Dana, 78, 114, 115, 141, 183, 197, 244, 246, 257, 271

Berman v. Parker, 98–102, 103, 105, 107, 108, 114, 117, 129–30, 131, 151, 152, 161, 181, 255

big-box stores, and tax revenue, 41, 124, 272, 273

Bill of Rights, 80, 86

Bird, Chief Justice Rose, 208

blight, designation of
    in *Aposporos v. Urban Redevelopment Commission of Stamford*, 258
    in California cases, 256–57
    of Chavez Ravine neighborhood, 204–5
    in Cottonwood Christian Center case, 173
    in Garden Grove, California, case, 32, 37, 39
    as justification for eminent domain, 7–9, 37, 39–40, 204
    in Lakewood, Ohio, case, 242–43
    legal standards for declaring, 126–28
    in 99 Cents Only stores case, 198
    in *Pequonnock Yacht Club, Inc. v. Bridgeport*, 257
    and urban renewal, 107, 108

Boston Business Journal, 207

Boston Red Sox stadium, 207

Boston's North End, 132–33, 134